Theory of Computation for Software Developers

The theory of computation is often viewed as one of the most abstract areas of computer science, mostly reserved for university courses. Yet its ideas power much of modern software: from regular expressions and compilers to animation systems and game AI. This book aims to bridge the gap between the formal world of the theory of computation and the realities of everyday programming practice.

Written in a clear, approachable style, it introduces the essential concepts of automata, formal languages, and computability. Through examples and practical connections, readers will see how theoretical models translate into the tools and systems developers work with every day. The book is designed for both students, taking basic computer science courses, and practicing developers who want to understand the theory behind the technologies they use but are not ready to dive into a fully formal academic text.

Covering material aligned with the ACM/IEEE Computer Science Curricula, this book can serve both as a gentle textbook and a self-contained crash course for curious professionals. Striking a balance between rigor and intuition, it presents the theory of computation as a practical foundation of how software and computation really work.

Maxim Mozgovoy is a senior associate professor at the University of Aizu, Japan. He earned his PhD in Applied Mathematics from St. Petersburg State University and his PhD in Computer Science from the University of Joensuu. His main research interests are focused on educational technologies, natural language processing, and artificial intelligence for games and interactive environments. Maxim has a record of over 100 published papers and industrial-level software development experience. He is a co-founder of Helium9 Games studio, a regular reviewer for IEEE Transactions on Games and Entertainment Computing, and a program committee member of the IEEE Conference on Games, FedCSIS, Foundations of Digital Games, and other international conferences.

Theory of Computation for Software Developers

Maxim Mozgovoy

CRC Press
Taylor & Francis Group
Boca Raton London New York

CRC Press is an imprint of the
Taylor & Francis Group, an **informa** business
A CHAPMAN & HALL BOOK

Designed cover image: Shutterstock

First edition published 2026
by CRC Press
2385 NW Executive Center Drive, Suite 320, Boca Raton FL 33431

and by CRC Press
4 Park Square, Milton Park, Abingdon, Oxon, OX14 4RN

CRC Press is an imprint of Taylor & Francis Group, LLC

ISBN: 978-1-032-61479-3(hbk)
ISBN: 978-1-032-61480-9 (pbk)
ISBN: 978-1-032-61499-1(ebk)

DOI: 10.1201/9781032614991

Typeset in Stix General Regular font
by KnowledgeWorks Global Ltd.

Contents

Preface xi

List of abbreviations xiii

Author xv

Chapter 1 Regular languages and regular expressions 1

1.1 Basic definitions 1
1.2 Introducing regular expressions 2
1.3 Practical regular expressions 4
1.4 String validation with regexes 4
1.5 Pattern matching with regexes 7
1.6 Capturing groups and backreferences 9
1.7 Takeaways 11

Chapter 2 Finite automata 12

2.1 Deterministic finite automata 12
2.1.1 Informal introduction 12
2.1.2 DFA as a graph 13
2.1.3 DFA Q&A 14
2.1.4 Describing formal languages 15
2.1.5 DFAs in Python 16
2.1.6 Minimizing DFAs 17
2.2 Nondeterministic finite automata 23
2.2.1 ε-automaton 26
2.2.2 Determinization of NFAs 27
2.2.3 NFA determinization algorithm 28
2.2.4 Determinization in Python 30
2.2.5 Simulating NFAs 35
2.2.6 NFA Q&A 37
2.3 State machines in JFLAP 38
2.4 Takeaways 42

Chapter 3 Bridging regular expressions and finite automata 44

3.1 Converting regular expressions to finite automata 44
3.2 Converting finite automata to regular expressions 48
3.3 Conversion functions in JFLAP 50

3.4 Matching patterns 51
3.4.1 From validation to matching 53
3.4.2 Kinds of pattern-matching engines 54
3.5 Takeaways 56

Chapter 4 State machines in software engineering 57

4.1 The State pattern and state machines 57
4.1.1 The problem of entangled behaviors 57
4.1.2 Disentangling behaviors 58
4.2 Vending machine 59
4.3 Markovian weather 62
4.4 Unity animation system 63
4.4.1 Animation clips and blending 64
4.4.2 Animator finite state machine 64
4.4.3 Sub-state machines 66
4.5 Takeaways 67

Chapter 5 Nonregular languages and context-free grammars 68

5.1 The pumping lemma 68
5.2 Languages and decision problems 69
5.3 Context-free grammars 71
5.4 Regular grammars 73
5.4.1 The benefits of constraints 73
5.4.2 Converting regular grammars to FAs 74
5.4.3 Converting FAs to regular grammars 76
5.4.4 Regular grammars in JFLAP 77
5.5 Takeaways 78

Chapter 6 Pushdown automata 80

6.1 Structure of a PDA 80
6.2 Recognizing nonregular languages 82
6.3 Converting context-free grammars to pushdown automata 82
6.4 Deterministic pushdown automata 84
6.5 Pushdown automata in JFLAP 86
6.6 Takeaways 88

Chapter 7 Parsing 89

7.1 Unambiguous and ambiguous grammars 89
7.2 Leftmost derivation and rightmost derivation 93
7.3 Directionality and lookahead 93
7.4 Properties of LL(k) and LR(k) grammars 94
7.5 Parsing LR(1) grammars 96
7.5.1 Preliminary notes 96

7.5.2 Removing ε-rules ... 97
7.5.3 Parsing procedure ... 98
7.5.4 *FIRST* sets ... 101
7.5.5 Set of items and its closure ... 102
7.5.6 Collection of sets of LR(1) items ... 104
7.5.7 Creating ACTION and GOTO tables ... 106
7.5.8 Testing the parser ... 108
7.5.9 The LR(1) parser as a pushdown automaton ... 110
7.6 Parsing LL(1) grammars ... 112
7.6.1 Recursive descent parser ... 113
7.6.2 Converting grammars to LL(1) form ... 116
7.7 Parsing arbitrary context-free grammars ... 117
7.7.1 Obtaining Chomsky normal form ... 118
7.7.2 Cocke-Younger-Kasami algorithm ... 120
7.8 Takeaways ... 123

Chapter 8 Building compilers ... 125

8.1 Translators, compilers, interpreters ... 125
8.2 The compiler pipeline ... 126
8.2.1 Scanner ... 126
8.2.2 Parser ... 128
8.2.3 Code generator ... 128
8.3 Developing TinyCode ... 130
8.3.1 Syntax of TinyCode ... 130
8.3.2 Parsing TinyCode ... 131
8.3.3 Testing the parser ... 134
8.3.4 Choosing an intermediate representation ... 136
8.3.5 Setting up code generation ... 137
8.3.6 Generating code ... 140
8.3.7 Executing code ... 144
8.4 Takeaways ... 150

Chapter 9 The Lindenmayer systems ... 151

9.1 Evolving plants ... 151
9.2 Generating strings ... 152
9.3 Visualizing strings ... 153
9.4 Fractal patterns ... 158
9.5 Beyond D0Ls ... 161
9.5.1 Stochastic L-systems ... 161
9.5.2 Context-sensitive rules ... 162
9.5.3 Parametric L-systems ... 163
9.6 Takeaways ... 164

Chapter 10 Turing machines 165

10.1 Beyond context-free languages 165
10.2 The pumping lemma for context-free languages 166
10.3 Two-stack PDAs 168
10.4 Deterministic Turing machines 168
10.5 Representing TMs with 2-PDAs 170
10.6 Recognizing languages with Turing machines 174
10.6.1 Recognizing a regular language 174
10.6.2 Recognizing a context-free language 174
10.6.3 Recognizing a context-sensitive language 175
10.7 TMs in Python 176
10.8 Computing with TMs 178
10.8.1 Subtracting numbers 178
10.8.2 Duplicating an input string 179
10.8.3 Sorting tape content 179
10.9 Subtracting numbers with a 2-PDA 180
10.10 Nondeterministic Turing machine 183
10.11 Multiple heads and tapes 184
10.12 Turing machines in JFLAP 186
10.13 Universal Turing machine 186
10.14 Takeaways 187

Chapter 11 Decidability and complexity 189

11.1 Decidability of languages 189
11.2 The halting problem 190
11.3 The Turing machine and decidability 191
11.3.1 The origins of the Turing machine 191
11.3.2 The Church-Turing thesis 193
11.3.3 Turing machines and computers 193
11.3.4 Checking code properties 195
11.3.5 The strong Church-Turing thesis 197
11.4 Church's formalism and functional programming 198
11.4.1 Lambda expressions 198
11.4.2 The β-reduction rule 199
11.4.3 Declarative computing 199
11.5 Functional programming in Python 201
11.5.1 Calculating the factorial 201
11.5.2 Conditional expressions 201
11.5.3 Processing lists 202
11.5.4 Mapping 204
11.6 Complexity 204
11.6.1 Time complexity 204
11.6.2 Complexity classes P and NP 206
11.6.3 Polynomial-time reductions 208

11.6.4 NP-hard and NP-complete problems ... 211
11.6.5 Complexity classes PSPACE and EXP ... 212
11.6.6 Computational irreducibility ... 213
11.7 Takeaways ... 215

References ... 217

Index ... 223

Preface

The theory of computation is one of those abstract foundations of computer science that rarely gets much attention from professional software developers. Its primary topics are often viewed as too theoretical or too specialized to be of interest to the general audience. For example, much of the traditional syllabus of this field is devoted to the study of properties of formal languages and parsing algorithms. In practice this comes useful, for example, in compiler design, which is certainly not what most of us do for a living.

This way, more abstract, foundational agenda of the theory of computation is mostly discussed within university-level computers science courses. In turn, as the world of software development became more complex and diverse, its typical practical applications came to be seen as niche specializations. On top of that, books on the subject are typically targeted at university students and might be hard to read for people not used to such literature.

However, the theory of computation discusses numerous topics, directly underpinning both our hardware and software. Here are just a few examples.

1. Imagine you have a deck of 100 cards labeled with some integers. How much time is needed to find a set of cards that add up to 42? Can we prove it cannot be accomplished faster?
2. There is a suspicion that a given Python code might end with a divide-by zero error on certain inputs. Is it possible to design a tool that analyzes the given source and finds out if such circumstances exist?
3. Imagine someone proposes a chip that combines a processor unit with read-only firmware and basic input-output capabilities. The chip is able to read input symbol by symbol, and to process data stored in its internal registers, but has no random-access memory at all. Can we define the exact scope of tasks this machine would be able to perform?
4. Suppose you need to describe a structure of a complex yet well-defined kind of data to be able to specify what constitutes a valid Python source or a JSON document. What is the right tool for the job?

These are the kinds of questions we are going to discuss in this book. They are directly addressed by the core branches of the field: *complexity theory* (what is easy and what is hard to compute), *computability theory* (what can be computed), *automata theory* (what different computational models can do), and *formal languages* (how to describe structured data). The answers to these questions underpin a variety of practical systems, such as type checkers for TypeScript or Rust, JSON and XML parsers, and network communication protocol drivers.

Some authors (e.g., Esparza and Blondin [24]) argue there is no need to adhere to the traditional way of teaching the elements of the theory of computation, which is largely focused on formal languages and their properties. While it certainly makes sense to discuss more recent application areas of this theory, and to give more attention to the common needs of professional software developers, we will generally follow the established narrative. This approach will help the readers to feel more at home if they turn to more in-depth literature for additional details or further topics. All Python sources and JFLAP configurations discussed in the book are available at

`https://github.com/rg-software/tscd`

Maxim Mozgovoy
The University of Aizu
Japan

List of abbreviations

2-PDA	Two-stack Pushdown Automaton
3-SAT	3-Satisfiability problem
CFG	Context-free grammar
CNF	Chomsky normal form
CSG	Context-sensitive grammar
CYK	Cocke-Younger-Kasami algorithm
DFA	Deterministic finite automaton
DPDA	Deterministic pushdown automaton
EBNF	Extended Backus-Naur Form
EXP	Exponential Time (complexity class)
EXPSPACE	Exponential Space (complexity class)
FA	Finite automaton
FSM	Finite state machine
IR	Intermediate Representation
KS	Knapsack problem
LALR	Lookahead LR
LBA	Linear bounded automaton
LL(k)	Left-to-right, Leftmost derivation, k symbols of lookahead
LR(k)	Left-to-right, Rightmost derivation, k symbols of lookahead
MST	Minimum spanning tree
NFA	Nondeterministic finite automaton
NP	Nondeterministic Polynomial time (complexity class)
P	Polynomial time (complexity class)
PDA	Pushdown automaton
PSPACE	Polynomial Space (complexity class)
RE	Regular expression
SAT	Boolean satisfiability problem
TM	Turing machine
TSP	Traveling salesman problem
UTM	Universal Turing machine

Author

Maxim Mozgovoy is a senior associate professor at the University of Aizu, Japan. He earned his PhD in Applied Mathematics from St. Petersburg State University and his PhD in Computer Science from the University of Joensuu. His main research interests are focused on educational technologies, natural language processing, and artificial intelligence for games and interactive environments. Maxim has a record of over 100 published papers and industrial-level software development experience. He is a co-founder of Helium9 Games studio, a regular reviewer for IEEE Transactions on Games and Entertainment Computing, and a program committee member of the IEEE Conference on Games, FedCSIS, Foundations of Digital Games, and other international conferences.

1 Regular languages and regular expressions

A message pops up on my phone: a smiley face and a link. Maybe it's just another funny cat video. Let's tap the link and find out.

Appreciate the simplicity of link sharing: the sender does not need to do anything to make the link tappable; the messenger app "knows" that a certain part of a message is a link and converts it into an interactive interface element.

Understanding the kind of data at hand is a common task in software engineering. An online shop makes sure the supplied sequence of characters is a valid credit card number. An email client app verifies that the receiver of your message is identified with a correct email address. A spreadsheet system recognizes user input as calendar dates or integers (with varying success [78]).

This seemingly mundane problem plays one of the central roles in the theory of computation, revealing a surprising complexity of related topics and challenges. For starters, consider the following question. We need to check whether an input string represents a particular kind of data (a valid credit card number, an email address, a day of the week). Which method can be used to specify the kind of data required?

Clearly, this is easy to do if the list of possible valid strings is short. For example, to check whether a given string represents a day of the week, we can simply compare it with "Monday", "Tuesday", and so on. The answer is merely seven comparisons away. However, this approach won't work for internet links, integer numbers, or valid JSON files. Maybe we need a special language for specifying what is valid and what is not?

Well, here our adventure begins.

1.1 BASIC DEFINITIONS

This book is not heavy on math. However, some formal notation will be handy: it saves space and allows us to speak the same language used in standard textbooks on the theory of computation. For starters, let's define several basic concepts.

An *alphabet* is any finite set of symbols. For example, the set $\{1, 2\}$ is the alphabet consisting of digits 1 and 2. The set $\{\mathtt{A}, \mathtt{B}, \ldots \mathtt{Z}\}$ is the alphabet of capital letters, and the set $\{a_1, a_2, a_3, a_4\}$ is an alphabet consisting of four unspecified elements. To avoid confusion, monospace font will be used to refer to explicit symbols rather than variables. Thus, `a` is a Latin letter, whereas a is a variable. Typically, alphabets are denoted by capital Greek letters, such as $\Sigma = \{0, 1\}$.

The symbols of a given alphabet can be pieced together to form strings. The expression *"a string over* Σ*"* is commonly used to indicate that the given string consists of symbols belonging to the alphabet Σ. For example,

DOI: 10.1201/9781032614991-1

`1001101` is a string over the alphabet {`1`, `0`}, and `computer` is a string over the alphabet of Latin letters. An *empty string*, containing no symbols, is usually denoted by the letter ε (epsilon). The length of such a string is zero.

The only string operation we will need is *concatenation*. When concatenating strings s_1 and s_2, we attach s_2 to the end of s_1. For instance, if s_1=`abcd` and s_2=`efg`, then their concatenation is $s_1 s_2$=`abcdefg`. The expression a^n denotes a string consisting of n copies of a concatenated together.

A set of all possible strings over a given alphabet Σ is denoted as Σ^*. For example, if Σ={`0`, `1`}, then Σ^*={ε, `0`, `1`, `00`, `01`, `10`, `11`, `000`, ...}. Any subset of this set constitutes a *language* (or a *formal language*). For example, the language L={`0`, `-1.5`, `1002.1135`, `-3.128`, ...} over the alphabet {`0`, `1`, ..., `9`, `-`, `.`} consists of strings that represent real numbers.

Typically, languages are denoted by capital Latin letters. Since languages are sets, the usual set notation applies. For example, instead of writing "string s belongs to language L", we will often use the shorter expression "$s \in L$". Similarly, $c \in \Sigma$ means that c is a symbol of the alphabet Σ.

A language can be either finite or infinite. For instance, a language over the alphabet {`a`, `b`}, consisting of all strings shorter than three symbols, includes only seven elements: ε, `a`, `b`, `aa`, `ab`, `ba`, and `bb`.

1.2 INTRODUCING REGULAR EXPRESSIONS

The definition of the term "language" in the last paragraph as a certain "interesting" set of strings brings us back to our previous question: what kind of language can be used to describe other languages? In daily conversation, English works fine: "all real numbers", "all web documents conforming to the HTML5 standard", "all array-sorting Python programs not larger than 1024 bytes". However, the situation becomes more complicated when language definitions must appear in a program. A software system might need to know whether a given string is a valid internet link or a JSON file, and it is our responsibility to equip our code with the right tool.

As noted above, describing a finite language is not particularly challenging: we can simply list all possible days of the week or available car brand names. For infinite languages, a more advanced instrument capable of specifying whole *families* of strings is required.

Now we will take a look at one of these instruments, known as *regular expressions* (REs). In the theory of computation, a regular expression over the alphabet Σ is any of the following constructions:

- The empty set symbol $\varnothing$ and the empty string symbol ε.
- Any element of the alphabet Σ.

A regular expression is also produced as a result of the following operations on regular expressions a and b:

- $(a \cup b)$ (*alternation*);

- (ab) (*concatenation*);
- (a^*) (*Kleene star* or *Kleene closure*).

Consider, for example, the alphabet $\Sigma = \{x, y, z\}$. Each of its elements is a regular expression over Σ. Since x and y are regular expressions over Σ, they can be combined to form the expression (xy), which is also a regular expression. This expression can be further transformed into $((xy)^*)$, and so on. Other examples of regular expressions over Σ include $((xz)y)^*$, $((((xy) \cup z)y)^*z)$, and $((x \cup y)(y \cup z)x)$.

Now that we know how to construct valid regular expressions, let's discuss their meaning.

Any regular expression r describes a certain language, denoted as $L(r)$.

The expression $\varnothing$ describes a language with no elements: $L(\varnothing) = \{\}$. The expression ε describes a language containing a single empty string: $L(\varepsilon) = \{\varepsilon\}$. Any alphabetic symbol produces a language made up of a single string created from this symbol: $L(\mathrm{x}) = \{\mathrm{x}\}$.

The regular expression $(a \cup b)$ describes a language that includes all the strings found in either $L(a)$ or $L(b)$. For example, if $L(a) = \{$`rain, snow, water`$\}$ and $L(b) = \{$`fall, drop`$\}$, then $L(a \cup b)$ is $\{$`rain, snow, water, fall, drop`$\}$.

The regular expression (ab) describes a language consisting of strings obtained by concatenating some string from $L(a)$ with some string from $L(b)$. For the previous examples of $L(a)$ and $L(b)$, $L(ab) = \{$`rainfall, snowfall, waterfall, raindrop, snowdrop, waterdrop`$\}$.

Finally, the Kleene star (a^*) describes a language $L(a^*) = \{\varepsilon, s_1, s_1s_2, s_1s_2s_3, ...\}$, where each s_i belongs to $L(a)$. Consider again the language $L(a) = \{$`rain, snow, water`$\}$. Then $L(a^*) = \{\varepsilon,$ `rain, snowrain, rainsnowrain, rainrainwater`, ...$\}$. Any concatenation of arbitrary strings from $L(a)$ is included in $L(a^*)$.

It is easy to see that complex regular expressions require many parentheses. To simplify reading, it is usually presumed that the Kleene star is applied before concatenation, and concatenation is applied before alternation. Thus, a cumbersome expression like $((a(b^*)) \cup (ba))$ can be rewritten simply as $ab^* \cup ba$. More parentheses can be removed thanks to the *associativity* of alternation and concatenation, meaning that $L((a \cup b) \cup c) = L(a \cup (b \cup c))$ and $L((ab)c) = L(a(bc))$. Thus, expressions like $a(b(cd))$ can be replaced with the more readable $abcd$.

Clearly, regular expressions fulfill the purpose of a language for describing languages, including infinite languages thanks to the Kleene star. They cannot, however, be used to specify *every* language imaginable. For instance, a seemingly uncomplicated language such as "all the strings where the letter `a` occurs as many times as `b`" is already beyond their capacity.

We will discuss the limitations of regular expressions later, but for now, let's note that any language that can be described with a regular expression is called a *regular language*. While the expressive capabilities of regular expressions are limited, many regular languages are practically useful. In particular, any finite language is regular. For example, the language $L = \{$`rain, snow, water`$\}$ can be described with the regular expression `rain` ∪ `snow` ∪ `water`.

1.3 PRACTICAL REGULAR EXPRESSIONS

Let's review the task of data validation. How difficult is it to check that a given input string represents a particular kind of data? Naturally, it depends on the kind of data. For example, it is very easy to check whether the input is a binary number:

```
def is_valid(s):
    for c in s:
        if c != '1' and c != '0':
            return False
    return True
```

In contrast, it is much harder to check whether an input string contains syntactically correct C++ code. In either case, writing a custom `is_valid()` function for every kind of data that needs to be checked is not an approach that can be called robust and scalable. For each kind of data, a separate validation function would be necessary, and every small change in requirements would mean code modifications.

A more advanced approach is to separate the validation task into two subtasks: (1) describing what kind of data is valid and (2) actually checking whether the current input matches the description of valid data.

The first subtask brings us back to the note at the beginning of the chapter: *maybe we need a special language for specifying what is valid and what is not.* Coincidentally, we have just discussed one such possible language: the language of regular expressions. Now we will focus on the ability of regular expressions to describe sets of strings, leaving the second subtask until the next chapter.

As already mentioned, the expressive power of regular expressions is limited to regular languages. It is less obvious that their capacity to describe languages is sufficient for the task of *string validation* but not for the task of *pattern matching*. For instance, a messenger app that makes internet links clickable must be able to identify them inside the input text, which is not the same task as figuring out whether the whole given string is a link. These limitations motivated the development of various extensions to the basic syntax of regular expressions (often called "regexes" among software developers), giving them more power for practical purposes.

1.4 STRING VALIDATION WITH REGEXES

Even if regular expressions had little practical use, they would still play an important role in the theory of computation. Regular expressions demonstrate that certain formal languages are somehow different from other formal languages. What kind of properties make a language regular? This is an interesting theoretical question to consider.

However, the practical merits of regular expressions were also understood quite early. Regular expressions were included in the QED text editor as a flexible and powerful instrument for pattern matching in 1968 [63]. In our time, they are readily available in nearly every mature programming language.

Now let's make a quick excursion into Python's regular expressions to see how far they depart from the basic theoretical version.

Most of the extensions (see Table 1.1) simply provide concise syntax or make it possible to refer to symbols not present on the keyboard. They are also sufficient for many typical data validation tasks.

TABLE 1.1: Basic elements of Python regular expressions[1].

<table>
<tr><th>Element</th><th>Description</th></tr>
<tr><td>Characters, except <code>^$.{[(|)]}*+?\</code></td><td>Represent themselves.</td></tr>
<tr><td><code>\r</code></td><td>Represents the carriage return character.</td></tr>
<tr><td><code>\n</code></td><td>Represents the newline character.</td></tr>
<tr><td><code>.</code></td><td>Represents any character except a newline. Equivalent to $0 \cup \cdots \cup 9 \cup a \cup \cdots \cup z \cup (other\ characters)$.</td></tr>
<tr><td>a*</td><td>Represents the Kleene star.</td></tr>
<tr><td>a+</td><td>A shortcut for aa* ("Kleene plus").</td></tr>
<tr><td>a?</td><td>Represents a or an empty string (equivalent to $a \cup \varepsilon$).</td></tr>
<tr><td>a{m}</td><td>Represents m repetitions of a (for example, a{3} is aaa).</td></tr>
<tr><td>a{m, n}</td><td>Represents from m to n repetitions of a. For example, a{2,4} is a shortcut for $aa \cup aaa \cup aaaa$. Both m and n are optional: a{m, } means "at least m repetitions", and a{, n} means "at most n repetitions".</td></tr>
<tr><td>[chars]</td><td>Represents a single character from the specified set. In addition to characters, it is possible to use character ranges. For example, <code>[cb0-9]</code> specifies a decimal digit, the letter <code>c</code>, or the letter <code>b</code>. A set $\{s_1, \ldots, s_n\}$ is equivalent to the expression $s_1 \cup \cdots \cup s_n$.</td></tr>
<tr><td>[^chars]</td><td>Represents a single character outside the specified set. For example, <code>[^0-9]</code> specifies any symbol that is not a decimal digit.</td></tr>
<tr><td><code>\</code></td><td>Used before a special character to specify its literal value. For example, <code>*</code> represents an asterisk, and <code>\[</code> stands for the left square bracket.</td></tr>
<tr><td>a | b</td><td>Represents the alternation operator: a | b is equivalent to $a \cup b$.</td></tr>
<tr><td><code>\d</code></td><td>Represents any decimal digit: $0 \cup 1 \cup \cdots \cup 9$.</td></tr>
<tr><td><code>\D</code></td><td>Represents any symbol that is not a decimal digit.</td></tr>
<tr><td><code>\s</code></td><td>Represents any whitespace character (including tabs, newlines, etc.)</td></tr>
<tr><td><code>\S</code></td><td>Represents any non-whitespace character.</td></tr>
<tr><td><code>\w</code></td><td>Represents any alphanumeric character.</td></tr>
<tr><td><code>\W</code></td><td>Represents any non-alphanumeric character.</td></tr>
</table>

[1] Full documentation is available at https://docs.python.org/3/library/re.html

As a simple example, consider again the process of validating a binary number, this time with the help of a regular expression:

```
import re


def is_valid(s):
    return re.fullmatch("[01]+", s) is not None
```

The function `re.fullmatch(pattern, string, flags=0)` returns `None` if the given `string` does not belong to the language $L(\texttt{pattern})$. If it does, a `Match` object containing additional information is returned.

Python's regular expression mechanism can be fine-tuned to activate certain useful conventions. This is done by passing a set of desired flags, combined with a bitwise OR operation, as a third argument to `re.fullmatch()`.

Three flags are used most commonly. The `re.IGNORECASE` flag instructs Python to treat uppercase and lowercase characters as equal. This works for non-Latin symbols as well. The `re.DOTALL` flag makes the dot `.` match the newline character. We will consider the remaining `re.MULTILINE` flag a bit later.

As a simple practical example, consider the task of DNA sequence validation. DNA sequences are represented as strings consisting of four possible characters: `A`, `T`, `C`, `G`. The following function will verify whether a given string represents a DNA sequence, regardless of character case:

```
# will return True for "AAAccCT"
def is_valid(s):
    return re.fullmatch("[atcg]+", s, re.IGNORECASE) is not None
```

For a slightly more complex example, let's check whether a given string represents a file name of an image in `png` or `gif` format:

```
# will return True for "income-histogram.png"
def is_valid(s):
    return re.fullmatch(r"\w+\.(gif|png)", s, re.IGNORECASE) is not None
```

A file name is a non-empty sequence of alphanumeric characters (`\w+`), followed by a dot and one of two admissible extensions, `png` or `gif`[1]. Both uppercase and lowercase names are valid. Since the dot is a special symbol meaning "any character", it must be prefixed with a backslash to be treated literally. Backslashes are also special characters, so every backslash must normally be prefixed with another backslash. However, this quickly makes regular expressions unwieldy. Python documentation recommends using r-prefixed *raw strings*, where backslashes are not treated as special characters.

[1] This is a simplification. In particular, valid file names may contain non-alphanumeric characters, such as `!` or `+`, and whitespace.

1.5 PATTERN MATCHING WITH REGEXES

As already mentioned, pattern matching was the first everyday task that made regular expressions a user-end feature of a text editor. This capability can still be found in modern tools. For example, the `Find` dialog in Visual Studio Code supports regex searches.

It should be clear, though, that regular expressions, as they are understood in the theory of computation, are not designed for this task. A regular expression describes a certain language, and the closest practical task requiring this ability is string validation, i.e., checking whether a given string s belongs to the language $L(r)$ described by the regular expression r.

Pattern matching requires additional capabilities, most notably the ability to control the general matching strategy. Suppose we need to identify binary numbers in the following string: `ab00101c`. Should the matching procedure report no results because the number `00101` is surrounded by letters? If not, should it report the longest found number, `00101`, or five single-digit numbers? Surprisingly, these seemingly minor requirements can only be addressed with considerably more complex machinery than that which is sufficient for string validation.

For now, let's discuss further extensions to the regular expression syntax that are indispensable for pattern matching (see Table 1.2).

TABLE 1.2: Extensions of regular expressions for pattern matching.

Element	Description
$a{*}?$, $a{+}?$, $a??$, $a\{m,n\}?$	*Lazy* versions of the respective constructions $a*$, $a+$, $a?$, $a\{m,n\}$.
$a{*}{+}$, $a{+}{+}$, $a?{+}$, $a\{m,n\}{+}$	*Possessive* versions of the respective constructions $a*$, $a+$, $a?$, $a\{m,n\}$[2].
$\hat{}a$	Represents the expression a at the beginning of a string.
$a\$$	Represents the expression a at the end of a string.
`\b`	Represents a position at the beginning or at the end of a word (a sequence of alphanumeric characters `\w`)
`\B`	Represents a position that is not at the beginning or at the end of a word.

[2] *Repetition operators* (`*`, `+`, `?`, `{m,n}`), as well as their lazy and possessive versions, are also called *quantifiers*.

One group of extensions restricts the place where a match must be found: at the beginning of the input string, at its end, or at a word border. By default, newline characters are treated as string boundaries, so `^a` can mean either "at the beginning of a string" or "at the beginning of a line". This convention can be turned off by passing the `re.MULTILINE` flag to the matching procedure.

A more interesting group of extensions controls the matching strategy, which can be *greedy*, *lazy*, or *possessive*.

The default *greedy matching* strategy will try to find the longest possible match. Suppose a certain text document contains a section with a list of people and their phone numbers, formatted as follows:

```
1. Leia Todd      206-342-8631
2. Damian Hartman 248-762-0356
3. Patrick Gomez  234-109-6626
...
```

Python's `re.search()` function will help in locating it:

```
s = """
These people are our primary contacts:
1. Leia Todd      206-342-8631
2. Damian Hartman 248-762-0356
3. Patrick Gomez  234-109-6626
Let's talk to someone tomorrow.
"""

m = re.search(r"1\..+\d{3}-\d{3}-\d{4}", s, re.DOTALL)
print(m.group()) # prints the entire phone book section
```

The function `re.search(pattern, string, flags=0)` returns a `Match` object describing the first found match for `pattern` in the given `string`. The actual matched text fragment can be retrieved by calling the `Match` object's `group()` method. Note that `re.search()` provides no way to obtain subsequent matches; we must rely on other functions for this purpose.

The phone book section starts with `1.` and ends with a telephone number (three dash-separated groups of digits). The first line of the section,

`Leia Todd      206-342-8631,`

perfectly satisfies this description. However, the greedy matching strategy causes the match to extend further until it hits the final telephone number, `234-109-6626`.

Certain tasks require a different approach. Internet documents (HTML files) support six levels of headings, denoted with `<h1>...<h6>` tags:

```
<h1>Heading 1</h1>
<h2>Heading 2</h2>
...
<h6>Heading 6</h6>
```

Suppose our goal is to extract all headings from a given document. As noted above, `re.search()` returns only the first match, so let's start by locating the first heading:

```
s = "<h1>This is title</h1><h2>This is subtitle</h2>This is body"

m = re.search(r"<h[1-6]>.+</h[1-6]>", s, re.DOTALL)
print(m.group())
```

The code might seem correct, but unfortunately, it extracts the entire text between `<h1>` and `</h2>`, i.e., the string `<h1>This is title</h1><h2>This is subtitle</h2>`. Greedy matching won't stop at `</h1>`, because that substring also matches `.+`. It will continue, extending the match until the last possible `</h[1-6]>`.

The job can be done by employing a *lazy matching* strategy:

```
s = "<h1>This is title</h1><h2>This is subtitle</h2>This is body"

m = re.search(r"<h[1-6]>.+?</h[1-6]>", s, re.DOTALL)
print(m.group()) # prints "<h1>This is title</h1>"
```

Lazy matching aims to match as few characters as possible for `.+?`, thus stopping at the first `</h[1-6]>`.

A less commonly used *possessive matching* strategy is "very greedy": it matches as many characters as possible for an expression marked with `*+`, `++`, or `?+`, without backing off, even if it causes the rest of the pattern to fail. Thus, the following code fails to match anything:

```
s = "<h1>This is title</h1><h2>This is subtitle</h2>This is body"
m = re.search(r"<h[1-6]>.++</h[1-6]>", s, re.DOTALL)
```

After matching the initial `<h1>`, the matching procedure consumes every subsequent character of `s` for `.++`, leaving nothing for the trailing `</h[1-6]>` part of the pattern to match.

1.6 CAPTURING GROUPS AND BACKREFERENCES

In the tasks of string validation and pattern matching, it can be useful to know how specific elements of a regular expression correspond to fragments of the found match. In the heading identification example, we reported the whole match, including the tags `<h1>` and `</h1>`. However, the goal is often to find the headings themselves, not their surrounding tags.

The resulting match can be split into meaningful fragments if the corresponding regular expression has *capturing groups*. Recall that the basic syntax of regular expressions includes parentheses to group expressions. A pattern `abc*` means "`ab`, then zero or more repetitions of `c`", whereas `(abc)*` means "zero or more repetitions of `abc`".

For pattern matching, parentheses are also used to mark the boundaries of a capturing group, identifiable by its cardinal number. By convention, the whole regular expression is group 0. The leftmost `(` character starts group 1, and so on. Groups can be nested.

A `Match` object `m`, returned by `re.search()`, provides access to each match fragment "captured" by a group. Earlier we used `m.group()` to retrieve the whole match; this call is equivalent to `m.group(0)`. The first group is returned by `m.group(1)`, and so on. Alternatively, groups can be addressed as list elements: `m[0]`, `m[1]`, ..., `m[N]`.

Using groups, we can, for example, retrieve a heading and its level number separately:

```
s = "<h1>This is title</h1><h2>This is subtitle</h2>This is body"

m = re.search(r"<h([1-6])>(.+?)</h[1-6]>", s, re.DOTALL)
print(f"level: {m[1]}, text: {m[2]}")
# prints "level: 1, text: This is title"
```

All non-overlapping matches in a given string can be retrieved with `re.finditer()`. This function takes the same arguments as `re.search()` and returns an iterator of all identified matches:

```
s = "<h1>This is title</h1><h2>This is subtitle</h2>This is body"

matches = re.finditer(r"<h([1-6])>(.+?)</h[1-6]>", s, re.DOTALL)
for m in matches:
    print(f"level: {m[1]}, text: {m[2]}")

# prints:
# level: 1, text: This is title
# level: 2, text: This is subtitle
```

The regular expressions of Python, Perl, and other programming languages include another powerful capability we cannot overlook: *backreferences*. Backreferences are used to specify the content of a previously matched group as part of a regular expression. The backreference `\1` refers to group 1, `\2` to group 2, and so on.

For example, the regular expression `(.*)-(\1)` can be used to check whether a given string consists of two identical substrings separated by a dash, such as `Baden-Baden`.

This neat instrument is mentioned here primarily to emphasize that nothing of this sort exists in the basic definition of regular expressions from the theory of computation. A language of dash-separated repeating strings is not regular and, from a theoretical perspective, cannot be described with a regular expression. Naturally, we are happy to benefit from any useful extensions, but let's keep the concepts of regular expressions that describe regular languages and their practical Python namesakes slightly apart in our mental map.

Backreferences are also vital to the search-and-replace functionality of Python's `re` module. Replacements are performed by calling the function

```
re.sub(pattern, repl, string, count=0, flags=0)
```

It returns a new string where matches of `pattern` in `string` are replaced by `repl`. At most `count` substitutions will be made; if `count` is 0, all matches are replaced. Since backreferences are allowed in `repl`, fairly advanced rearrangements of the source string can be achieved. As a simple example, suppose we want to "flatten" all headings in our HTML document, converting all of them to level 1. This can be done as follows:

```
s = "<h1>This is title</h1><h2>This is subtitle</h2>This is body"

r = re.sub(r"<h[1-6]>(.+?)</h[1-6]>", r"<h1>\1</h1>", s, 0, re.DOTALL)

# prints "<h1>This is title</h1><h1>This is subtitle</h1>This is body"
print(r)
```

1.7 TAKEAWAYS

1. Regular expressions provide one method for declaring a formal language, i.e., a finite or an infinite set of strings.
2. In a sense, regular expressions divide all formal languages into two classes: regular languages (those that can be described with regular expressions) and *nonregular languages* (everything else).
3. In programming languages and various tools, regular expressions are used for string validation and pattern matching. The purpose of validation is to check whether a given string belongs to the language described by a regular expression. The goal of pattern matching is to find a "match" for a given "pattern" (a substring satisfying the regular expression) within a given string.
4. Somewhat confusingly, pattern matching is done in Python by calling functions with "search" or "find" in their names, such as `search()`, `findall()`, and `finditer()`. Conversely, validation (matching a pattern against an entire string) is done by calling `fullmatch()`.[3]
5. Since more than one substring may satisfy the same regular expression, the found matches depend on the specific strategies used for matching individual elements of the regular expression.
6. Syntactical means for denoting the desired matching strategy (greedy, lazy, possessive) and extensions, such as backreferences, make Python regular expressions more versatile and capable of describing even some nonregular languages.

[3]A function called `match()` will check for a match for the given pattern only at the beginning of the given string.

2 Finite automata

Let's recap the story that unfolded in the last chapter. To make sense of data, we need to understand whether the given data represents the type of data we are interested in. For this reason, it would be handy to have a specialized language describing various possible kinds of input. Regular expressions were then offered as an option for such a language. Granted, they can only describe regular languages, but one has to start somewhere.

What makes using regular expressions in practical tasks tricky is their *declarative* nature. While they are perfectly capable of describing formal languages, they do not offer any concrete procedure to carry out the task of string validation. In our examples, Python functions like `re.search()` or `re.fullmatch()` worked "automagically," and we never discussed their internals.

In this chapter, we will attack the task of describing formal languages from another angle. We will consider a virtual machine capable of performing string validation. This machine and its variations will serve as a foundation for practical string validation and pattern matching routines.

2.1 DETERMINISTIC FINITE AUTOMATA

2.1.1 INFORMAL INTRODUCTION

Let's start with a simple virtual device called a *deterministic finite automaton* (DFA) or *deterministic finite state machine* (DFSM). Its operation can be understood from the sketch shown in Figure 2.1.

A DFA always resides in a certain *state* (pointed to by a movable needle in the sketch). The number of states can be large but is always *finite*, and this is why this device is called a *finite state* machine. One state of the machine must be designated as the *start* (or *initial*) state, i.e., pointed to by the needle before the device starts doing

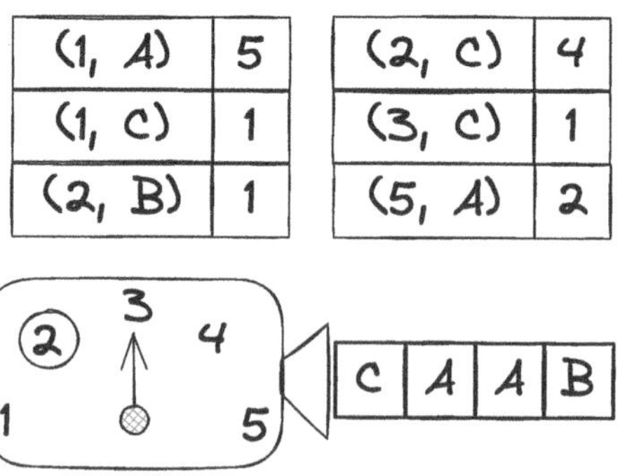

FIGURE 2.1: A DFA processing the input string CAAB.

DOI: 10.1201/9781032614991-2

any work. Some states may also be chosen as *favorable* (or *accept*) states.\index{finite automaton (FA)!accept state|see {favorable state} In the sketch, the start state is 3, and the only favorable state is 2 (circled). Favorable states are simply marked as such; they have no other special properties.

A DFA is equipped with a reading device, able to process tapes of finite length. Input tapes are partitioned into cells containing certain symbols. A cell cannot be empty in the sense that it has to contain *something*, at least a whitespace character.

The machine operates according to a set of *transitions*, specifying the destination state for each possible combination of the current state and the next input symbol. The DFA reads its input string symbol by symbol and switches between states as mandated by the transitions. Transitions must be unambiguous: if there is a rule that the input symbol `A` switches the device from state 1 to state 5, there should be no other rules for state 1 and the input symbol `A`. This is why this automaton is called *deterministic*.

The machine in Figure 2.1 is about to process the input tape containing the string `CAAB`. This will be done as follows:

```
# start state is 3
read symbol        # result is C
switch to state 1 # use rule (3, C) -> 1
read symbol        # result is A
switch to state 5 # use rule (1, A) -> 5
read symbol        # result is A
switch to state 2 # use rule (5, A) -> 2
read symbol        # result is B
switch to state 1 # use rule (2, B) -> 1
end
```

After processing its input, the automaton will be in its ordinary (non-favorable) state 1, and this is all we are going to get from a DFA: it can read strings and switch between states, nothing more. This functionality is, however, sufficient for some scenarios of string validation. A DFA essentially sorts input strings into two classes: the ones that leave the DFA in one of its favorable states, and the ones that do not.

2.1.2 DFA AS A GRAPH

Figure 2.1 emphasizes the "hardware" aspect of a DFA but does not really help to comprehend its most complex part, the system of transitions. A better way to sketch a DFA is to represent its states with circles and its transitions with directed arrows (see Fig 2.2). For example, a `C`-labeled arrow from state 3 to state 1 represents the rule $(3, \mathtt{C}) \rightarrow 1$. An arrow coming "from the outside" points to the start state. Favorable states are represented with double-lined circles.

Coincidentally, this drawing is a common visual representation of a *directed graph*: circles are graph vertices, and arrows are (directed) edges. Indeed, the transitions of a DFA form a graph, which is good news, meaning that DFAs can be analyzed with established methods of graph theory.

Formally speaking, a DFA consists of the following five elements:

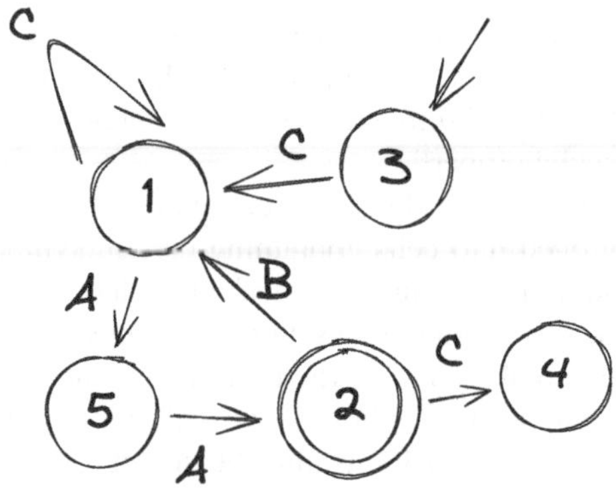

FIGURE 2.2: A DFA as a directed graph.

1. A finite set of states $Q = \{q_1, q_2, \dots, q_n\}$.
2. A finite set of input symbols (the alphabet) $\Sigma = \{a_1, a_2, \dots, a_m\}$.
3. The start state $q_s \in Q$.
4. A set of favorable states $F = \{f_1, f_2, \dots, f_k\}$. All favorable states are simply states, meaning that F is a subset of Q.
5. A *transition function* $\delta(q_i, a) = q_j$, mapping a pair (*state*, *symbol*) to a new state. Thus, δ represents the set of transitions.

A deterministic finite state machine is often defined as a tuple of these five elements: DFA = $(Q, \Sigma, \delta, q_s, F)$.

2.1.3 DFA Q&A

Before moving on, let's fill some gaps with a quick Q&A.

Q: The states of the example DFA are labeled with numbers, and the input tape seems to contain only capital Latin letters. Why?

A: No particular reason. States can be labeled in any convenient way (q_0, q_1, and so on, or `StartState`, `CentralState`, ...). Similarly, each cell of the input tape should contain exactly one symbol of a particular finite alphabet, but there are no restrictions on the nature of the alphabet to be used.

Q: Can a finite automaton have no start state? What about favorable states?

A: The start state must be specified. A set of favorable states can be empty, but favorable states provide the only possible feedback to the user in the DFA version we are currently discussing.

Q: Does this feedback include the specific state label at the end of input processing?

A: No. A DFA only reports whether its last state is favorable or not.

Q: Just in case, let's make it clear: can a DFA transition from a favorable state back to a "regular" (non-favorable) state?

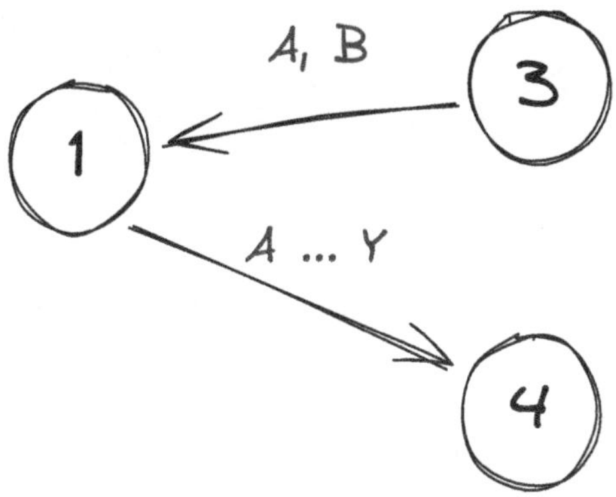

FIGURE 2.3: Shortcut notation in DFA transition rules.

A: Yes, it can. Some sources call favorable states "final states," which might be slightly misleading. A favorable (also known as final) state is simply marked as such and works just like any other state.

Q: What would happen if we add several transitions that contradict each other? For instance, $(5, \texttt{A}) \rightarrow 1$ and $(5, \texttt{A}) \rightarrow 2$?

A: We can't add such transitions because this is prohibited. The resulting device will not be a deterministic finite state machine.

Q: What happens in case of an abnormal situation? Suppose our DFA (Figure 2.2) is currently in state 2, and the next input symbol is `A`. This case is not covered by the rules!

A: Great question. Theoretically, this should never happen because we are supposed to take into account every conceivable combination of the current state and the next input symbol. If our ultimate goal is to implement a DFA as actual hardware or a virtual device, a missing transition rule should be treated as an error. This error can be handled differently. The easiest option would be to skip the rest of the input string and report a "non-favorable" result, but in some cases, it might be better to raise an exception or call some designated error-processing code.

Q: Hmm... suppose we have a rule $(1, \texttt{A}) \rightarrow 2$, which means we need to draw an arrow between vertices 1 and 2. If we add a rule $(1, \texttt{B}) \rightarrow 2$, we'll have two arrows between the same vertices, and if we do the same for the remaining letters except `Z`, there will be 25 arrows?!

A: Drawings like the one shown in Figure 2.2 are made for people, so any reasonable shortcut notation is acceptable (see Figure 2.3).

2.1.4 DESCRIBING FORMAL LANGUAGES

Now it's time to see how a DFA can be used to describe a formal language. Let's start with something simple: our input alphabet will consist of the characters `0` and `1`, and the target language will include strings that represent even binary numbers. A binary

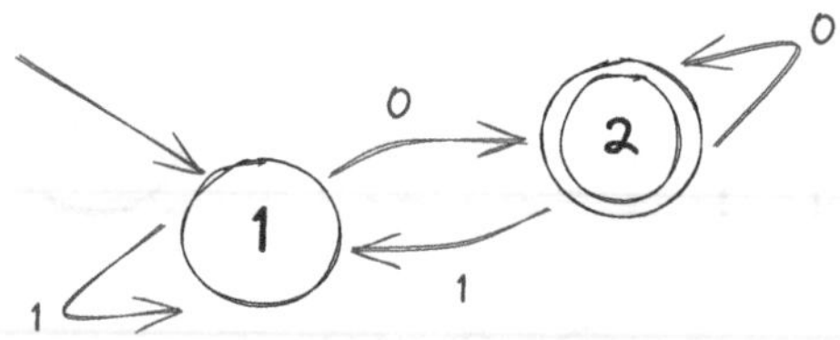

FIGURE 2.4: A DFA for recognizing even binary numbers.

number is even if it ends with 0, so we need to make sure zeros switch the DFA into its favorable state, while ones do the opposite (see Figure 2.4).

Suppose the input tape contains the sequence 0110100. Then the DFA would perform the following operations:

```
# start state is 1
read 0, switch to state 2
read 1, switch to state 1
read 1, stay in state 1
read 0, switch to state 2
read 1, switch to state 1
read 0, switch to state 2
read 0, stay in state 2
```

The resulting state is favorable, so we can conclude that 0110100 is an even binary number.

According to established terminology, a finite state machine *accepts* a certain string if this string leaves the machine in one of its favorable states. In the opposite case, the machine *rejects* the string. The set of strings accepted by the finite state machine forms the language that is *recognized* by the machine.

Therefore, every possible input string is either accepted or rejected by the DFA. Abnormal situations (a missing transition rule) can be handled in any reasonable manner, but let's at least agree that troublemaking input strings will not be accepted.

2.1.5 DFAS IN PYTHON

There is still much to be discussed about deterministic finite state machines, but now let's make a brief stop and appreciate how remarkably easy it is to simulate a DFA in Python. The DFA that recognizes the language of even binary numbers, for instance, can be written in just a few lines of code:

```
def accepts(rules, favstates, start, input):
    state = start
    try:
        for c in input:
            state = rules[(state, c)]
        return state in favstates
    except KeyError:
        return False
```

```
rules = {
    (1, "0"): 2,
    (1, "1"): 1,
    (2, "0"): 2,
    (2, "1"): 1,
}

favs = {2}
start = 1

print(accepts(rules, favs, start, "011011")) # prints False
print(accepts(rules, favs, start, "010110")) # prints True
```

Note that the actual DFA is encoded in `rules`, `favs`, and `start`, so the simulation of another machine is merely a question of supplying a different configuration to `accepts()`.

The Python code makes it easier to notice another remarkable feature of DFAs: string processing takes place in a `for` loop, traversing the input string character by character. This makes the total running time of the program proportional to the length of its input, meaning that the underlying algorithm has *linear* time complexity.

Strictly speaking, this particular Python code is not linear, because inside the `for` loop we also perform a dictionary lookup. This is a very fast operation on average, but it might get slower in certain unlucky situations. In any case, it is possible to implement a DFA without dictionary lookups, obtaining indisputably linear complexity.

2.1.6 MINIMIZING DFAS

It is no secret that bloated and inefficient programs sometimes deliver functionality that can be achieved with more compact and faster code. Similarly, two different DFAs may happen to recognize the same formal language. If that's the case, there is no reason to prefer a device with a large and complicated system of states and transitions when a simpler option is available.

The notion of "efficiency" is not clear-cut in general programming tasks. It is common, for example, to trade memory for speed and vice versa. The case of DFAs is simpler: we already know that every input string is going to be processed symbol by symbol, so there is no room for improving performance in terms of speed, making size the only target for optimization.

In the theory of computation, the "size" of a DFA is measured by its number of states, so the goal of optimization is to reduce the number of states to the minimum. Any software developer knows how difficult it is to optimize a program, so it might be surprising that a DFA can be optimized simply by following a well-defined formal algorithm.

We'll consider this algorithm in a moment, but before that, I should note that DFA optimization (more precisely, *minimization*) is a common step in systems working with autogenerated DFAs. So far, we have only dealt with handcrafted deterministic finite state machines, but DFAs may also be created by a "DFA generator." Such tools are commonly designed to be simple and straightforward and, as a result, often

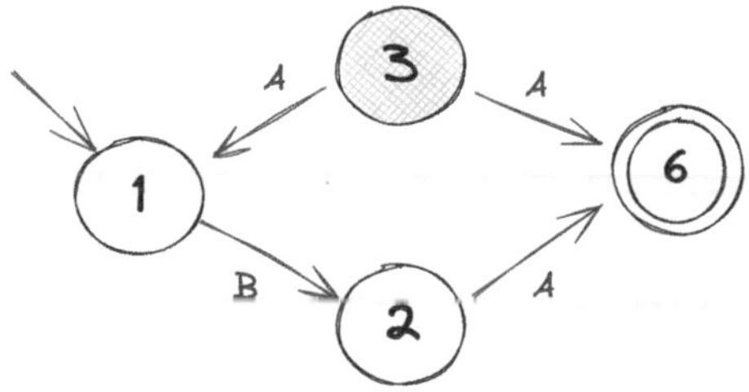

FIGURE 2.5: An unreachable state (3) in a DFA.

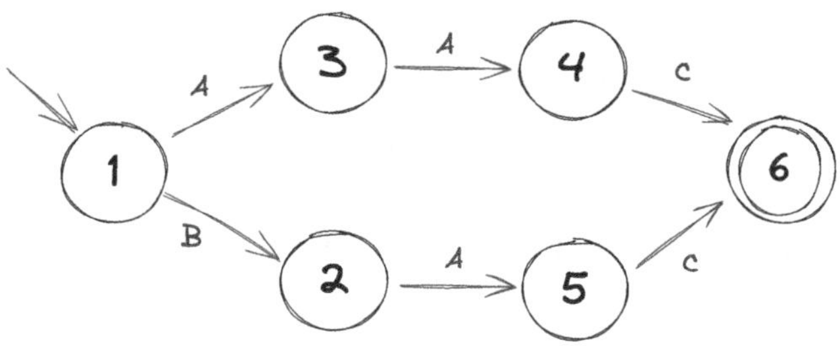

FIGURE 2.6: An example of equivalent states.

produce DFAs with more states than necessary. A conventional approach is to treat generation and minimization as two related yet independent tasks.

The simplest DFA minimization procedure (*Moore's algorithm* [49]) relies on the concepts of *unreachable states* and *state equivalence*.

An unreachable state is simply a state that cannot become current regardless of input (see Figure 2.5). I wouldn't expect anyone to introduce unreachable states into a handcrafted DFA, but a DFA generator might occasionally produce one.

The concept of state equivalence is a bit more advanced. Informally speaking, two states are considered equivalent if the DFA starting from either of them accepts and rejects the same set of input strings. In other words, it would not be possible to guess which of two equivalent states was chosen as a start state merely by analyzing the results of input string processing.

Figure 2.6 shows a concrete example. States 2 and 3 are equivalent: once the DFA is in either of these states, any subsequent input data will be treated in the same manner.

In a nutshell, DFA minimization consists of three operations: 1) removing unreachable states, 2) identifying pairs of non-equivalent states, and 3) merging equivalent states into single states:

```
remove unreachable states and related transitions
create a list of all unordered pairs (p, q) of DFA states, where p ≠ q
mark pairs containing one favorable and one non-favorable state

WHILE a previously unmarked pair of non-equivalent states can be found
```

```
    mark the identified pair

replace each set of equivalent states with a single new state
modify the transition table accordingly
```

Removal of unreachable states is a straightforward process:

```
add the start state to a set Q

WHILE Q is not empty
    take out an arbitrary element S from Q
    mark S as reachable
    FOR EACH alphabet symbol c
        add δ(S, c) to Q if it is not yet marked as reachable

remove all unreachable states and related transitions
```

The main step of the minimization algorithm separates state pairs into two classes, "marked" and "unmarked." The ultimate goal is to mark all pairs made up of non-equivalent states. Initially, the algorithm marks all pairs consisting of one favorable and one non-favorable state, since they cannot be equivalent. This process has to continue as long as the algorithm is able to identify new pairs to be marked:

```
FOR EACH state p
    FOR EACH state q
        FOR EACH alphabet symbol c
            IF (p, q) is not marked, but (δ(p, c), δ(q, c)) is marked
                # p and q are not equivalent, so mark (p, q)
                ...
```

Suppose our DFA has two transition rules: $(p, a) \rightarrow p'$ and $(q, a) \rightarrow q'$. If the pair (p', q') is already marked as non-equivalent, it implies that p and q cannot be equivalent either, so the pair (p, q) must also be marked. This process has to continue as long as the algorithm is able to identify new pairs to be marked.

Note that the algorithm presumes that the DFA is *complete*, i.e., there exists a transition rule for any combination of the current state and input symbol. We have already discussed that in practice it is perfectly fine to treat missing rules as errors, leading, for example, to immediate rejection of input. The right way to process such errors during minimization is to create a new non-favorable "sink" state and to direct all the missing transitions there (see Figure 2.7).

Finally, it is necessary to combine groups of equivalent states into single states. Since each unmarked pair contains two equivalent states, we can analyze these pairs to identify larger groups:

```
let each DFA state s belong to its own "group of s"
FOR EACH unmarked pair (p, q)
    merge the group of p and the group of q
```

This way, every time two states are found to be equivalent, their groups are merged. When this process is done, these groups will become the states of the minimized DFA.

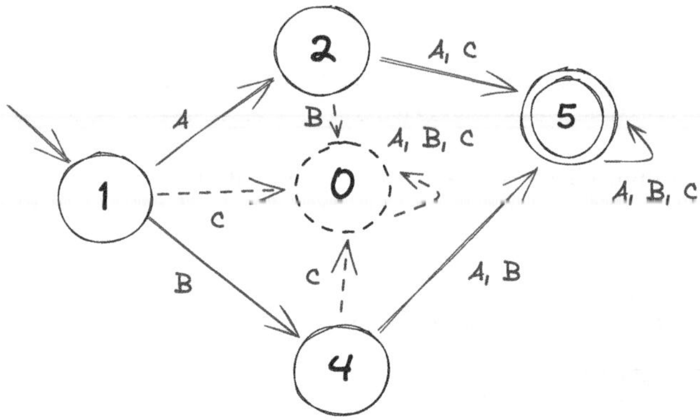

FIGURE 2.7: Handling missing rules in a DFA with $\Sigma = \{A, B, C\}$.

A Python implementation of the DFA minimization algorithm is shown in Listing 2.1.

Listing 2.1: DFA minimization.

```
from collections import defaultdict
from dataclasses import dataclass

FS = frozenset


@dataclass
class FA:
    rules: defaultdict
    favs: set
    start: int

    def states(self):
        src = {s for (s, _) in self.rules.keys()}
        dst = {self.rules[(s, c)] for s in src for c in self.symbols()}
        return src | dst

    def symbols(self):
        return {c for (_, c) in self.rules.keys()}

    def remove_unreachable(self):
        Q = {self.start}
        reachable = set()

        while Q:
            S = Q.pop()
            reachable.add(S)
            new_states = {self.rules[(S, c)] for c in self.symbols()}
            Q.update(new_states - reachable)

        for s, c in list(self.rules.keys()):
            if s not in reachable or self.rules[(s, c)] not in reachable:
```

```
                del self.rules[(s, c)]

        self.favs &= reachable

    def all_pairs(self):
        return {FS((p, q)) for p in self.states() for q in self.states()
         if p != q}

    def to_mark(self, marked):
        for p, q in self.all_pairs() - marked:
            for c in self.symbols():
                if FS((self.rules[(p, c)], self.rules[(q, c)])) in marked:
                    return FS((p, q))
        return None

    def merge_states(self, marked_pairs):
        group = {s: s for s in self.states()}

        for p, q in self.all_pairs() - marked_pairs:
            p_group, q_group = group[p], group[q]
            for s in self.states():
                if group[s] == p_group:
                    group[s] = q_group

        self.start = group[self.start]
        self.favs = {group[s] for s in self.favs}
        self.rules = {(group[p], c): group[self.rules[(p, c)]] for (p, c)
         in self.rules}

    def minimize(self):
        self.remove_unreachable()

        marked = {
            FS((p, q))
            for p in self.states()
            for q in self.states()
            if (p in self.favs) != (q in self.favs)
        }

        while new_pair := self.to_mark(marked):
            marked.add(new_pair)

        self.merge_states(marked)


dfa = FA(...) # define DFA here

dfa.minimize()
print(dfa.states())
print(dfa.start)
print(dfa.favs)
print(dfa.rules)
```

This code follows the algorithm described above quite closely. The input DFA has to be specified with three elements: a dictionary of transition rules, such as `(1, "A"): 3`, a set of favorable states, and a start state. The DFA does not have to be complete. Its transitions are stored in a `defaultdict(int)` dictionary, which returns

0 for a missing key. Thus, a non-favorable state 0 is reported as the destination for any missing transition.

The complete list of states and alphabet symbols can be retrieved directly from the rules. Retrieving states is not a very straightforward process, because we have to combine source and destination states:

```
def states(self):
    src = {s for (s, _) in self.rules.keys()}
    dst = {self.rules[(s, c)] for s in src for c in self.symbols()}
    return src | dst
```

Since we check all possible combinations of (s, c), the set of target states `dst` will contain the value 0 if it is ever retrieved from `self.rules` in the case of a missing transition.

Fortunately, Python supports set operations, which makes it easy to obtain, for example, unmarked pairs by subtracting marked pairs from the complete collection of pairs:

```
for p, q in self.all_pairs() - marked:
    ...
```

Note that pairs in this algorithm have to be *unordered*: (p, q) must be treated as the same pair as (q, p). For this reason, it is not possible to rely on built-in tuples; a `frozenset` must be used instead.

Let's try minimizing an example DFA (Figure 2.8) to see this program in action:

```
dfa = FA(
    defaultdict(
        int,
        {
            (8, "A"): 2,
            (7, "A"): 6,
            (7, "B"): 2,
            (1, "A"): 7,
            (1, "B"): 2,
            (2, "B"): 7,
            (2, "A"): 3,
            (3, "A"): 5,
            (3, "B"): 4,
            (4, "A"): 6,
            (4, "B"): 5,
            (5, "A"): 2,
            (5, "B"): 4,
            (6, "B"): 5,
            (6, "A"): 1,
        },
    ),
    {6},
    7,
)

# output
```

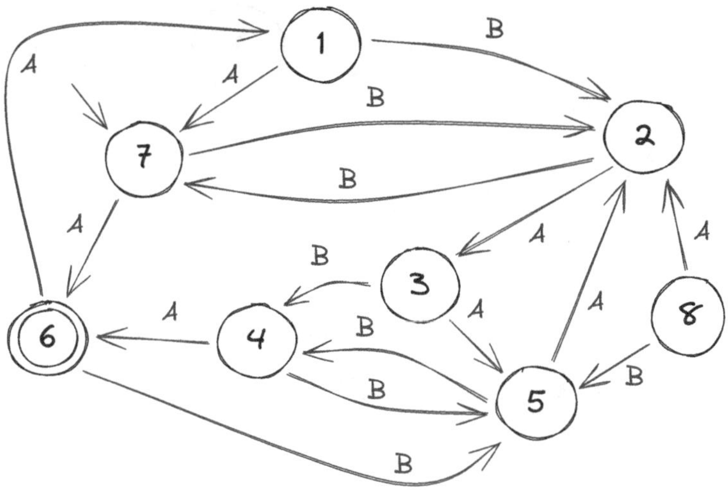

FIGURE 2.8: An example DFA to be minimized.

```
{1, 3, 6, 7}
7
{6}
{(7, 'A'): 6, (7, 'B'): 3, (1, 'A'): 7, (1, 'B'): 3, (3, 'B'): 7, (3, 'A'): 3,
 (6, 'B'): 3, (6, 'A'): 1}
```

The resulting DFA has only four states instead of the original eight (Figure 2.9).

2.2 NONDETERMINISTIC FINITE AUTOMATA

The only practically useful DFA we have considered so far is the even binary number detector, shown in Figure 2.4. Its simplicity is deceptive: while it is sometimes possible to design a DFA that recognizes a target language by spending a few minutes with pencil and paper, the task may also turn out to be significantly more challenging.

An obvious source of difficulty in engineering design is the limitations imposed by a designer's toolset. We can achieve more by using more powerful, less restricted instruments. In the case of DFAs, one such limitation is the requirement of determinism: if there is a rule $(1, \mathtt{A}) \rightarrow 2$, it is not allowed to have a conflicting rule, such as $(1, \mathtt{A}) \rightarrow 3$. *Nondeterministic finite automata* (NFAs) do not impose such limitations.[1]

I think the easiest way to understand how such a machine operates is to rely on the concept known as the *many-worlds interpretation* in physics, conceived within the discourse on quantum mechanics. Our everyday life mostly takes place in a classical Newtonian environment, which has a deterministic nature: when flipping a coin,

[1]Either of these devices can be called simply a *finite automaton* (FA) or a *finite state machine* (FSM).

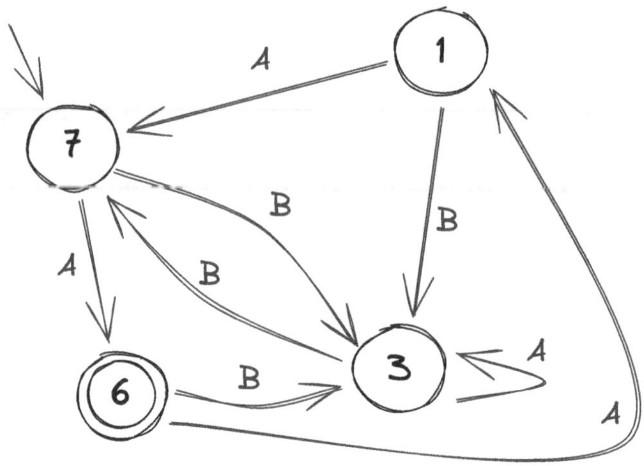

FIGURE 2.9: The minimized example DFA.

we understand that the outcome is not really random. Theoretically, if we know all the physical properties of the coin, of the surface it hits, and the values of the acting forces, we can predict the resulting coin side. In contrast, quantum-level interactions are believed to be random by nature. Furthermore, it is not possible to find out ("observe") the outcome of an interaction without interfering with the process.

One way to deal with a nondeterministic system is to treat its state after the interaction but before the observation as a combination of possible outcomes. When observed, the system "collapses" into a certain state, discarding the rest of the potential outcomes. The most popular example of what this kind of thinking entails is the Schrödinger's cat thought experiment. A radioactive source is placed next to a Geiger counter, rigged to break a flask of poisonous gas if radioactivity is detected. This whole contraption is placed into a sealed box along with a cat. The release of a radioactive particle is a quantum-level process, so according to the logic above, we must treat the state of the box as a combination of both potential outcomes (cat dead / cat alive) until an actual observation is made. Therefore, Schrödinger's cat is dead and alive simultaneously while the box is still closed.

Another option is the "multiverse," a concept based on the ideas of Hugh Everett and popularized by Bryce DeWitt [22]: each quantum interaction triggers the birth of several new universes, each realizing one of the possible outcomes. In DeWitt's words, *"This universe is constantly splitting into a stupendous number of branches, all resulting from the measurement-like interactions between its myriads of components. Moreover, every quantum transition taking place on every star, in every galaxy, in every remote corner of the universe is splitting our local world on earth into myriads of copies of itself."*

Whatever reservations we might have about this view applied to the real world, it is quite handy in the world of nondeterministic finite state machines. Suppose our NFA is facing a situation where three rules, $(5, \mathtt{A}) \to 3$, $(5, \mathtt{A}) \to 7$, and $(5, \mathtt{A}) \to 1$,

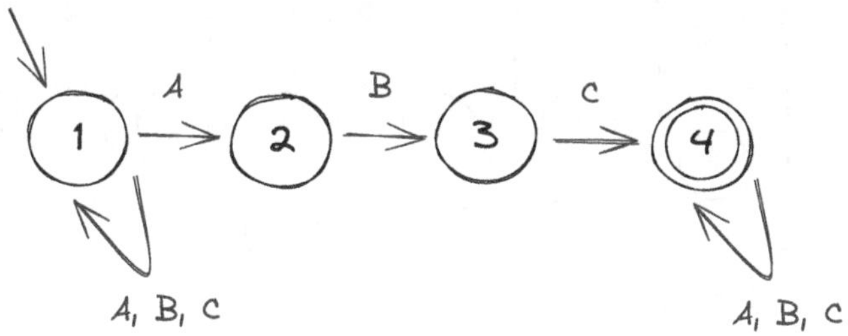

FIGURE 2.10: The NFA-based solution.

require switching to three different states. In a deterministic world, this is a problem, but in a multiverse, such things happen all the time: we'll have three new universes, reflecting three possible decisions. In the first timeline, the NFA will continue operating from state 3. In the second and third timelines, it will continue from states 7 and 1, respectively.

The input is considered to be accepted by an NFA if it is accepted *in at least one* of the timelines. Conversely, the input is rejected if it is rejected *in each* timeline.

Now let's consider a simple example where an NFA is easier to design than a DFA. The task is to create an automaton that accepts all strings over the alphabet $\{\mathtt{A}, \mathtt{B}, \mathtt{C}\}$ containing the substring `ABC`. For instance, the automaton must accept `ABAABCAA` and `AABCCC` but reject `AABBCC` and `ABBBACC`. Here I would ask you to put the book aside and try designing a DFA-based solution. It is not overly complex: only four states are needed.

We will discuss the solution a bit later, and now let's examine the NFA version (Figure 2.10). As an example, consider how this NFA processes the strings `AABBCC` and `AABCCC` (see Figure 2.11), presuming that missing transition rules are treated as rejection of input.

When processing the string `AABBCC`, the NFA has to make a choice at the very first step: move to state 2, according to the rule $(1, \mathtt{A}) \rightarrow 2$, or stay in state 1, as per the rule $(1, \mathtt{A}) \rightarrow 1$. In a multiverse, it can do both. In the first world, the NFA would switch to state 2 and face a missing transition rule for the next input character. In the second world, the NFA would stay in state 1 to face another fork on the road. Both of these new options (state 1 and state 2) turn out to be dead ends: the NFA either stays in state 1 until the end of the input string or shortly faces another missing transition rule.

In contrast, there is a "happy path" for the input string `AABCCC`: the NFA has to choose the rule $(1, \mathtt{A}) \rightarrow 1$ at the first fork and the rule $(1, \mathtt{A}) \rightarrow 2$ immediately after that.

To prove that a certain string is accepted by a given NFA, it is enough to demonstrate the existence of such a "happy path." Some authors talk about "magic" or "clairvoyant" capabilities of NFAs rather than the multiverse [23]. In this mental model, the NFA always chooses the right option when facing a choice. Both ways of thinking are equally good; just pick the one that works best for you. Proving the rejection of

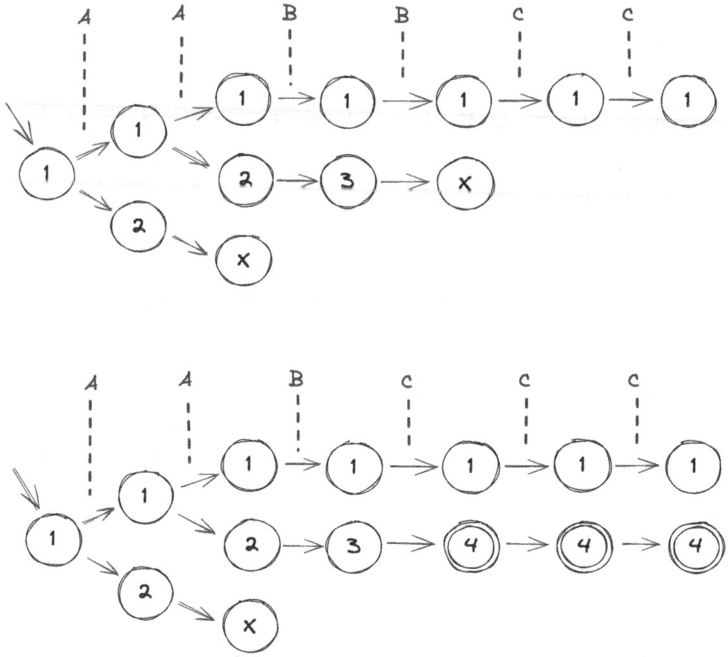

FIGURE 2.11: The strings AABBCC and AABCCC processed by the NFA.

FIGURE 2.12: Connecting the “Even binary” and “ABC substring” automata.

a given input string is harder: in this case, we have to analyze all possible paths and show that none of them is “happy.”

2.2.1 ε-AUTOMATON

Nondeterministic behavior is not the only capability that makes NFAs more convenient than DFAs as design tools. Another useful feature, normally considered to be available in NFAs, is *ε-transitions*.

We have already designed a machine for detecting strings that represent even binary numbers (Figure 2.4). We also have a machine for detecting strings containing the substring ABC (Figure 2.10). Now imagine we are interested in strings that start with an even binary number followed by a sequence containing a substring ABC. Since we already have devices for detecting both these components, it makes sense to connect them in sequence (see Figure 2.12).

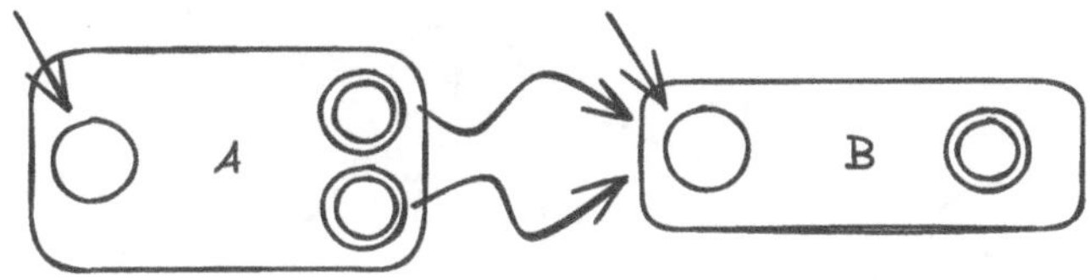

FIGURE 2.13: Connecting automata with multiple favorable states.

What makes this work difficult is the fact that each transition must be labeled with a certain symbol. However, the goal is to connect the two automata seamlessly: no input character should be consumed by the connector transition.

In this particular example, one can simply combine the favorable state of the first automaton and the start state of the second automaton into a single new state. Unfortunately, this approach can be used only if there is a single favorable state. A good solution should work equally well in more complex situations (see Figure 2.13).

An easy way out is to introduce the notion of ε-transitions: since ε stands for an empty string, an ε-labeled transition will denote a transition performed without consuming any input symbols. An automaton containing at least one ε-transition is sometimes called an *ε-automaton*. Such automata are nondeterministic because each ε-transition offers a choice: stay in the current state or move to the new destination state.

An NFA, just like a DFA, can be defined as a five-element tuple: NFA $=$ $(Q, \Sigma, \delta, q_s, F)$. Nondeterministic transitions extend this notion only slightly. In the case of DFAs, the transition function maps a pair (*state*, *symbol*) to a new state: $\delta(q_i, a) = q_j$. In NFAs, ε becomes a legitimate value for a, and the transition function maps a pair (*state*, *symbol*) to a *set* of destination states: $\delta(q_i, a) = \{\tilde{q}, \bar{q}, \hat{q}, \ldots\}$.

2.2.2 DETERMINIZATION OF NFAS

The impressive capabilities of NFAs are undermined by a notable snag: to figure out whether a given input is accepted or rejected, it is necessary to visit every world in the multiverse. DFAs are easy to simulate, but what about NFAs? One way to do it is to draw a chart of all possible timelines and examine them independently, just as we did in Figure 2.11. Another possible solution is to convert the given NFA into an equivalent DFA that recognizes the same language.

It might sound surprising that a clairvoyant or multiverse-backed computational device can be transformed into a mere DFA, but the general idea of this process is actually quite simple [61].

Consider what happens when the NFA from Figure 2.10 processes the string `CABCA`:

```
initially: in state 1
after C: in state 1
after CA: can be in either state 1 or state 2
after CAB: can be in either state 1 or state 3
after CABC: can be in either state 1 or state 4
after CABCA: can be in state 1, 2, or 4
```

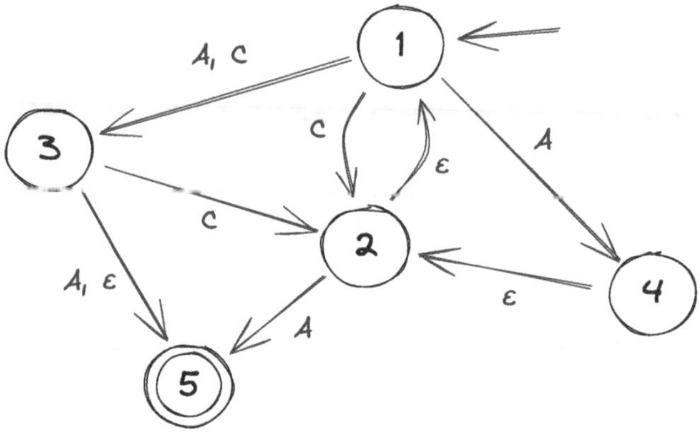

FIGURE 2.14: An example NFA for determinization.

Here we examine all the timelines in the multiverse simultaneously, keeping an updated set of possible states after each subsequent step: $\{1\}$, $\{1\}$, $\{1,2\}$, $\{1,3\}$, $\{1,4\}$, $\{1,2,4\}$. Since $\{1,2,4\}$ includes the accepting state 4, we can conclude that the string CABCA is accepted by the NFA.

Now imagine a DFA with states labeled "$\{1\}$", "$\{1, 2\}$", "$\{1, 3\}$", "$\{1, 4\}$", and "$\{1, 2, 4\}$". Our walk through the timelines is equivalent to the operation of this DFA, switching from "$\{1\}$" to "$\{1, 2\}$" and so forth. If we mark "$\{1, 2, 4\}$" as an accepting state (because it includes 4), the DFA will accept CABCA.

Traversing timelines is more tricky for ε-automata, but the general algorithm, which we will consider in more detail now, remains the same.

2.2.3 NFA DETERMINIZATION ALGORITHM

Let's assume that the states of the source NFA are labeled with integer numbers from 1 to N. The first step of the conversion algorithm would be to generate the states of the DFA to be constructed. These states will represent all possible subsets of the set $\{1, 2, \dots, N\}$, excluding the empty set:

$$\{1\}, \{2\}, \dots, \{N\}, \{1,2\}, \{1,3\}, \dots, \{1,N\}, \dots, \{1,\dots,N\}$$

Now we need to introduce the concept of the *set of states reachable with a certain symbol*. Suppose s is a state and c is a symbol from the input tape. In a DFA, only one destination state corresponds to the combination of a source state and an input symbol, (s, c). In an NFA, conflicting transitions are allowed, so there can be a whole set of states $P(s, c)$, reachable from s by the input symbol c. Another useful set, denoted as $P'(s, c)$, is obtained by extending $P(s, c)$ with all the states reachable from the elements of $P(s, c)$ via one or more ε-transitions.

Figure 2.14 illustrates these concepts. The example NFA can transition from its start state to states 3 and 4 by reading A from the input. Therefore, $P(1, \mathtt{A}) = \{3, 4\}$. States 1 and 2 are reachable from state 4 with ε-transitions. Similarly, an ε-transition leads from state 3 to state 5. Therefore, $P'(1, \texttt{A}) = \{1, 2, 3, 4, 5\}$. By examining transitions in the same way, we can conclude that $P(3, \texttt{C}) = \{2\}$, $P'(3, \texttt{C}) = \{1, 2\}$, $P(1, \texttt{C}) = \{2, 3\}$, and $P'(1, \texttt{C}) = \{1, 2, 3, 5\}$.

Note that P' is constructed by extending P with states reachable from P via ε-transitions. This is why $P'(3, \texttt{C})$, for instance, does not include state 5, even though state 5 is directly reachable from state 3 via an ε-transition. If an NFA does not contain ε-transitions, the corresponding sets P and P' are equal.

If s is the start state of the original NFA, then the start state of the target DFA will be the state labeled with the *ε-closure* of s:

$$\{s\} \cup \{\text{all states reachable from } s \text{ via } \varepsilon\text{-transitions}\}$$

The start state of the NFA shown in Figure 2.14 is state 1. The start state of the corresponding DFA will be $\{1\}$, since state 1 has no outgoing ε-transitions. If the NFA had a rule $(1, \varepsilon) \to 3$, the start state of the corresponding DFA would have been $\{1, 3, 5\}$.

Favorable states of the target DFA are the states constructed from at least one favorable state of the original NFA. The example NFA (Figure 2.14) has only one favorable state, 5. Hence, the following states have to be favorable in the DFA: $\{5\}$, $\{1, 5\}$, $\{2, 5\}$, $\{3, 5\}$, $\{4, 5\}$, $\{1, 2, 5\}$, $\{1, 3, 5\}$, $\{1, 4, 5\}$, $\{2, 3, 5\}$, $\{2, 4, 5\}$, $\{3, 4, 5\}$, $\{1, 2, 3, 5\}$, $\{1, 2, 4, 5\}$, $\{1, 3, 4, 5\}$, $\{2, 3, 4, 5\}$, and $\{1, 2, 3, 4, 5\}$.

The transitions of the DFA are generated with the following procedure:

```
FOR EACH state S of the DFA
    FOR EACH alphabet symbol c
        R = {}
        FOR EACH state component si of S
            R = R ∪ P'(si, c)
        generate rule (S, c) → R
```

The obtained DFA will most likely not be optimal, so it should be processed further with a minimization algorithm.

The rule-generation procedure is designed to perform the following task. We have a certain alphabet symbol c and state S of the target DFA. State S is labeled with a set of states from the original NFA: $S = \{s_1, \ldots, s_k\}$. The goal is to find the states of the original NFA accessible from states $s_1, \ldots, s_k$ via c-labeled transitions and their subsequent ε-transitions. The resulting set of states will form the label of a single target state R of the DFA in the rule $(S, c) \to R$.

As an example, consider two rules obtained during determinization of the NFA shown in Figure 2.14.

Let $S = \{1, 3\}$, $c = \texttt{A}$. Since $P'(1, \texttt{A}) = \{1, 2, 3, 4, 5\}$ and $P'(3, \texttt{A}) = \{5\}$, we'll have $R = P'(1, \texttt{A}) \cup P'(3, \texttt{A}) = \{1, 2, 3, 4, 5\}$. A rule $(\{1, 3\}, \texttt{A}) \to \{1, 2, 3, 4, 5\}$ is generated.

Let $S = \{2, 3, 5\}$, $c = \texttt{C}$. Since $P'(2, \texttt{C}) = \varnothing$, $P'(3, \texttt{C}) = \{1, 2\}$, and $P'(5, \texttt{C}) = \varnothing$, we'll have $R = P'(2, \texttt{C}) \cup P'(3, \texttt{C}) \cup P'(5, \texttt{C}) = \{1, 2\}$. A rule $(\{2, 3, 5\}, \texttt{C}) \to \{1, 2\}$ is generated.

2.2.4 DETERMINIZATION IN PYTHON

Now let's extend our existing minimization code to support both minimization and determinization algorithms.

The easiest way to describe nondeterministic NFA transitions would be to specify a set of possible destination states instead of a single state and to allow empty strings as input characters:

```
dfa = FA(
    defaultdict(
        int,
        {
            (8, "A"): 2,
            (8, "B"): 5,
            ...
        },
    ),
    {6},
    7,
)

nfa = FA(
    defaultdict(
        set,
        {
            (1, ""): {3}, # epsilon-transition
            (1, "A"): {3, 4}, # nondeterministic transitions
            (1, "C"): {3, 2},
            ...
        },
    ),
    {5},
    1,
)
```

Note that we need `defaultdict` to produce an empty set instead of zero in case of a missing transition, so we'll have to store NFA rules in a `defaultdict(set)` object.

We will also have to modify the `states()` method to support both types of automata:

```
class FA:
    ...

    def states(self):
        src = {s for (s, _) in self.rules.keys()}
        all_dst = (self.rules[(s, c)] for s in src for c in self.symbols())
        all_dst_sets = ({d} if isinstance(d, int) else d for d in all_dst)
        dst = set().union(*all_dst_sets)

        return src | dst
```

Here each element of `all_dst` can be either an integer or a set, so we convert integers to sets and combine the resulting sets into the final set of possible destination states dst. Since union() takes the elements to be combined as separate arguments, it is necessary to unpack all_dst_sets into arguments using the asterisk operator (*).[2]

The complete determinization algorithm is shown in Listing 2.2.

Listing 2.2: DFA determinization.

```
@dataclass
class FA:
    rules: defaultdict
    favs: set
    start: int

    def states(self):
        ...

    def symbols(self):
        ...

    def e_reachable_by(self, state, symbol):
        r = set()
        for s in self.rules[(state, symbol)]:
            r.add(s)
            r.update(self.e_reachable(s))
        return r

    def e_reachable(self, state):
        Q = {state}
        reachable = {state}
        checked = set()
        while Q:
            S = Q.pop()
            checked.add(S)
            new_reachable = self.rules[(S, "")] - reachable
            reachable.update(new_reachable)
            Q.update(new_reachable - checked)
        return reachable

    def dfa_states(self, nfa_states, dfa_state):
        if not nfa_states:
            yield dfa_state
        else:
            x = nfa_states.pop()
            yield from self.dfa_states(nfa_states, dfa_state)
            yield from self.dfa_states(nfa_states, dfa_state | {x})
            nfa_states.add(x)

    def determinize(self):
        cnt = 1
        R = {}
        stateid = {}

        for s in self.dfa_states(self.states(), set()):
            stateid[FS(s)] = cnt
```

[2]See https://docs.python.org/3/reference/expressions.html#expression-lists

```
            cnt += 1
            for c in self.symbols() - {""}:
                rlist = [self.e_reachable_by(si, c) for si in s]
                R[(FS(s), c)] = FS().union(*rlist)

        nstart = {self.start} | self.e_reachable(self.start)
        nrules = {(stateid[s], c): stateid[v] for (s, c), v in R.items()}

        self.favs = {v for k, v in stateid.items() if k & self.favs}
        self.start = stateid[FS(nstart)]
        self.rules = defaultdict(int, nrules)
```

The core of this program is just a few lines long. It corresponds to the rule-generating procedure shown in the pseudocode above:

```
for s in self.dfa_states(self.states(), set()):
    ...
    for c in self.symbols() - {""}:
        rlist = [self.e_reachable_by(si, c) for si in s]
        R[(FS(s), c)] = FS().union(*rlist)
```

Here we generate a rule for every combination of `s` and `c`, excluding the empty string. The destination state `R` is obtained by calling `e_reachable_by()`, which calculates $P'(s_i, c)$. Note that sets are converted into frozensets where necessary.

Now let's proceed to the more tricky parts. The function `dfa_states()` generates all the states of the resulting DFA. They are represented with sets of integers, which is fine for the algorithm but inconvenient as a final output. To convert these sets into integers, we'll assign each set a unique ID:

```
stateid[FS(s)] = cnt
cnt += 1
```

These IDs will replace sets at the final stages of determinization. Generating the resulting start state is easy. It is simply the union of the original start state and all ε-reachable states from it:

```
nstart = {self.start} | self.e_reachable(self.start)
self.start = stateid[FS(nstart)]
```

Obtaining the resulting favorable states is a bit less straightforward:

```
self.favs = {v for k, v in stateid.items() if k & self.favs}
```

Here `k` is a set of integers representing a temporary DFA state label. If it produces a non-empty intersection with `self.favs`, the corresponding state `stateid[k]` has to become a favorable state of the resulting DFA.

The value of $P(s, c)$ in our case is produced directly by `self.rules[(s, c)]`. Consequently, to obtain $P'(s, c)$ in `e_reachable_by()`, we combine the states taken from `self.rules` with their ε-reachable neighbors. The approach employed by `e_reachable(state)` is similar to the one used in the unreachable state detection routine of the minimization algorithm. We check the immediate ε-reachable neighborhood of `state` and add the retrieved neighboring states to the set `Q` for further inspection, excluding previously checked states. The resulting set of visited ε-reachable states is returned to the caller.

The temporary states of the resulting DFA are created by the generator function `dfa_states()`. It is somewhat tricky because 1) it is a generator, and 2) it is recursive.

The task of a generator function is to obtain the next element in the requested sequence and `yield` it back to the caller. When the sequence ends, nothing needs to be generated. In our case, each `yield` has to return a previously unseen element from the sequence

$$\varnothing, \{1\}, \{2\}, \ldots, \{N\}, \{1,2\}, \{1,3\}, \ldots, \{1,N\}, \ldots, \{1,\ldots,N\}$$

The generator receives two arguments: the set of NFA states to be processed (`nfa_states`) and the (initially empty) set `dfa_state` that will become the next element in the sequence of generated DFA states. When all NFA states are processed, `nfa_states` becomes empty, and the obtained `dfa_state` can be yielded to the caller. In the opposite case, we have to do the following:

```
create a copy of nfa_states for subsequent operations
take out one (arbitrary) element from the copy of nfa_states
consider sequences that do not include this element
consider sequences that include this element
```

The set `nfa_states` is like a bag of colored balls, and our task is to produce every possible combination of them. The algorithm picks a ball and faces a choice: either include it in the resulting combination or leave it out. To generate all possibilities, both options are explored recursively for every ball until the bag is empty. Choosing to include no balls generates an empty set, while always including every ball yields the complete collection. All other choices lead to a partial combination. In our case, the state corresponding to the empty set is not strictly necessary, but any redundant states will be removed by the minimization algorithm. Note that calling a generator from another generator in Python requires the `yield from` expression.[3]

It is important to make sure that manipulations with `nfa_states` do not affect its content in alternative branches. For example, suppose we have a half-empty bag of balls and a partial resulting combination of balls on the table. We take the next ball from the bag and examine both paths—with and without this ball in the resulting combination. However, this is not the end: the bag was originally half-empty because we were exploring the consequences of a certain choice made before that. Therefore, we have to place the ball back in the bag and return to the previous step to examine alternatives.

The combination of determinization and minimization works great for the example device shown in Figure 2.14. It gets trimmed down from five to merely two states:

---

[3]More details at https://docs.python.org/3/whatsnew/3.3.html#pep-380

```
...
nfa = FA(
    defaultdict(
        set,
        {
            (1, "A"): {3, 4},
            (1, "C"): {3, 2},
            (2, ""): {1},
            (2, "A"): {5},
            (3, "A"): {5},
            (3, "C"): {2},
            (3, ""): {5},
            (4, ""): {2},
        },
    ),
    {5},
    1,
)

nfa.determinize()
nfa.minimize()
print(nfa.start) # 17
print(nfa.favs) # {30}
print(nfa.rules) # {(17, 'C'): 30, (17, 'A'): 30, (30, 'C'): 30, (30, 'A'): 30}
```

Now let's consider a more interesting example: the NFA for detecting ABC-containing strings (Figure 2.10). By applying determinization and minimization, we obtain the device shown in Figure 2.15:

```
...
nfa = FA(
    defaultdict(
        set,
        {
            (1, "A"): {1, 2},
            (1, "B"): {1},
            (1, "C"): {1},
            (2, "B"): {3},
            (3, "C"): {4},
            (4, "A"): {4},
            (4, "B"): {4},
            (4, "C"): {4},
        },
    ),
    {4},
    1,
)

nfa.determinize()
nfa.minimize()
print(nfa.start) # 9
print(nfa.favs) # {14}
print(nfa.rules) # {(9, 'B'): 9, (9, 'A'): 10, (9, 'C'): 9, (10, 'B'): 13,
# (10, 'A'): 10, (10, 'C'): 9, (14, 'B'): 14, (14, 'A'): 14, (14, 'C'): 14,
# (13, 'B'): 9, (13, 'A'): 10, (13, 'C'): 14}
```

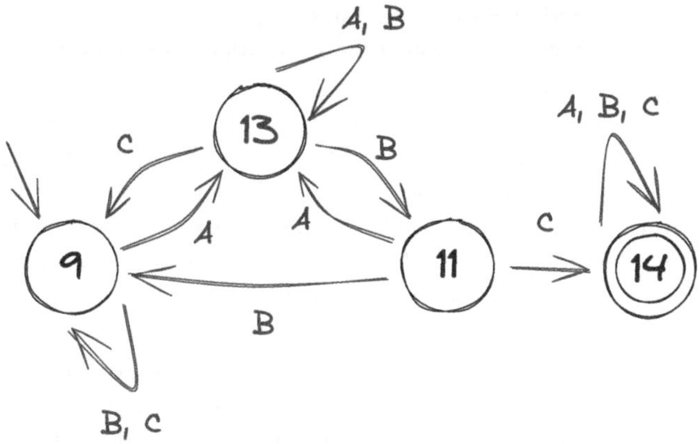

FIGURE 2.15: A DFA for detecting strings with the substring ABC.

While it has only four states, the task of designing it manually is far from trivial, so the intermediate NFA version is quite helpful here. Let's also note that we were lucky to get such a small resulting solution: a DFA equivalent of a four-state NFA may require up to $2^4 - 1 = 15$ states.

2.2.5 SIMULATING NFAS

Determinization opens the possibility of running NFAs on a regular computer: we need to convert an NFA to a DFA, minimize it, and then use the DFA simulator described above. Another option would be to simulate an NFA directly by visiting all alternative timelines to find out their outcomes. This method is similar to the one used to generate all the subsets of the set of NFA states. Every splitting world is like a crossroad, but instead of following just one path, the simulator has to examine all of them.

Imagine a natural way to investigate every nook in a maze. An adventurer would move along the chosen path to the next crossroad, place a "breadcrumb" there, and start methodically exploring all possible directions, for example, in a clockwise order. If a certain path ends with another crossroad, it would have to be explored in the same manner. Alternatively, if the path leads to a dead end or to a breadcrumb-marked crossroad (meaning it was explored before), the adventurer would backtrack to the previous crossroad and choose the next path to try.

Breadcrumbs are essential to this method of exploration (known as *depth-first search*). It might seem they merely save some legwork, but their primary purpose is to prevent going in circles. Suppose the adventurer arrives at a crossroad and chooses the leftmost path to continue. How to make sure it is not the same crossroad and not the same path as the one taken ten minutes ago? There is no way to tell without breadcrumbs.

To apply depth-first search to the task of simulating NFAs, we need to understand what kinds of entities represent "paths" and "crossroads" in this case. Intuitively, paths are transitions and crossroads are states, but this is not quite right. Note, for example, that an automaton can revisit the same state over and over again during its normal operation (Figure 2.4).

Consecutive visits to the same state are different because the content of the input tape changes over time. In a DFA, each step removes one symbol from the input tape, so there is no danger in circular routes: eventually, all the symbols are going to be processed, ending the simulation. Stretching the maze metaphor further, imagine that the goal of our adventurer is to find a certain mysterious artifact that appears only at a very specific time of day. In such a situation, it would be reasonable to revisit an empty crossroad at some later time because, in a sense, it would not be the same crossroad.[4] This observation helps to see that the real crossroad is a combination of the current state and the current content of the input tape, represented by the pair (*state*, *tape*). The only way to revisit the same crossroad would be to "teleport" using one or more ε-transitions.

Listing Listing 2.3 shows a simple depth-first-search-based NFA simulator with breadcrumbs guarding ε-transitions. Its "heart" is the generator function `accepts_gen()` that returns the outcome of the next explored NFA timeline. Its caller, `accepts()`, returns `True` as soon as it identifies a path ending in a favorable state. `False` is returned if no such path exists.

Listing 2.3: NFA simulation with depth-first search.

```
from dataclasses import dataclass
from collections import defaultdict


@dataclass
class FA:
    rules: defaultdict
    favs: set
    start: int

    def accepts(self, input):
        return any(self.accepts_gen(input, self.start, 0, set()))

    def accepts_gen(self, input, state, i, visited):
        visited.add((state, i))
        for s in self.rules[(state, "")]:
            if (s, i) not in visited:
                yield from self.accepts_gen(input, s, i, visited)
        visited.remove((state, i))

        if i == len(input):
            yield state in self.favs
        else:
            for s in self.rules[(state, input[i])]:
                yield from self.accepts_gen(input, s, i + 1, visited)
```

[4] I have to add that backtracking to the previous crossroad in this new metaphor would also mean *going back in time*.

```
# NFA for detecting strings containing "ABC"
nfa = FA(
    defaultdict(
        set,
        {
            (1, "A"): {1, 2},
            (1, "B"): {1},
            (1, "C"): {1},
            (2, "B"): {3},
            (3, "C"): {4},
            (4, "A"): {4},
            (4, "B"): {4},
            (4, "C"): {4},
        },
    ),
    {4},
    1,
)

print(nfa.accepts("ACBAAA"))  # prints False
print(nfa.accepts("ACBABCAA"))  # prints True
```

The NFA simulator is a good example of a classic time-memory tradeoff. The determinization algorithm has *exponential* time complexity: for an NFA of N states, it might need to produce up to $2^N - 1$ states for the resulting DFA, meaning it has to perform at least this number of operations. The DFA itself would consume exponentially more memory than the original NFA. On the other hand, it processes input strings in linear time. In contrast, direct NFA simulation does not require determinization or extra memory, but following all possible timelines in the multiverse might take exponential time.

2.2.6 NFA Q&A

Nondeterministic devices deserve their own quick Q&A section.

Q: What do nondeterministic transitions provide apart from making the task of designing finite state machines a bit easier?

A: Some FA-generating algorithms can be made simpler if nondeterministic transitions are allowed. Simulating a certain NFA directly might be the only viable option to run it if the corresponding DFA requires too much memory.

However, since any NFA can be theoretically converted to a DFA, nondeterministic transitions do not give NFAs any extra string-recognition power. If a certain language can be recognized by an NFA, it can be recognized by a DFA as well.

Q: We usually talk about languages "consisting of even binary numbers" or "consisting of strings containing the substring ABC." Is it possible to design a device that accepts every string *except* an even binary number or every string that *does not* contain the substring ABC?

A: This is an excellent but surprisingly simple exercise. If a certain language L is recognized by a given DFA, the *complement* language $\Sigma^* - L$ is recognized by a "complement" DFA that can be constructed as follows:

1. Make sure the original DFA is complete.
2. Swap its favorable and non-favorable states.

Note that this approach only works for DFAs, so if your source automaton is nondeterministic, it has to be determinized first. If the source automaton is incomplete, you'll need to complete it with a non-favorable "sink" state that will become favorable in the resulting device.

Q: The NFA simulator has to take special care of ε-transitions. Is it possible to leverage the power of NFAs without having to deal with them?

A: Indeed, some algorithms can be made simpler if we presume that each transition reads exactly one symbol from the input tape. A compromise between a DFA and an NFA would be an NFA without ε-transitions. Some variations of the NFA determinization algorithm include ε-transition removal as a preliminary step, but it is also possible to consider it as a separate useful procedure [24, Sec. 1.4.2].

2.3 STATE MACHINES IN JFLAP

Python is a handy tool for exploring basic FSM-related algorithms, but a more specialized solution can often provide greater convenience. For instance, the capability to simulate and transform state machines *drawn* on the screen rather than represented as Python data structures would have been convenient. This feature, along with other useful instruments designed specifically for students of the theory of computation, is implemented in the open-source software JFLAP.[5] Let's explore some of its FA-related capabilities.

At the time of writing, the most up-to-date version of JFLAP is 7.1. When launched, it displays the start screen, shown in Figure 2.16. For now, let's proceed with the **Finite Automaton** option.

The next screen shows a working area for placing states and transitions. Nondeterministic and ε-transitions are allowed. The circular toolbar button activates **State Creator** mode. Every mouse click in this mode creates one additional automaton state. By right-clicking a state in **Attribute Editor** mode (the "pointer" toolbar button), it is possible to make it **Final** (favorable) or **Initial** (see Figure 2.17). To delete a state, click it while in **Deleter** mode (the "skull and crossbones" toolbar button).

The "arrow" toolbar button activates **Transition Creator** mode. To make a transition, click and hold the left mouse button on the source state, drag the mouse to the destination state, release the button, and input a transition label. An empty label corresponds to an ε-transition, actually called a lambda (λ) transition in JFLAP. To make a transition from a certain state back to the same state, you'll need to perform a simple trick: hold the left mouse button, drag the mouse a bit, and release it over

[5] Available at https://www.jflap.org. You'll need to have Java 8 installed to run JFLAP.

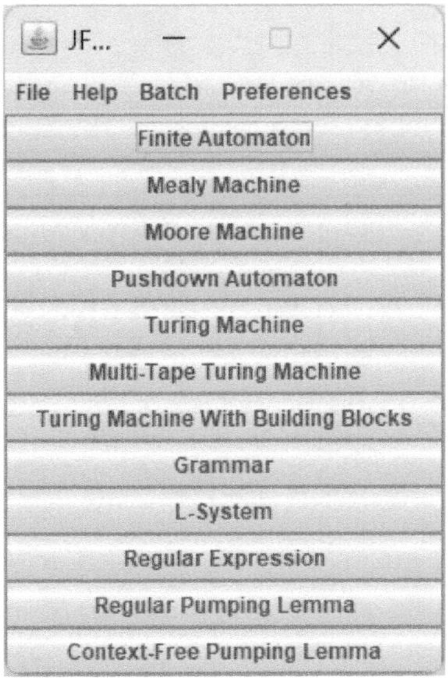

FIGURE 2.16: The JFLAP start screen.

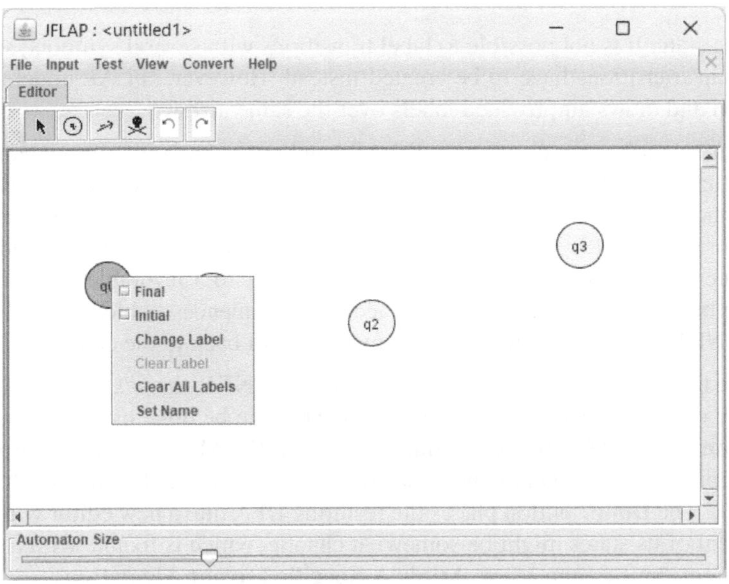

FIGURE 2.17: Creating states in JFLAP.

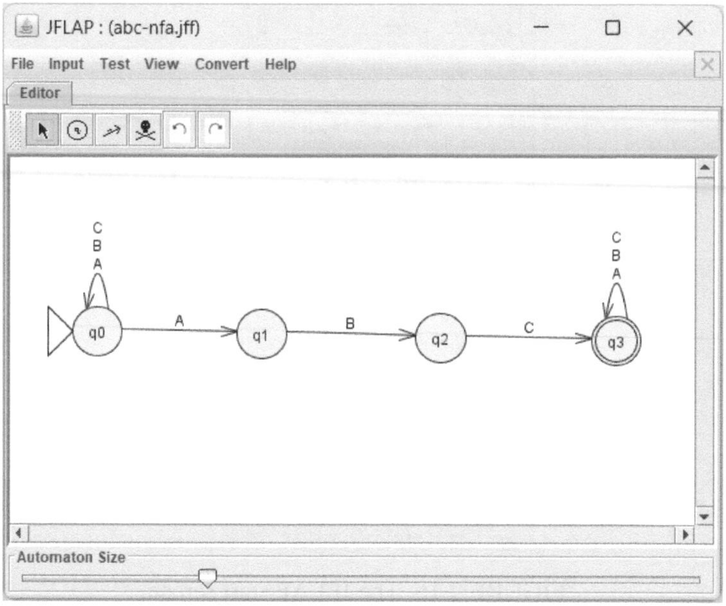

FIGURE 2.18: An NFA for detecting strings with a substring `ABC` (JFLAP version).

the same state. It is not possible to label transitions with several symbols; several independent transitions have to be created instead. However, JFLAP understands the intention and draws all provided labels over the same arrow.

As an example, let's check how JFLAP handles the `ABC` substring-detecting NFA (see Figure 2.18). To make it process an input string, use the **Input, Fast Run** menu option and enter the tape content. The result of processing the input string `AAABCCA` is shown in Figure 2.19. JFLAP both informs the user about the outcome and displays the sequence of transitions moving the automaton into a favorable state. The **Keep looking** button tries to find alternative accepting sequences (which is possible in the case of NFAs). The **I'm done** button returns control back to the editor.

Since the device we are experimenting with is an NFA, the next natural step would be to try out the determinization algorithm. This can be done using the menu **Convert, Convert to DFA**. Being an educational tool, JFLAP visualizes the process step by step, but you can just click the **Complete** button to obtain the final result (see Figure 2.20). The **Done?** button places the resulting DFA into a new editor window. The placement of its states might be somewhat chaotic, which is fixable with a choice of layout algorithms (menu **View, Apply A Specific Layout Algorithm**).

After determinization, it makes sense to minimize the obtained DFA. In JFLAP, this is done via the menu **Convert, Minimize DFA**. DFAs with missing transitions will be automatically completed. This is not necessary in our case, so we can proceed straight to minimization. This process can be performed step by step as well, but you

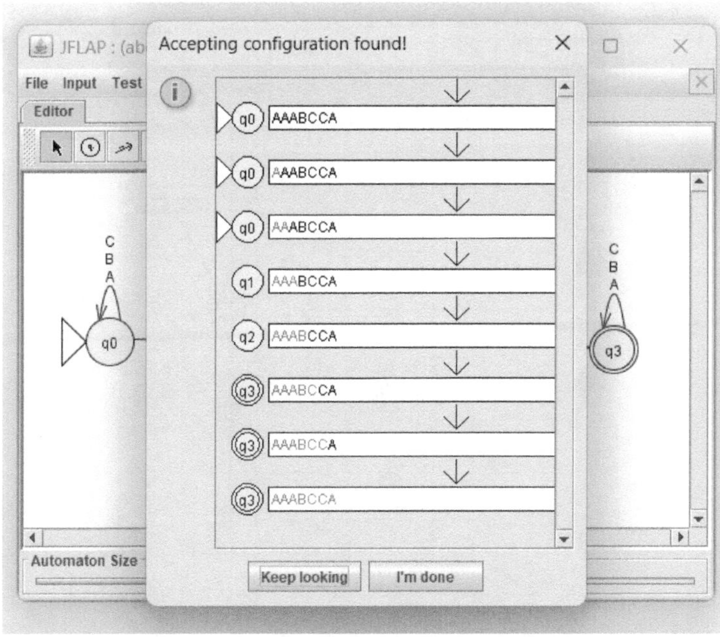

FIGURE 2.19: Processing the input string AAABCCA.

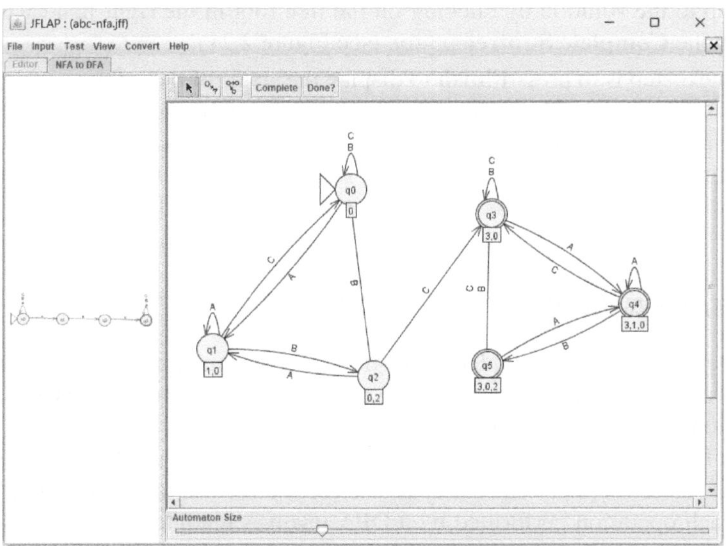

FIGURE 2.20: NFA determinization with JFLAP.

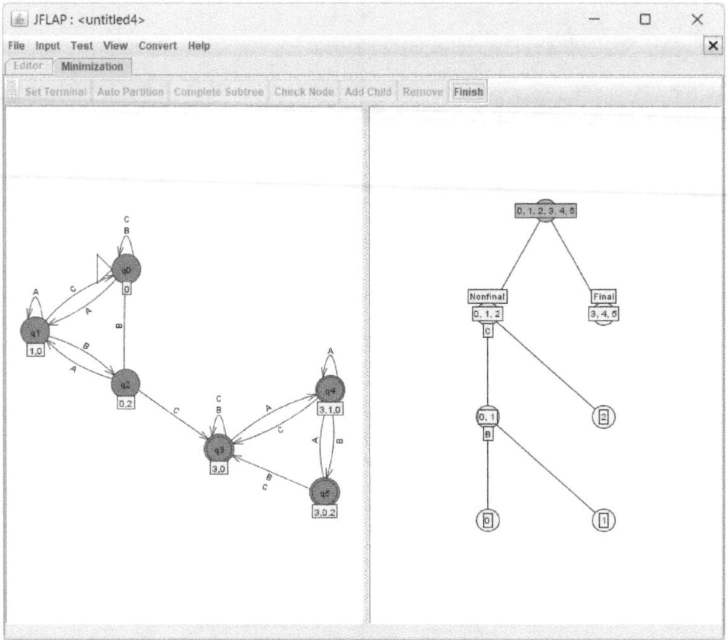

FIGURE 2.21: DFA minimization in JFLAP.

can jump to the solution by clicking on the tree root in the right-hand window and pressing the **Complete Subtree** button (see Figure 2.21).

The next step is to press **Finish** to display the states of the minimized DFA. Once again, JFLAP offers an interactive exercise, which can be skipped by pressing **Complete**. Finally, the **Done?** button places the resulting DFA into a new editor window (see Figure 2.22). Note that the resulting automaton is an exact copy of the version obtained with our Python program (Figure 2.15).

2.4 TAKEAWAYS

1. Deterministic and nondeterministic finite automata are our new tools for describing formal languages. The only other option we have discussed previously was regular expressions.
2. A DFA can be treated as a kind of "computer-like" device. It can be designed on a sheet of paper and easily transformed into a runnable program.
3. Each operation performed by a DFA involves reading exactly one symbol from the input tape, meaning that processing the whole tape takes linear time (proportional to the length of the input).
4. Nondeterministic behavior, surprisingly, does not increase the expressive power of finite state machines: NFAs recognize the same class of languages

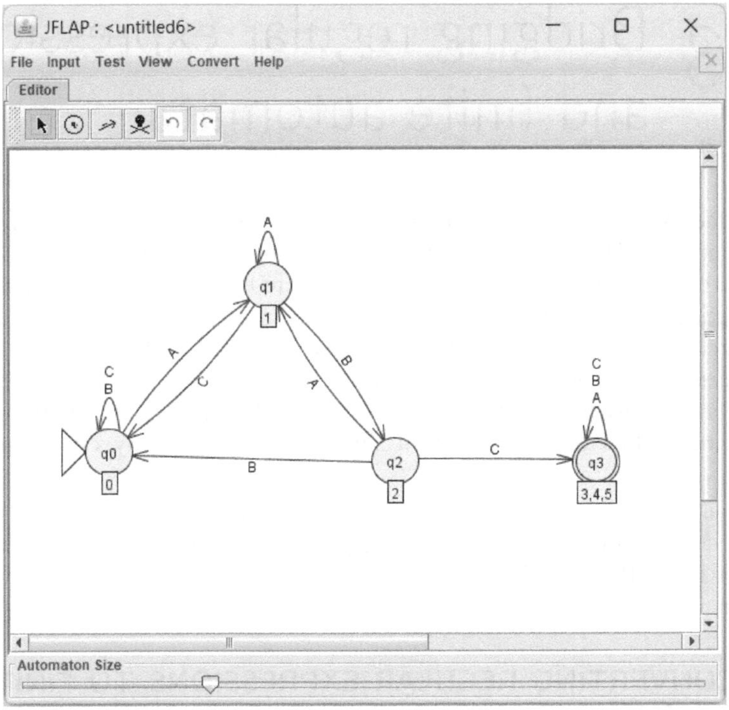

FIGURE 2.22: The minimized DFA in JFLAP.

as DFAs. However, nondeterministic transitions can help to obtain smaller and simpler automata.

5. A DFA can be minimized (in terms of its state count) using a well-defined formal procedure. Minimization does not affect the DFA's functionality.
6. An NFA can be executed on a computer directly, but in the worst case, one run of such a simulator might take exponential time (proportional to 2^N, where N is the length of the input).
7. An NFA can be determinized. This operation may result in a significant (exponential) increase in the number of states, but the execution time of the obtained DFA is guaranteed to be linear.

3 Bridging regular expressions and finite automata

One of the examples in the previous chapter featured a DFA for recognizing even binary numbers. The language of even binary numbers is also easy to describe with a regular expression: `[01]*0`. This case shows there is a certain overlap between regular languages, describable with regular expressions, and the languages that can be recognized by finite state machines. An important result in the theory of computation, *Kleene's theorem* [40], asserts that there is a *complete equivalence* rather than a mere overlap between these language classes. In other words, any language that can be described with a regular expression can also be recognized by a finite automaton, and vice versa.[1]

Formal proofs are generally outside the scope of this book. However, in this case, the equivalence of these language classes can be shown by developing actual procedures for FA-to-RE and RE-to-FA conversion. These procedures are well worth our attention.

3.1 CONVERTING REGULAR EXPRESSIONS TO FINITE AUTOMATA

According to the definition from the first chapter, regular expressions are:

- The elements $\varnothing$, ε, and any source alphabet symbols.
- The expressions $(a \cup b)$, (ab), and (a^*), where a and b are regular expressions.

Using these "atoms," it is possible to construct any complex regular expression. Therefore, to convert regular expressions into FAs, we have to learn how to represent each "atom" as a finite state machine separately.

The devices corresponding to $\varnothing$, ε, and individual alphabet symbols are simple (see Figure 3.1). Now imagine we have two finite automata, a and b, and we need to combine them to obtain $(a \cup b)$, (ab), and (a^*).

Alternation is achieved by creating ε-transitions to both a and b from a newly created start state S (see Figure 3.2). All favorable states of a and b remain favorable in the resulting automaton.

Suppose the input of this FA can be accepted by b. Nondeterministic ε-transitions create a multiverse of two timelines. In the first timeline, the input is processed and rejected by a. In the second timeline, it is processed and accepted by b and, therefore,

[1]Naturally, this is true for "theoretical" regular expressions, which have no additional means such as backreferences.

DOI: 10.1201/9781032614991-3

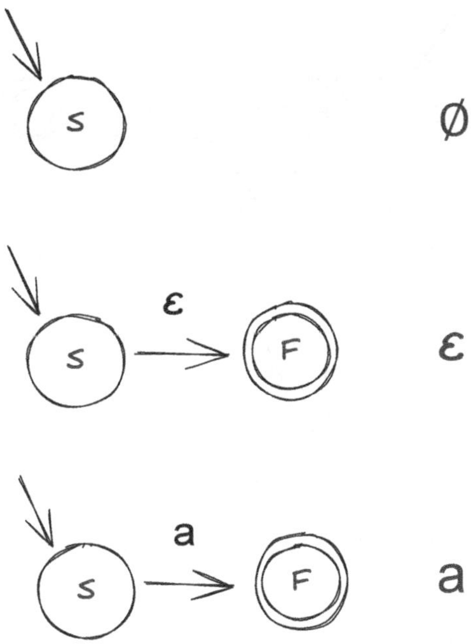

FIGURE 3.1: FAs recognizing ∅, ε, and single alphabet symbols.

is accepted by the FA. As a result, the combined FA accepts any string that is accepted either by *a* or by *b*.

Concatenation is achieved by connecting *a* and *b* sequentially: all favorable states of *a* are made non-favorable and are connected to the start state of *b* with ε-transitions, then the start state of *a* becomes the start state of the combined FA (see Figure 3.3).

The last remaining operation (Kleene star) is a bit more tricky. Since it means "zero or more occurrences of *a*," the start state of the combined FA must be favorable. Every occurrence of *a* has to leave the FA in a favorable state as well. This is achieved by creating a new state *S* (both start and favorable) and connecting it to *a*. All favorable

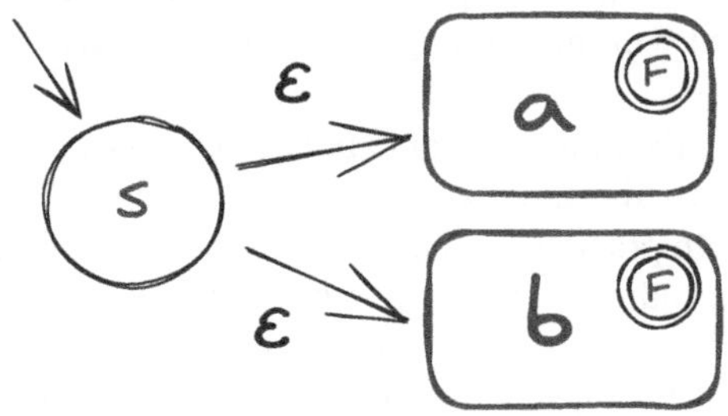

FIGURE 3.2: The FA for the expression $(a \cup b)$.

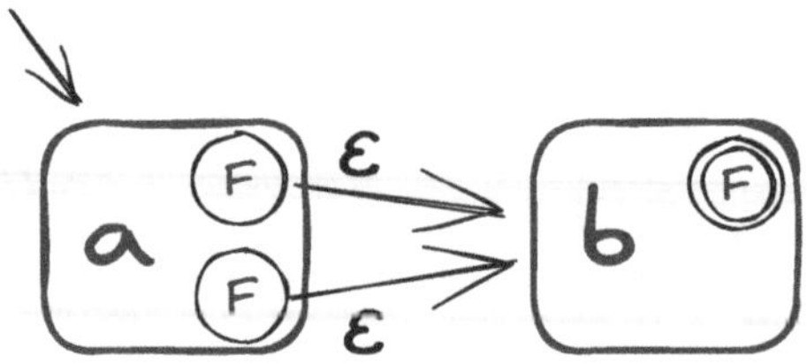

FIGURE 3.3: The FA for the expression (ab).

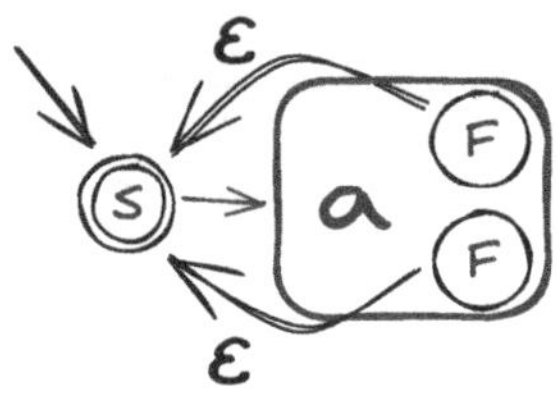

FIGURE 3.4: The FA for the expression (a^*).

states of a are marked as non-favorable and connected to S with ε-transitions (see Figure 3.4).

Equipped with these diagrams (forming the *McNaughton-Yamada-Thompson algorithm* [2, Sec. 3.7.4]), we can consider a simple conversion example. Let's build a finite automaton corresponding to the regular expression $(\mathtt{x} \cup \mathtt{y})^* \mathtt{z}$. According to the rules of precedence, the first operation to be performed here is alternation, followed by the star, and, finally, by concatenation. It is easiest to add new parts to our FA in the same order.

We'll start with two automata, recognizing the individual symbols x and y. In the next step, they are joined according to Figure 3.2, forming a device able to recognize $\mathtt{x} \cup \mathtt{y}$. Following the procedure for the remaining operations, we'll obtain the resulting FA (see Figure 3.5).

The design of this FA is far from exemplary, but determinization and minimization with JFLAP make wonders, producing a state machine of merely two states (see Figure 3.6).

Our Python version of the same procedure generates three states because it builds a complete automaton with no missing transitions. In effect, it produces the device shown in Figure 3.7.

The constituents of the input regular expression can be processed in any order, but it is necessary to identify the argument(s) of each operation that appears in the regular expression correctly. In practice, this means that the converting procedure should be able to recognize parentheses and take into account the precedence of operations. This task of *parsing* the input regular expression is not considered to be a part of the McNaughton-Yamada-Thompson algorithm. We will discuss parsing in Chapter 7.

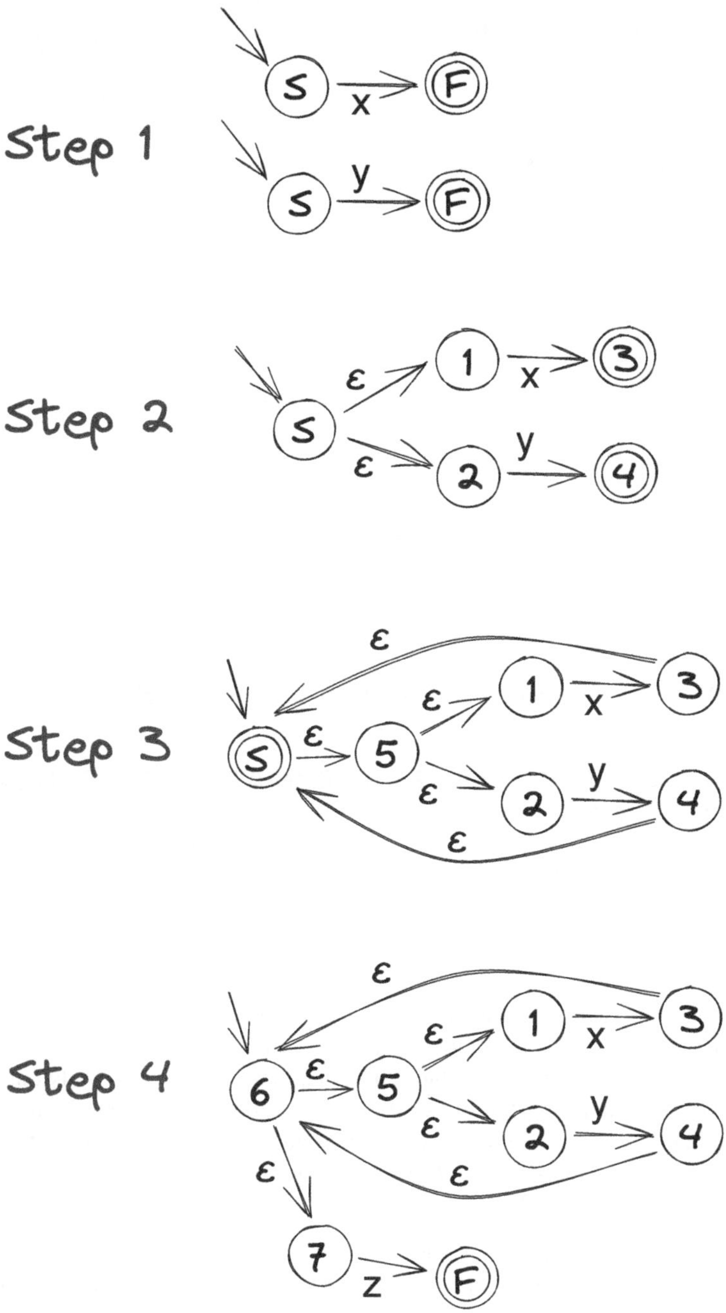

FIGURE 3.5: The FA for the expression $(x \cup y)^*z$.

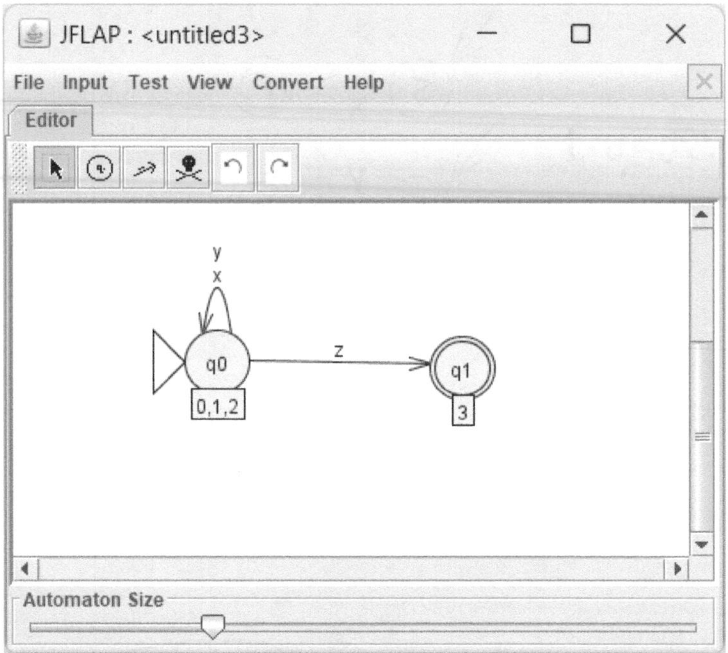

FIGURE 3.6: The minimized DFA for the expression $(\mathrm{x} \cup \mathrm{y})^*\mathrm{z}$ (JFLAP version).

3.2 CONVERTING FINITE AUTOMATA TO REGULAR EXPRESSIONS

The inverse process of deriving a regular expression from a given FA is not as straightforward but is still quite simple.

It starts with two preprocessing steps:

1. Removing transitions to the start state. The original FA must not contain transitions to its start state S. If this rule is violated, it is necessary to create a new start state S' and add the transition rule $(S', \varepsilon) \to S$.
2. Removing extra favorable states. The original FA must have only one favorable state, and this state must not have outgoing transitions. If this rule is violated, it is necessary to create a new favorable state F', mark the original favorable states $F_1, \ldots, F_n$ as non-favorable, and add the transition rules $(F_1, \varepsilon) \to F', \ldots, (F_n, \varepsilon) \to F'$.

Note that a transition from a state to itself is considered both incoming and outgoing, so FAs with a transition from the start state back to the start state or from a favorable state back to a favorable state require the steps described above.

The general idea of the conversion algorithm is to remove FA states (except S' and F') one by one, replacing the associated transitions according to the following rules:

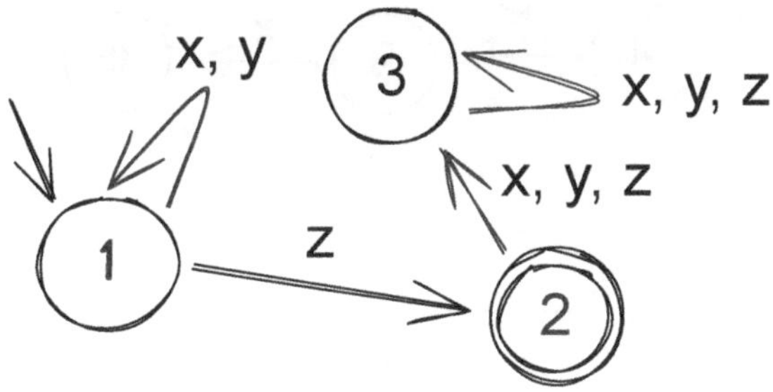

FIGURE 3.7: The minimized DFA for the expression $(x \cup y)^*z$ (complete version).

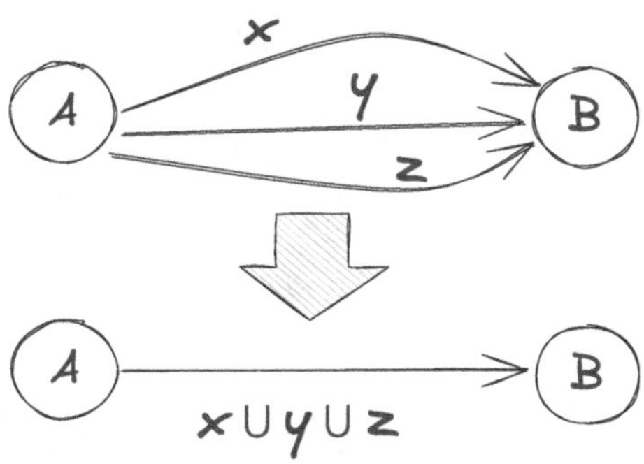

FIGURE 3.8: "Compressing" multiple transitions.

1. Multiple transitions from A to B are "compressed" into a single transition labeled with an alternation of the original labels (see Figure 3.8).
2. A pair of transitions $(A, x) \to B$ and $(B, z) \to C$ is replaced with a transition $(A, xz) \to C$ (see Figure 3.9).
3. A triple of transitions $(A, x) \to B$, $(B, y) \to B$, and $(B, z) \to C$ is replaced with a transition $(A, xy^*z) \to C$ (see Figure 3.10).
4. A state with no associated transitions is removed.

As soon as the resulting diagram has only one transition left (it should connect S' with F'), the conversion procedure is over. The label of this remaining transition is the final regular expression. It can be simplified further by removing any ε symbol that is part of a concatenation (because $\varepsilon s = s\varepsilon = s$). Further simplifications are possible, but they are not as easy to achieve.

Let's consider the process of FA-to-RE conversion using the automaton shown in Figure 3.5 as an example (recall that it was obtained from the regular expression $(x \cup y)^*z$). The states to be removed on each step are shown in gray (see Figure 3.11 and Figure 3.12).

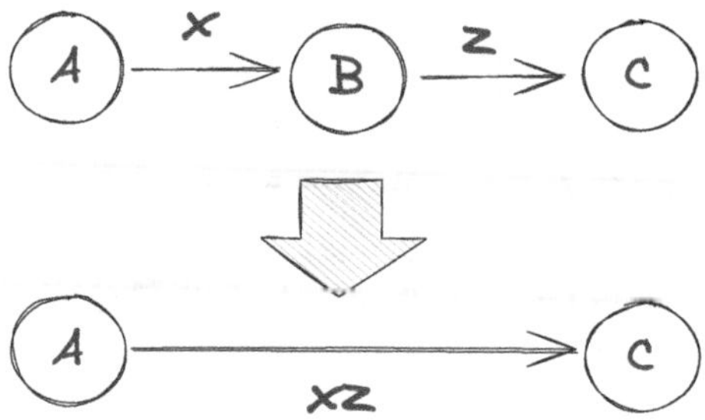

FIGURE 3.9: Replacing transitions A → B and B → C with a regular expression.

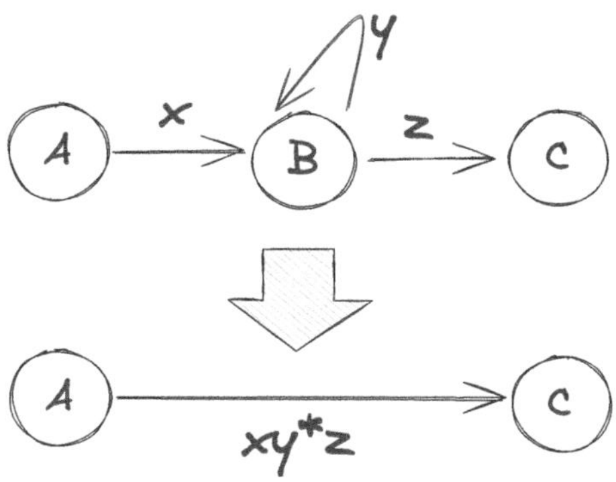

FIGURE 3.10: Replacing transitions A → B, B → B, and B → C with a regular expression.

3.3 CONVERSION FUNCTIONS IN JFLAP

If you want to experiment a bit more with FA-to-RE and RE-to-FA conversion procedures, you can rely on JFLAP. As an example, let's convert the `ABC` substring-detecting NFA (Figure 2.10) into a regular expression. Choose **Finite Automaton** in the JFLAP start screen and create the NFA to be converted. Next, select the **Convert, Convert FA to RE** menu option and keep pressing **Do It** until you see the message "Generalized Transition Graph Finished!" If you press **Do It** once again, JFLAP will respond with a less polite message box: "You're done. Go away." Press **Export** to open the resulting regular expression in a new window (see Figure 3.13).

Note that JFLAP uses + to denote alternation, so the resulting regular expression is actually $(\texttt{A} \cup \texttt{B} \cup \texttt{C})^*\texttt{ABC}(\texttt{A} \cup \texttt{B} \cup \texttt{C})^*$.

To convert a regular expression to a finite state machine, go back to the start screen and select **Regular Expression**. Type your expression in the input field and select **Convert, Convert to NFA**. If you need to input the empty string symbol ε (or λ, in JFLAP conventions), just type an exclamation mark instead. For example, `(A+!)*` is the JFLAP version of $(\texttt{A} \cup \varepsilon)^*$. Press **Do All** in the next window and **Export** to copy the obtained machine into a new working area.

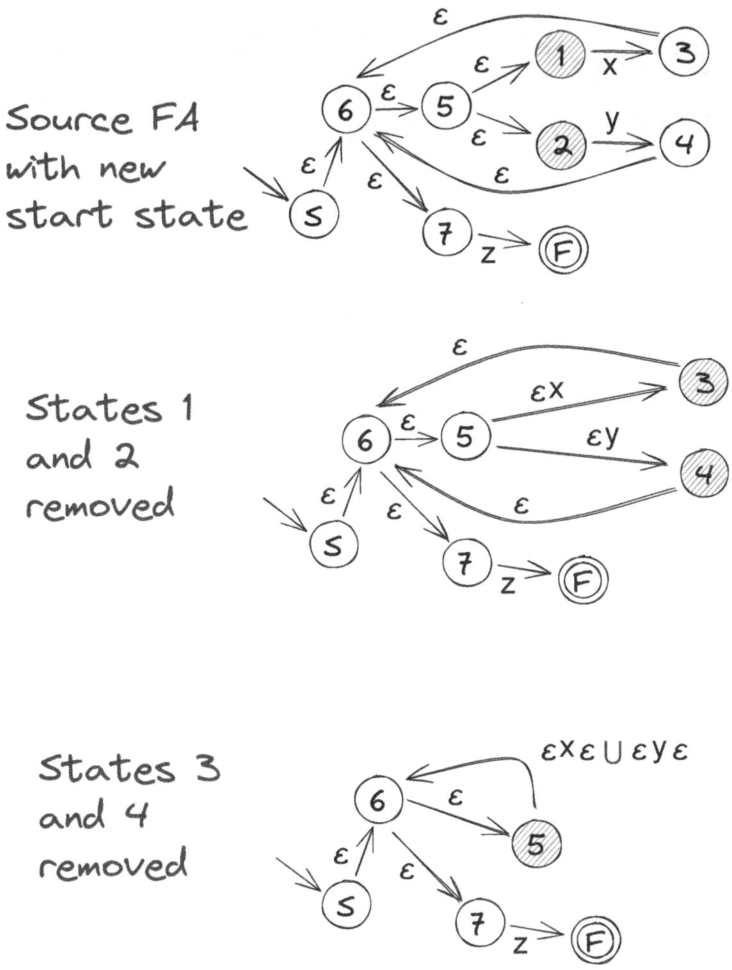

FIGURE 3.11: FA-to-RE conversion (part 1).

The result will most likely not look great (see Figure 3.14), but determinization and minimization should help.

3.4 MATCHING PATTERNS

The conversion procedures described in this chapter might seem somewhat incomplete: while their general organization should be clear, the ultimate description in the form of Python code is not provided. I think implementation details in this case may distract from the main message of the chapter: it is *possible* to convert a regular expression to an equivalent finite automaton and vice versa. Therefore, both of these instruments describe the same class of formal languages, namely regular languages.

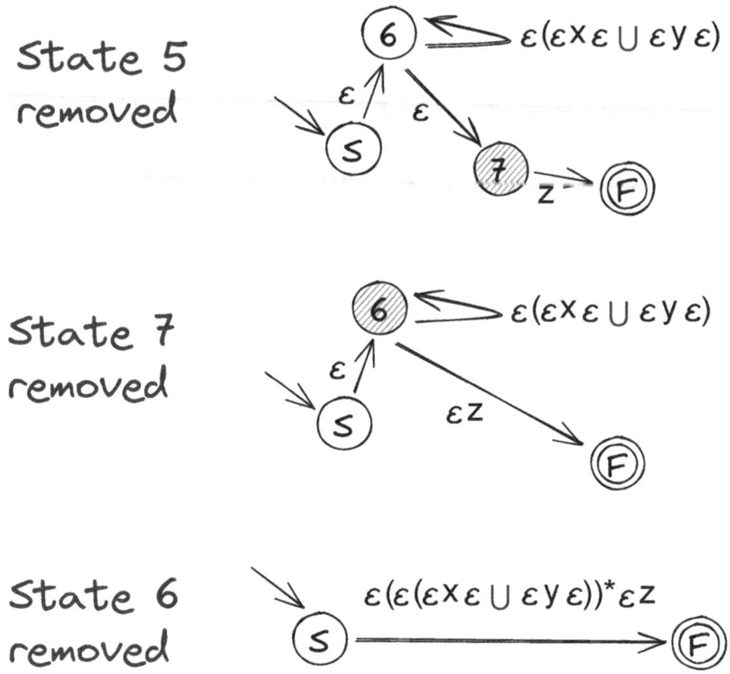

FIGURE 3.12: FA-to-RE conversion (part 2).

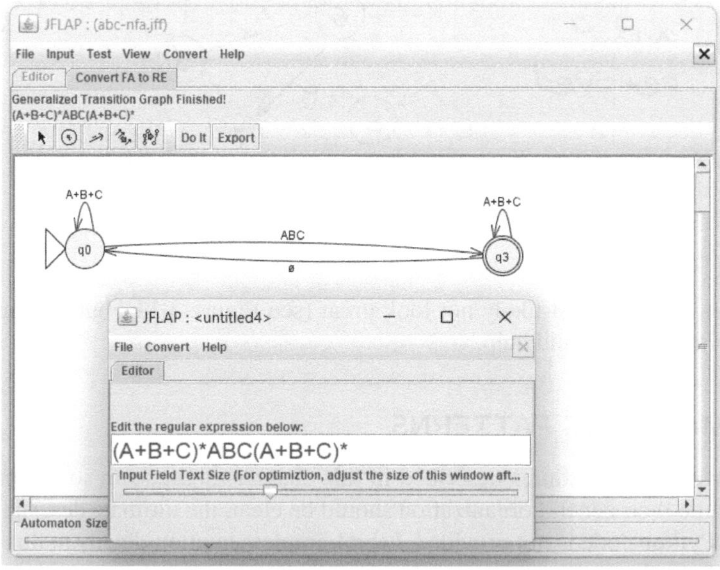

FIGURE 3.13: FA-to-RE conversion in JFLAP.

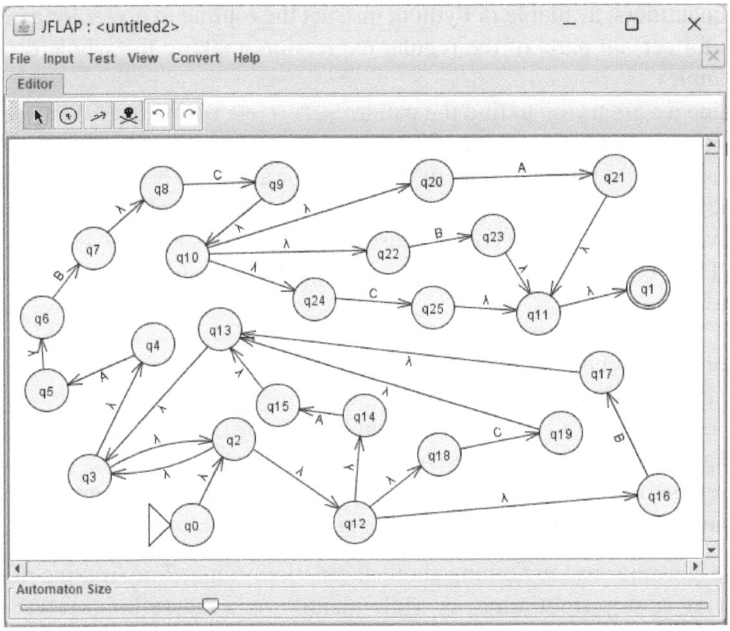

FIGURE 3.14: An NFA obtained from the regular expression `(A+B+C)*ABC(A+B+C)*`.

This equivalence is not coincidental. Stephen Kleene, who developed the original notation for regular expressions, studied sequences of events in the *McCulloch-Pitts nerve net*, an early abstract computational device that had features of both neural networks and finite automata [40]. The notions of regular expressions and finite state machines evolved over the years, but their original connection remained solid.

Generally, regular expressions offer a clean and compact method for describing regular languages. However, they do not provide any practical means for testing whether a given string belongs to the language described by a given regular expression. The equivalence between REs and FAs resolves this shortcoming: we can simply create an equivalent FA for the given RE and run it with a certain input string.

From the perspective of the theory of computation, describing formal languages is the only purpose of regular expressions. However, as already noted in the first chapter, regular expressions came into wide use as a tool for pattern matching. I think pattern matching is mostly outside the scope of this book, but let's take a quick look at some challenges that arise in this task. A more thorough discussion can be found, for example, in [26] and [18].

3.4.1 FROM VALIDATION TO MATCHING

In a nutshell, pattern matching is a harder problem than validation because the matching routine should be able to locate both the start and the end of the pattern and to decide which match to choose if there are several eligible candidates. Lazy and possessive quantifiers, available in Python, instruct the routine to prefer longer or shorter matches for certain parts of the regular expression, making the whole process even more complex.

Imagine we are trying to find the pattern `yell.+(cat|caterpillar)` inside the input string `yelling yellow caterpillar`. Should the resulting match start at `yelling` because it is closer to the beginning of the string, or at `yellow` because it is closer to the end? Should the match end after `cat` because it is the first of the two user-specified alternatives, or after `caterpillar` because this fragment is longer?

Friedl [26, Ch. 4] identifies only two universally respected conventions of regular expression engines:

1. Earlier matches have priority over later matches (thus, it is `yelling` rather than `yellow` in our case).
2. The quantifiers `*`, `+`, `?`, and `{m,n}` are greedy by default, which is evident in engines that offer *both* greedy and lazy versions. Greediness of `?` means it prefers to match one character over zero. Consequently, when applying the pattern `ab?c` to the string `abc`, the engine includes `b` in its match.

These conventions say nothing about alternation. A matching routine might report `caterpillar` or stop right after `cat` while identifying a match for `(cat|caterpillar)`. Naturally, this choice is not random: it depends on the type of the underlying matching mechanism.

3.4.2 KINDS OF PATTERN-MATCHING ENGINES

Consider the following idea for building a routine for matching the pattern `r` in the input text `s`:

```
build a DFA for r
FOR EACH i from 0 to length(s) - 1
    run the DFA with the input string, starting at the i-th character of s

    IF the DFA was ever in its favorable state(s)
        report the last input symbol that triggered
        a favorable state as the end of the match
```

An approach of this kind was apparently used in the original implementation of the AWK programming language. Running the DFA for every subsequent character of `s` is not efficient and can be improved [18], but let's focus on the way this method handles the Kleene star and alternation.

The regular expression `a*` is converted to a DFA consisting of a single (both start and favorable) state S and a single transition rule $(S, \text{a}) \to S$. An input string like `aaab` will be processed until `b` causes the DFA to halt due to a missing transition rule, and `aaa` will be reported as the resulting match. This way, `*` is treated as a greedy quantifier. Similarly, the alternation `(cat|caterpillar)` favors `caterpillar` because it corresponds to the most recently seen favorable state of the DFA shown in Figure 3.15.

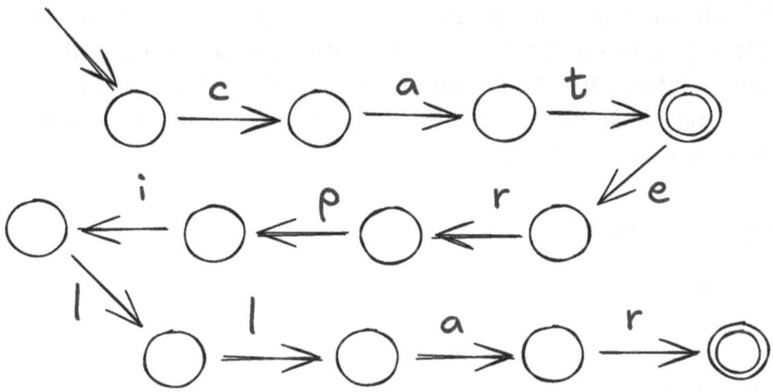

FIGURE 3.15: Handling the alternation `(cat|caterpillar)` with a DFA.

The "AWK approach" (also used in the `egrep` tool) can be contrasted with Thompson's NFA-based matching routine that directly simulates an NFA, resorting to *backtracking* when necessary. In this method, alternatives are explored in left-to-right order, until the first successful match is found. Such NFA-based engines would report different matches for `(cat|caterpillar)` and `(caterpillar|cat)`:

```
import re

# Python uses an NFA-based engine
print(re.search("cat|caterpillar", "caterpillar").group()) # 'cat'
print(re.search("caterpillar|cat", "caterpillar").group()) # 'caterpillar'
```

Unlike Python, `egrep` will always choose `caterpillar`:[2]

```
c:\test>echo "caterpillar" | egrep "cat|caterpillar" -o
caterpillar

c:\test>echo "caterpillar" | egrep "caterpillar|cat" -o
caterpillar
```

The choice between these approaches is an attempt to balance requirements. The NFA-based approach is more flexible, allowing for the implementation of advanced extensions, such as submatches (groups) and *backreferences*. However, its backtracking mechanism can be extremely inefficient in certain edge cases. For example, the following code takes a *very* long time to complete [26, Ch. 4]:

```
import re
re.search("X(.+)+X", "=XX========================================")
```

[2]This pattern-matching utility is included in Linux and macOS. A Windows build can be downloaded at https://gnuwin32.sourceforge.net/packages/grep.htm

The NFA-based approach, chosen by Ken Thompson for QED, avoids the costly NFA-to-DFA conversion step [1, Sec. 3.9]. Consequently, features like lazy quantifiers have been a hallmark of NFA engines found in Perl, Ruby, and PHP [26, Ch. 4]. However, recent works have shown that lazy quantification can be implemented in highly efficient, non-NFA-based engines as well, such as Google's RE2.[3]

3.5 TAKEAWAYS

1. Finite automata and regular expressions describe the same class of languages. FAs can be converted to REs, and vice versa. This fact gives us practical tools for string validation.
2. The role of regular expressions in the theory of computation is to describe formal languages. However, regular expressions are often used for pattern matching in various practical instruments.
3. The two primary methods of pattern matching are based on RE-to-DFA conversion and direct NFA simulation. The former method is fast but requires time and space to perform the conversion and is generally less capable. The latter method might get very slow in certain cases but is faster to set up and allows for the implementation of advanced extensions like backreferences.

[3] Available at https://github.com/google/re2

4 State machines in software engineering

The theory of computation relies on a very specific notion of a finite state machine. In the previous chapters, we discussed finite automata, their computational capabilities, and their connection to regular expressions. Software engineers, however, typically use the term "state machine" to refer to literally any system based on the idea of "states and transitions." The idea of representing the logic of a certain process as a state machine turned out to be a powerful engineering tool, applicable in a wide variety of projects.

In this chapter, we will discuss some possible use cases for state machines beyond the task of implementing regular expressions. We will see how the basic notion of a finite automaton can be extended to include all sorts of useful instruments capable of modeling various aspects of the system to be designed.

4.1 THE STATE PATTERN AND STATE MACHINES

4.1.1 THE PROBLEM OF ENTANGLED BEHAVIORS

Decoupling and *decomposition* are among the foundational principles of nearly every well-designed software system.[1] Our minds are not really well suited to comprehending structures consisting of dozens and hundreds of interconnected components. Ideally, any part of the system that needs to be understood as a whole should consist of only a handful of loosely coupled elements. By localizing ("encapsulating") any complex logic within the bounds of a single component, we make the system simpler to understand. A lack of decomposition leads to a "spaghetti code," hard to understand and maintain.

Imagine a component that does different things under different circumstances. On one hand, being an identifiable component, it should be implemented within a single logical unit (e.g., a class). On the other hand, bringing distinct behaviors together without introducing "spaghetti code" can be quite a challenge.

A fun example of such a case is discussed by Nystrom [54]:

"We're working on a little side-scrolling platformer. Our job is to implement the heroine that is the player's avatar in the game world. That means making her respond to user input. Push the B button and she should jump. Simple enough:[2]

```
def handleInput(Input input)
```

[1] Decoupling is *"any systematic method or technique by which modules can be made more independent"* [77, Sec. 6.3]. Decomposition is the process of *"break[ing] things into manageable chunks"* [42].

[2] The original examples in Nystrom's book are written in C++. The versions here are adapted to a more Python-like pseudocode for consistency with other listings in this book.

DOI: 10.1201/9781032614991-4

```
    if input == PRESS_B:
        yVelocity_ = JUMP_VELOCITY
        setGraphics(IMAGE_JUMP)
```

Spot the bug? There's nothing to prevent 'air jumping': keep hammering B while she's in the air and she will float forever. The simple fix is to add an `isJumping_` *Boolean field to Heroine that tracks when she's jumping, and then do:*

```
def handleInput(Input input)
    if input == PRESS_B:
        if not isJumping_:
            isJumping_ = True
            # Jump...
```

There should also be code that sets `isJumping_` *back to* `False` *when the heroine touches the ground. I've omitted that here for brevity's sake.*

Next, we want the heroine to duck if the player presses down while she's on the ground, and stand back up when the button is released:

```
def handleInput(Input input)
    if input == PRESS_B:
        # Jump if not jumping...
    elif input == PRESS_DOWN:
        if not isJumping_:
            setGraphics(IMAGE_DUCK)
    elif input == RELEASE_DOWN:
        setGraphics(IMAGE_STAND)
```

Spot the bug this time? With this code, the player could:

1) Press down to duck.

2) Press B to jump from a ducking position.

3) Release down while still in the air.

The heroine will switch to her standing graphic in the middle of the jump. Time for another flag... "

Nystrom's story goes on and on in the same manner until it is clear that every new capability or bug fix makes the code even more brittle and harder to understand. The source of this complexity lies exactly in the attempt to bring together distinct behaviors, resulting in complicated logic that activates this or that code fragment in accordance with the current combination of Boolean flags.

4.1.2 DISENTANGLING BEHAVIORS

One possible solution for Nystrom's predicament is to employ the *State pattern*, a design pattern intended to *"Allow an object to alter its behavior when its internal state changes. The object will appear to change its class."* [27, Sec. 5]. The general idea is to replace Boolean flags with a single "state" value and to choose the active behavior according to the current state.

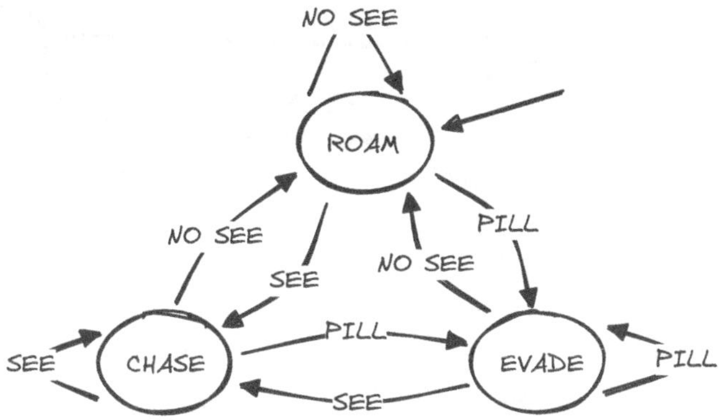

FIGURE 4.1: A state machine for a Pac-Man ghost.

This approach is commonly employed in game programming, especially for creating autonomous non-player characters. For example, Pac-Man ghosts[3] switch between "roaming," "chasing," and "evading" states (see Figure 4.1) [6]. On every timer tick, the system checks state variables (whether Pac-Man is visible and whether a "power pill" is active) and possibly switches the ghost to another state. The switching logic can be quite flexible. For example, what should be done if the current state is "evade," a power pill is active, and the ghost sees Pac-Man? We can prioritize conflicting rules by checking the pill status first, so the ghost will stay in the "evade" state until the pill is inactive, without even checking whether Pac-Man is visible.

Clearly, the Pac-Man ghost control system has a lot in common with a finite state machine. It has states and transitions that define the state-switching logic. There are also notable differences: transitions are labeled with general "events," and states are associated with various kinds of behavior. The "Gang of Four" book [27] summarizes the differences between the State pattern and state machines as follows: *"the State pattern models state-specific behavior, whereas the table-driven approach focuses on defining state transitions."*

However, this difference is too subtle for many authors. Numerous sources, including the already-cited [54] and [6], and Unity courses [21], use the term "finite state machine" for nearly any design consisting of states and transitions. That said, the actual behavior of non-player characters is indeed bound to states, while the system of transitions tends to be relatively simple.

4.2 VENDING MACHINE

Game AI systems are interesting to discuss, but they involve relatively complex behaviors (even in the case of Pac-Man ghosts). Instead, we will consider the design of a "vending machine" system, which is closer to a table-driven finite state machine than to a typical State pattern-based solution.

[3] https://en.wikipedia.org/wiki/Pac-Man

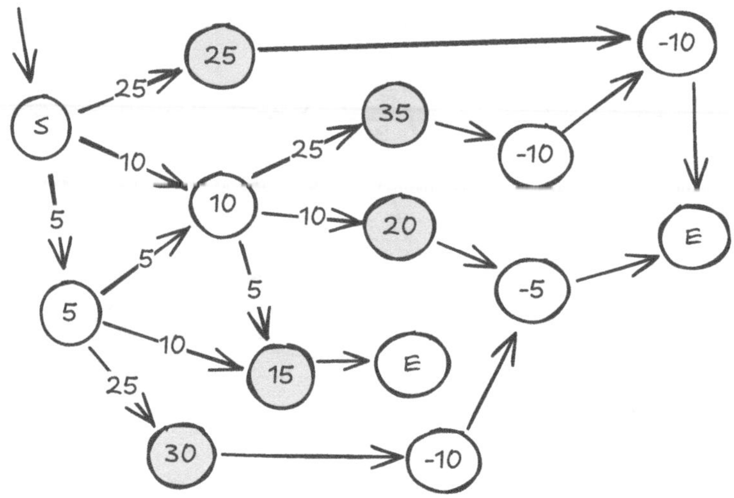

FIGURE 4.2: A "vending" finite state machine.

Imagine a vending machine that sells drinks. One bottle costs 15 cents. The machine accepts 5-, 10-, and 25-cent coins. As soon as the user has inserted enough coins for a drink, the machine dispenses one bottle and returns the change.

One possible implementation of the vending machine logic is shown in Figure 4.2. Initially, the machine is in state *S*. By accepting a coin, the machine transitions into state *5*, *10*, or *25*. Eventually, the machine reaches one of the gray-colored states (*15*, *20*, *25*, *30*, or *35*) and dispenses a bottle of the drink. Subsequent states instruct the machine to return change of the specified value (*10* or *5*) until one of the final *E* states is reached (then the machine can be reset to *S*).

This kind of design offers several advantages. First, it encodes a very simple logic that can potentially be implemented with basic electronic components, such as logic gates and flip-flops. No microprocessor or memory is needed. This factor may not have much weight in our time of cheap hardware, but let's still acknowledge it. Next, it clearly indicates the connections between physical and logical operations. Inserting coins triggers transitions between the states on the left-hand side of the chart. The gray-colored states activate the dispenser unit. The states on the right-hand side of the chart activate the change-returning mechanism. It is easy to imagine, for example, that a state like *-10* is connected to a dispenser filled with 10-cent coins. Finally, it is not difficult to check that the device works correctly. Only three types of coins can be inserted, and we can verify that each state on the left-hand side has three outgoing transitions. We know exactly how much money should be returned in every "dispensing" state and can trace the actual process of returning coins.

To wrap up the vending machine example, consider its Python implementation shown in Listing 4.1. It reads input data until one of the "gray" states is reached. Next, it dispenses a drink and returns change until the state `E` becomes active. Note that there are three independent "-10" states, labeled as `10a`, `10b`, and `10c` in Python.

All "return change" states have a trailing letter in their names, so the actual change value can be obtained using expression `state[:-1]`.

Listing 4.1: Vending machine.

```
def vend(rules, graystates):
    state = "S"
    while state not in graystates:
        c = input("Insert coin: ")
        state = rules[(state, c)]
        print(f"Collected: {state}c")

    print("Dispensing drink")
    state = rules[(state, "")]

    while state != "E":
        print(f"Returning change: {state[:-1]}c")
        state = rules[(state, "")]


vend(
    {
        ("S", "25"): "25",
        ("S", "10"): "10",
        ("S", "5"): "5",
        ("25", ""): "10a",
        ("10a", ""): "E",
        ("10", "25"): "35",
        ("10", "10"): "20",
        ("10", "5"): "15",
        ("35", ""): "10b",
        ("10b", ""): "10a",
        ("20", ""): "5a",
        ("5a", ""): "E",
        ("15", ""): "E",
        ("5", "5"): "10",
        ("5", "10"): "15",
        ("5", "25"): "30",
        ("30", ""): "10c",
        ("10c", ""): "5a",
    },
    {"25", "35", "20", "15", "30"},
)
```

The following printout shows one possible vending session:

```
> python vending.py
Insert coin: 5
Collected: 5c
Insert coin: 5
Collected: 10c
Insert coin: 25
Collected: 35c
Dispensing drink
Returning change: 10c
Returning change: 10c
```

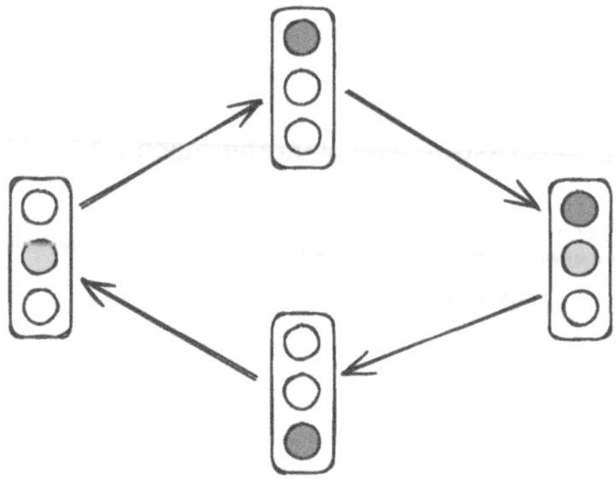

FIGURE 4.3: A state diagram for a traffic light system.

4.3 MARKOVIAN WEATHER

The "vending machine" is still conceptually very similar to a classic finite state machine, merely extending the "states and transitions" scheme with state-associated events.

The basic FSM formula can be modified in all kinds of ways. Consider, for example, the task of modeling autonomous processes that unfold over time. Suppose that our system receives no input data, but its state changes as the clock ticks. This situation can be modeled with a finite state machine, with each transition labeled "clock tick." Deterministic state machines can represent relatively simple deterministic systems, such as traffic lights, which switch according to the same pattern over and over again (see Figure 4.3). (Note that the duration of the pause before the next tick occurs should be stored in the current state.)

The idea of uncertainty can be expressed with probabilistic rules. The FSM-like device shown in Figure 4.4 represents a simple model of weather changes. We start with sunny weather. The next clock tick keeps the weather sunny with a 60% probability or switches it to cloudy (30% probability) or rainy (10% probability).

This kind of device is known as a *Markov process* or *Markov chain*.Like FSMs, Markov processes have no memory: when the system resides in a certain state, it does not "remember" how it arrived there. Thus, this instrument is suitable for modeling processes that satisfy the *Markov property*: the future evolution of a process should not depend on its history.

A simple implementation of the "weather automaton" is shown in Listing 4.2. It outputs a sequence of weather types, such as

```
sunny
sunny
cloudy
sunny
...
```

Listing 4.2: Markovian weather.

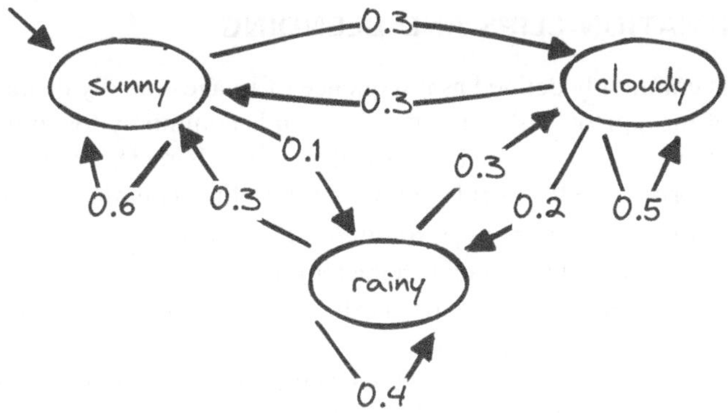

FIGURE 4.4: A Markov chain-based weather model.

```
from random import choices

DAYS = 20


def next_day(state):
    rules = {
        "sunny": (("sunny", "rainy", "cloudy"), (0.6, 0.1, 0.3)),
        "cloudy": (("cloudy", "sunny", "rainy"), (0.5, 0.3, 0.2)),
        "rainy": (("rainy", "sunny", "cloudy"), (0.4, 0.3, 0.3)),
    }
    states, weights = rules[state]
    return choices(states, weights)[0]


state = "sunny"
colors = {"sunny": "gold", "cloudy": "gray", "rainy": "black"}

for day in range(DAYS):
    print(state)
    state = next_day(state)
```

4.4 UNITY ANIMATION SYSTEM

An interesting case of FSM-based design can be found in the Mecanim animation system of the Unity game engine.[4] While the topic of game animation is beyond the scope of this book, Mecanim is a good example of how the idea of "states and transitions" can be used to build an advanced animation system capable of meeting all kinds of practical needs. Let's briefly discuss some of its basic elements.

[4] https://docs.unity3d.com/6000.2/Documentation/Manual/AnimationOverview.html

4.4.1 ANIMATION CLIPS AND BLENDING

Animation is commonly defined as a sequence of images rapidly displayed to create an illusion of movement. This type of animation is commonly found in 2D pixel art games, where various movement phases of a game character are represented with independent sprites. In 3D worlds, an animation clip *"contains information about how a character (...) changes its position, rotation, or other properties over time"*.[5]

For example, a typical humanoid character consists of a virtual skeleton, made of individual interconnected bones, and a mesh, "rigged" to the skeleton and responsible for the character's outward appearance. A *skeletal animation* clip is a sequence of numerical parameters describing how the orientation of bones changes over time.

A skeleton has a "root bone" that defines the overall position and orientation of the character. Any other bone has a "parent bone" it connects to. These connection points, or joints, are the places where orientation values are applied. Given the position and orientation of the root bone and the orientation of each other bone, it is possible to calculate the resulting pose of the skeleton.

This approach makes it possible to create animation clips that are applicable to a wide variety of humanoid characters. It also enables *blending*: several animation clips can be combined into a single "blended" clip, incorporating the features of the original clips with specified weights. Blending is the key to smooth animation: there is no need to switch abruptly, say, between walking and running. Instead, we can gradually move from a (100% walking, 0% running) blended clip to a (0% walking, 100% running) blended clip.

4.4.2 ANIMATOR FINITE STATE MACHINE

Let's return to Heroine's behavior example discussed by Nystrom. It is very likely that different states of the player character will be represented with different animation clips, such as "idle" for the standing state, "jumping" for the jumping state, and so on.

The system of transitions between states is important for animation, in particular, because of blending: it should be possible to adjust blending options for each transition between a pair of animation clips independently. In Unity, these transitions are handled by an Animator component, configurable via a visual editor (see Figure 4.5). By clicking on a transition, it is possible to modify the parameters of that particular blend (see Figure 4.6).

The primary purpose of the Unity Animator is to define transitions rather than states. A notable distinction between the Animator and more conventional FSM-based designs is introduced by time: since transitions between animation clips are not instant, it takes time to fully switch from a source to a target state. By observing "on state enter" and "on state exit" events, it is easy to find cases where a new "head" state is activated before an old "tail" state has been exited.

[5] https://docs.unity3d.com/6000.2/Documentation/Manual/AnimationOverview.html

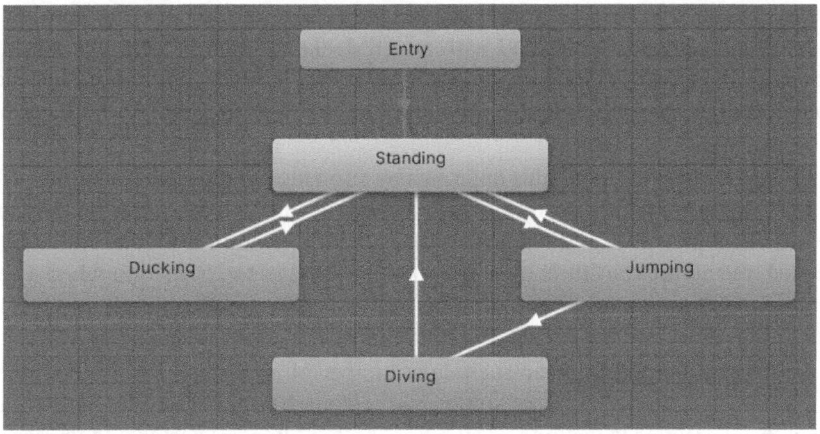

FIGURE 4.5: A simple Unity Animator configuration.

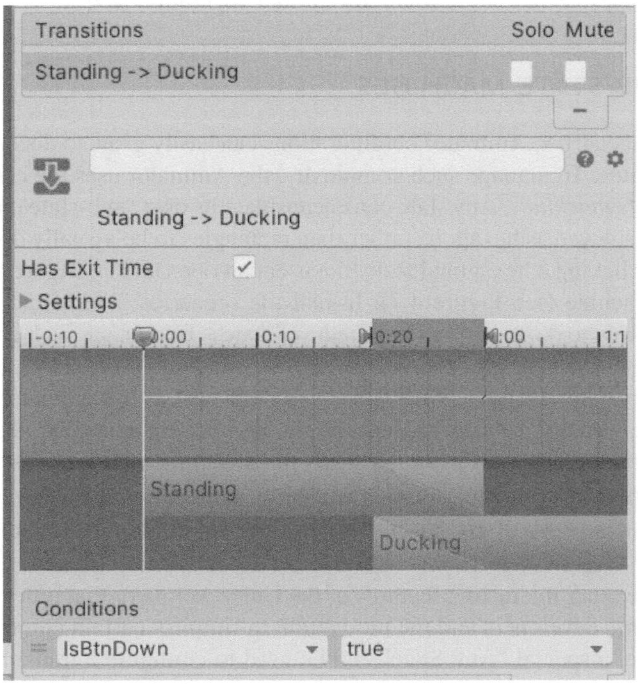

FIGURE 4.6: Adjusting blending parameters for a transition.

State events can be used to trigger behaviors. Let's recall that the heroine's behavior is conveniently described with an FSM-like system. It feels like a pointless duplication of effort to design a similar system for Heroine's animation. Instead, we can incorporate behavior into the Animator, making it responsible for both animation and logic.

Unity Animator supports this approach by allowing conditional transitions. A transition between animation A and animation B can be unlabeled: once A is about to end, the transition activates, and A blends into B. Another option is to make A loop (once finished, the animation starts over again) and to trigger the transition when a certain condition becomes true. Figure 4.6 shows this setup: the "Standing" to "Ducking" transition is activated only when the Boolean variable `IsBtnDown` becomes true.

Animator configuration can include a number of *animation layers*. Imagine that your game character consists of somewhat independent upper and lower body parts. When the characters is walking or standing, both body parts perform their respective "walking" or "idle" animations. However, imagine that the character is also able to use a gun in both states, meaning that a "shooting" animation can be activated separately for the upper body part. This functionality can be implemented by introducing separate "layers" for both body parts. Each layer will be controlled by its own state machine that reacts only to events relevant to its operation [29].

4.4.3 SUB-STATE MACHINES

In real-life scenarios, Animator configurations can easily grow to dozens, if not hundreds, of states. To manage such complexity, the Animator uses the concept of *hierarchical state machines*. Any state can encapsulate its own "sub-state machine." Such states are displayed as hexagons rather than rectangles to be visually distinguishable. By double-clicking a hexagonal state, the user can open and configure the associated sub-state machine (see Figure 4.7). In real-life scenarios, Animator configurations can easily grow to dozens, if not hundreds, of states. To manage such complexity, the Animator uses the concept of *hierarchical state machines*. Any state can encapsulate its own "sub-state machine." Such states are displayed as hexagons rather than rectangles to be visually distinguishable. By double-clicking a hexagonal state, the user can open and configure the associated sub-state machine (see Figure 4.7).

A transition from the "base layer" machine can lead to any specified state in the sub-state machine. Similarly, a transition leading out of the sub-state machine can be connected to any state of the base layer.

There are other interesting features of the Unity Animator that reflect the practical needs of game developers and the motivation to simplify certain common scenarios. For example, a special "Any State" can be used to configure a transition that might happen at any time. For instance, if we presume that the heroine may take damage in any state, we technically have to create a separate transition from every single state in the Animator to the "Damaged" state. If the same blending is acceptable for all of them, we can instead create and configure a single transition from "Any State" to "Damaged," which will be triggered by the `IsDamaged` condition.

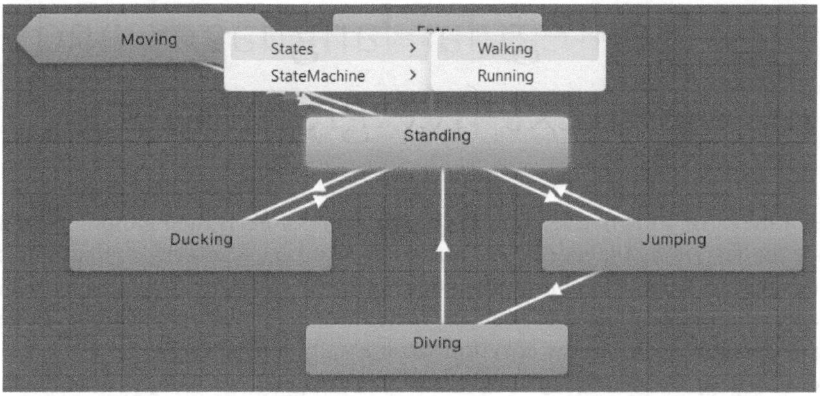

FIGURE 4.7: Configuring a sub-state machine in Unity.

Unity state machines can be also viewed as a domain-specific adaptation of an established instrument for representing complex systems, known as *Harel statecharts* [33]. Statecharts extend the basic FSM formula with familiar capabilities, such as events, actions, sub-state machines, and "orthogonal regions" that roughly correspond to animation layer controllers. Harel statecharts were adopted in the Unified Modeling Language (UML) under the name of *behavioral state machines*.

4.5 TAKEAWAYS

1. The broad concept of "states and transitions" is widely applied in practical software development. In particular, it is at the heart of the State pattern, described in the "Gang of Four" book [27] as a recipe for "switching" between the different possible behaviors of the same object.
2. In this context, finite state machines can be treated as "thinking tools," offering an efficient way to manage complexity in certain well-defined cases.
3. While the State pattern is mostly focused on states rather than transitions, certain kinds of software systems need carefully designed networks of transitions. Our "vending machine" is a good example.
4. The basic finite state machine formula can be extended in various ways. For example, probabilistic rules are found in Markov chains, while hierarchical state machines reduce the complexity of Unity Animator components.

5 Nonregular languages and context-free grammars

One of the most attractive features of regular expressions is their simplicity as a language for describing languages. A short string like `[01]*0` describes an infinite set of strings that all share the same valuable property (in this case, being an even binary number). Similarly, finite state machines offer a very simple representation of a computational process. It is very easy to reason about their behavior: now we are right here; if X happens, we will get there, and if Y happens, we will get over there. Automata lack memory, which is a common source of complexity in code. There is no need to think about the content of this or that variable affecting the current branching instruction.

However, these tools have a well-defined scope, and some tasks simply lie outside of it. Regular expressions describe regular languages, but not all languages are regular, meaning we have to explore other instruments to deal with them. Chapter 1 mentions the language of dash-separated repeating strings (such as `Baden-Baden`) as an example, but why is it not regular? Let's find out and then discuss appropriate tools capable of handling such cases.

5.1 THE PUMPING LEMMA

The traditional way to prove the existence of nonregular languages is to employ the *pumping lemma for regular languages* (Lemma 8 in [61]). It establishes that any infinite regular language L possesses the following property:

There exists an integer p (the *pumping length*) such that any string s in L with a length of at least p can be represented as a concatenation of three strings xyz in such a way that:

1. the substring y is not empty;
2. the length of the substring xy does not exceed p;
3. the strings xz, xyz, $xyyz$, $xyyyz$, and so on (i.e., xy^iz for any $i \geq 0$) also belong to L.

In other words, any sufficiently long string of a regular language contains a substring y that can be removed or repeated ("pumped") any number of times to produce strings that also belong to L.

The pumping lemma establishes a *necessary* rather than *sufficient* property of regular languages: strings of a regular language must be "pumpable."[1] Therefore, if a

[1]Because this is not a sufficient condition, some non-regular languages can still satisfy the pumping lemma's requirements. A more powerful technique for proving non-regularity involves showing that a language has an *infinite fooling set* [8].

DOI: 10.1201/9781032614991-5

certain language is not "pumpable," it is not regular. For some languages, this is easy to show.

For example, consider the language $L = \{\mathtt{a}^n\mathtt{b}^n\}$, which is composed of strings ε, `ab`, `aabb`, `aaabbb`, and so on.

To show L is not regular, we can use a proof by contradiction. Assume L is regular and has a pumping length p. Consider a string $s = \mathtt{a}^p\mathtt{b}^p$, which belongs to L. According to the pumping lemma, we should be able to split s into three substrings xyz so that the length of xy does not exceed p, and y is nonempty and pumpable.

However, we know that the first p characters of s are all `a`s. Therefore, pumping y increases the number of `a`s without increasing the number of `b`s, so $xyyz$ cannot be in L.

This contradiction proves that our assumption was false, and L is not regular.

It might not be immediately obvious why regular languages are pumpable. Recall that any regular language can be recognized by a finite state machine. Suppose a machine that recognizes language L consists of N states. Since its current state is updated after reading every subsequent input symbol, processing a string of length N or more will cause the machine to pass through at least $N + 1$ states (including the start state). By the *pigeonhole principle*[2], the machine must revisit one of its earlier states on the way. Therefore, a certain substring of the input string (y) causes the machine to loop. This means that y can be either removed entirely or repeated any number of times without affecting the machine's final verdict.

5.2 LANGUAGES AND DECISION PROBLEMS

We have spent considerable time discussing the problem of language recognition. The tasks of string validation and pattern matching served as motivation: a systematic approach is required to address the practical need to highlight URLs, extract email addresses, or validate even binary numbers. Regular expressions, backed by finite automata, provide practical tools for describing such string patterns and identifying them in data streams.

Next, we have identified some nonregular languages. Nonregular patterns cannot be described with regular expressions, so we need more powerful instruments for string validation and pattern recognition. Apparently, the next logical step would be to explore such instruments.

However, at this point, the original motivation starts to lose its footing. It seems that regular expressions and even more limited `glob` expressions[3] are the only methods of describing textual patterns universally adopted in popular programming languages. I think the reason is quite simple: nonregular languages typically describe something more advanced than just patterns to be found in the input. For example, it is rarely enough to know whether a given XML file is valid or not; it is more common to *parse* it, identifying its elements and handling possible errors. Both validation and parsing

[2] "If $n \geq m$ pigeons are put into m pigeonholes, there's a hole with more than one pigeon" [5].

[3] See https://docs.python.org/3/library/glob.html

of a complex entity such as XML require a specialized solution, which is often easily available.[4] Thus, advanced universal instruments for describing textual patterns built into a language like Python would not have as much practical value as one might think.

Such instruments would help, for example, if you decide to create your own XML parser or C compiler. While tasks of this kind are obviously important, are they relevant to a typical software developer or interesting from a theoretical perspective?

It turns out that they are, and the role of formal languages extends beyond the task of describing certain kinds of strings. Languages are closely connected with *computational problems*, which we will briefly discuss now.

Informally speaking, a computational problem is a task that can be solved by means of *computation*, i.e., a process of producing the desired output from the given input in a finite number of steps. For example, "sort the given input array of numbers" or "find the roots of the equation $x^2 + a = 10$ for the given a" are computational problems. Computational problems are characterized by their *complexity classes*, which we will discuss later. One important type of computational problem is the *decision problem*. A decision problem is formulated as a yes/no question: sorting a given array is not a decision problem, while finding whether a given array is sorted is one. Decision problems exist in all complexity classes and are often used to study various properties of these classes.

Any kind of data that forms the input of a computational problem can be encoded as a sequence of symbols. This point can be elaborated on more formally, but in our case, it is enough to note that any program that gets input from a stored file actually reads a sequence of symbols.

Now consider what the input and output of the decision problem *"is the given array of numbers sorted?"* might look like. Its input is an array encoded as a string, such as `10 45 1 53`. Its output is a Boolean yes/no value. Does this ring any bells?

Compare the following statements:

1. A certain subset of Σ^* forms the language L. To find whether a certain string s belongs to L, we need a procedure that would accept or reject any given s.
2. The subset of strings representing space-separated sorted integers forms the language L. To find whether a certain sequence of integers is sorted, we need a procedure that would print "yes" or "no" for any given input sequence.

Decision problems *are* formal languages, and the study of formal languages is actually the study of decision problems, extending far beyond the task of pattern matching. We have seen that some interesting patterns can be described with regular expressions and recognized by finite state machines, and some other patterns require more powerful tools. The same can be said about decision problems: certain problems can be solved by finite state machines, and certain problems cannot.

What makes automata so limited? What kind of improvements can be introduced, and how much additional power will they bring? Questions of this sort belong to the

[4]Python provides XML processing capabilities; see https://docs.python.org/3/library/xml.html

very core of the theory of computation, and yet they are easy to overlook in our age of ubiquitous, universal computing machines. For us, the conventional notion of computation is what a digital computer does, but imagine being a computer pioneer trying to construct an early computational device. What kinds of capabilities are essential, and what kinds are merely conveniences? What kinds of tasks will be solvable and how?

Summing up, nonregular languages open the door to the world of more advanced computational problems, and this is sufficient motivation to give them proper consideration.

5.3 CONTEXT-FREE GRAMMARS

Our next instrument, *context-free grammars* (CFGs), was originally conceived as a method for describing the structures of human language [9]. The field of natural language processing ultimately switched to more powerful tools, but context-free grammars remained an important instrument for describing formal languages.

Consider the following set of rules:

$$
\begin{aligned}
S &\rightarrow A\_N \\
A &\rightarrow \texttt{brave} \\
A &\rightarrow \texttt{lazy} \\
A &\rightarrow \texttt{hungry} \\
A &\rightarrow \texttt{cat} \\
A &\rightarrow \texttt{dog} \\
A &\rightarrow \texttt{bear}
\end{aligned}
$$

They state that S can be replaced with the sequence A_N, where A can be `brave`, `lazy`, or `hungry`, and N can be `cat`, `dog`, or `bear`. This way, S can be transformed into phrases like `brave_dog` or `hungry_bear`.

Each rule (called a *production rule*) specifies a certain allowed way to replace a *nonterminal* symbol (or *variable*) with a sequence of other nonterminal and *terminal* symbols. Terminal symbols form the basic alphabet of the language. In our case, the alphabet consists of words like `cat` or `lazy` and an underscore character, found in the rule $S \rightarrow A\_N$. To avoid confusion, nonterminals are usually represented with uppercase letters, and terminals with lowercase letters or other symbols. The *start symbol* (traditionally, S, as in "sentence") defines the top-level structure of the resulting string. Rules with S on the left-hand side are usually listed first.

Note that production rules specify what is *allowed* rather than *required*. In a string like A_A_N, it is allowed to replace any symbol A with `hungry`, `lazy`, or `brave`. Thus, we can replace the first A with `brave`, the second A with `hungry`, and N with `dog`, obtaining `brave_hungry_dog`.

More formally, a context-free grammar is defined as a tuple (Σ, V, R, S), where Σ is a set of terminals (the alphabet), V is a set of variables, R is a set of production rules, and $S \in V$ is the start symbol. Each production rule has a single variable on its left-hand side and a string over the alphabet $\Sigma \cup V$ on its right-hand side:

$$X \rightarrow (\Sigma \cup V)^*, \text{where } X \in V$$

Such a grammar is called "context-free" because production rules can be applied to replace any nonterminal in a given string regardless of its local context, i.e., the neighborhood formed by surrounding symbols.

Production rules having the same left-hand side can be combined to save space:

$$S \rightarrow A\_N$$
$$A \rightarrow \texttt{brave} \mid \texttt{lazy} \mid \texttt{hungry}$$
$$N \rightarrow \texttt{cat} \mid \texttt{dog} \mid \texttt{bear}$$

This notation is merely a shorthand: it still lists seven separate rules, not three.

The language described by this grammar is finite, but grammars can be used to describe infinite languages as well. As an example, let's consider a simplified language of correct email addresses, corresponding to the following regular expression:

```
[a-zA-Z0-9._-]+@[a-zA-Z0-9_-]+(\.[a-zA-Z0-9_-]+)+
```

Let's break it down into pieces. My own email address, `mozgovoy@u-aizu.ac.jp`, consists of a username `mozgovoy`, followed by the `@` symbol, and a number of dot-separated domain parts (`u-aizu`, `ac`, and `jp`). The username and domain parts must be nonempty (hence `+` after each element), and the list of domains must include at least two parts.

The same language can be described with a context-free grammar:

$$S \rightarrow H\texttt{@}BT$$
$$C \rightarrow \texttt{a} \mid \ldots \mid \texttt{z} \mid \texttt{A} \mid \ldots \mid \texttt{Z} \mid \texttt{0} \mid \ldots \mid \texttt{9} \mid \texttt{\_} \mid \texttt{-}$$
$$D \rightarrow C \mid \texttt{.}$$
$$H \rightarrow D \mid DH$$
$$B \rightarrow C \mid CB$$
$$T \rightarrow \texttt{.}B \mid \texttt{.}BT$$

This notation is harder to read, so let's try to understand what is going on:

1. An email address consists of a "head" H, followed by the `@` symbol, a "body" B, and a "tail" T.
2. The nonterminal C corresponds to the set of characters `[a-zA-Z0-9_-]`.
3. The nonterminal D includes all the characters of C and the dot character.
4. The head symbol H consists of either a single character from the set defined by D or a single character from D followed by another head.
5. Similarly, the body B is either a single character from the set defined by C or a single character from C followed by another body.
6. Finally, the tail T is either a dot followed by the body B or a dot followed by the body and another tail.

FIGURE 5.1: Forming the head fragment `cat`.

Recursive definitions like $H \to D \mid DH$ take time to get used to, but they represent the only method of describing strings of potentially infinite length in context-free grammars. For example, consider how to obtain the word `cat` (see Figure 5.1). We start with a single nonterminal H. By applying the rule $H \to DH$ twice, we get the string DDH. Next, by applying the rule $H \to D$, we obtain DDD. Finally, each D can be replaced with any lowercase letter, resulting in `cat`. In the same way, we can generate a whole email address.

Clearly, context-free grammars are able to describe email addresses. However, this is still a regular language. Let's now consider a grammar for the language $L = \{\mathtt{a}^n\mathtt{b}^n\}$, which was shown above to be nonregular:

$$S \to \mathtt{a}S\mathtt{b} \mid \varepsilon$$

For example, by taking the start symbol S and applying the rule $S \to \mathtt{a}S\mathtt{b}$ three times, we obtain the string `aaaSbbb`. Next, by applying the rule $S \to \varepsilon$, we create the string `aaabbb`, which belongs to language L.

5.4 REGULAR GRAMMARS

5.4.1 THE BENEFITS OF CONSTRAINTS

We have seen that context-free grammars can describe a certain class of *context-free languages* that includes at least some regular and some nonregular languages. Before digging deeper into the world of nonregular languages, let's discuss the following beautiful property of context-free grammars: by applying certain constraints to the structure of the available rules, we can obtain *regular grammars* that can only describe regular languages.

Regular grammars can be further classified into *right-linear* and *left-linear* grammars. Right-linear grammars include only rules of the form $A \to w$ or $A \to wB$, where A, B are nonterminals and w is a string of terminals (possibly empty). In these rules, a nonterminal on the right-hand side can only appear at the very end.

Left-linear grammars impose similar limitations: rules must be of the form $A \to w$ or $A \to Bw$. In these rules, a nonterminal on the right-hand side can only appear at the very beginning. Having two or more nonterminal symbols on the right-hand side of a rule is not allowed in either grammar type.

5.4.2 CONVERTING REGULAR GRAMMARS TO FAS

The best way to prove that regular grammars describe regular languages is to show how to convert any given regular grammar to a finite state machine. For right-linear grammars,[5] this can be accomplished with the following algorithm [34, Sec. 5.4]:

1. Create a state for each nonterminal symbol in the grammar. Label the states with the nonterminal symbols.
2. Designate the state labeled with the grammar's start symbol (likely, S) as the start state.
3. Create a single, dedicated favorable state and label it F'.

Next, process every rule of the grammar as follows:

1. For a rule of the form $A \to aB$, add the transition $(A, a) \to B$.
2. For a rule of the form $A \to a_1 a_2 \ldots a_n B$, add $n-1$ new states (let's label them here as $S_1, \ldots, S_{n-1}$) and create the transitions $(A, a_1) \to S_1$, $(S_1, a_2) \to S_2, \ldots, (S_{n-1}, a_n) \to B$.
3. For a rule of the form $A \to a_1 a_2 \ldots a_n$, add new states and transitions as described above, but instead of the transition $(S_{n-1}, a_n) \to B$, create the transition $(S_{n-1}, a_n) \to F'$.
4. For a rule of the form $A \to B$, add the transition $(A, \varepsilon) \to B$.
5. For a rule of the form $A \to a$, add the transition $(A, a) \to F'$.
6. For a rule of the form $A \to \varepsilon$, add the transition $(A, \varepsilon) \to F'$.

Some of these rules can be easily grouped together to form fewer, more general rules (for example, $A \to a$ is merely a special case of $A \to a_1 a_2 \ldots a_n$), but this can make them even harder to read. Fortunately, the actual conversion procedure is much simpler than it might seem, as Figure 5.2 shows.

As an example, let's convert the following right-linear grammar to a finite state machine:

$$S \to \mathtt{a}S \mid \mathtt{b}B \mid \varepsilon$$
$$B \to \mathtt{b}B \mid \varepsilon$$

[5] It can be shown that any left-linear grammar can be converted to an equivalent right-linear grammar and vice versa [35, Sec. 9.1].

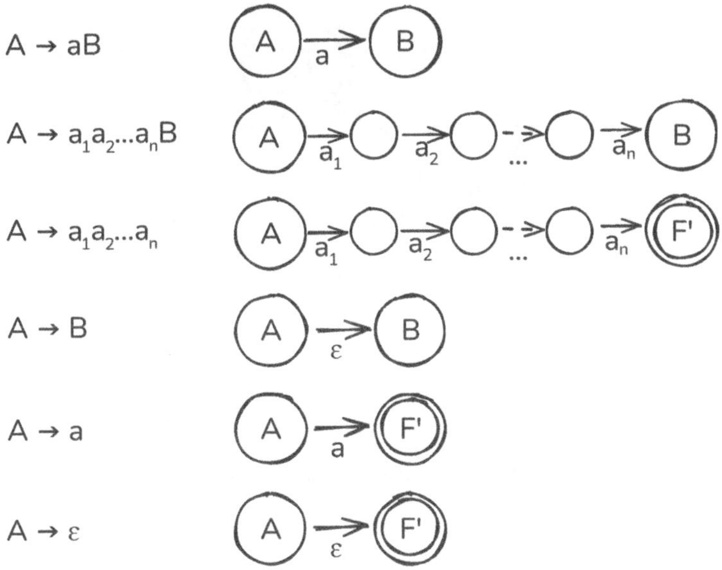

FIGURE 5.2: Generating FA transitions from the rules of a right-linear grammar.

This grammar describes the language of strings consisting of any number of `a`s followed by any number of `b`s (i.e., corresponding to the regular expression `a*b*`). Let's write down each rule on its own line:

$$S \rightarrow \mathtt{a}S$$
$$S \rightarrow \mathtt{b}B$$
$$S \rightarrow \varepsilon$$
$$B \rightarrow \mathtt{b}B$$
$$B \rightarrow \varepsilon$$

The next step is to create a state for each nonterminal symbol of the grammar and a separate favorable state F'. In our case, this means creating three states: S, B, and F'.

Finally, let's add transitions corresponding to each rule:

1. Rule $S \rightarrow \mathtt{a}S$: transition $(S, \mathtt{a}) \rightarrow S$.
2. Rule $S \rightarrow \mathtt{b}B$: transition $(S, \mathtt{b}) \rightarrow B$.
3. Rule $S \rightarrow \varepsilon$: transition $(S, \varepsilon) \rightarrow F'$.
4. Rule $B \rightarrow \mathtt{b}B$: transition $(B, \mathtt{b}) \rightarrow B$.
5. Rule $B \rightarrow \varepsilon$: transition $(B, \varepsilon) \rightarrow F'$.

As a result, we will obtain the finite state machine shown in Figure 5.3.

Note that up to this point, context-free grammars were used to *generate* strings, such as correct email addresses. Our finite state machine is able to *recognize* strings

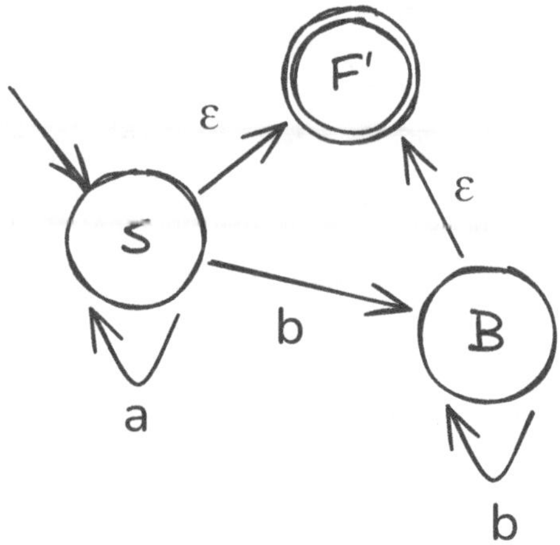

FIGURE 5.3: An FSM obtained from the example right-linear grammar.

described by the given grammar. The problem of language recognition remains central to this book, so we will focus mostly on this aspect.

5.4.3 CONVERTING FAS TO REGULAR GRAMMARS

We have demonstrated that any regular grammar can be transformed into a finite state machine, which means that in terms of expressive power, finite state machines are at least as powerful as regular grammars. To demonstrate equivalence, let's discuss how to construct a regular grammar corresponding to a given finite state machine. This can be done with the following procedure [34, Sec. 5.4]:

1. Label all states of the given FA with unique uppercase letters. These will be the nonterminals.
2. Designate the nonterminal corresponding to the start state of the FA as the start symbol of the resulting grammar.
3. For each favorable state F, add the production rule $F \to \varepsilon$ to the resulting grammar.
4. For each ε-transition $(A, \varepsilon) \to B$, add the production rule $A \to B$ to the resulting grammar.
5. For each transition $(A, \mathrm{c}) \to B$, add the production rule $A \to \mathrm{c}B$ to the resulting grammar.

Let's take the FA for detecting strings containing the substring abc as an example input (Figure 5.4).

Its nine transition rules will be converted to nine production rules of the resulting grammar as follows:

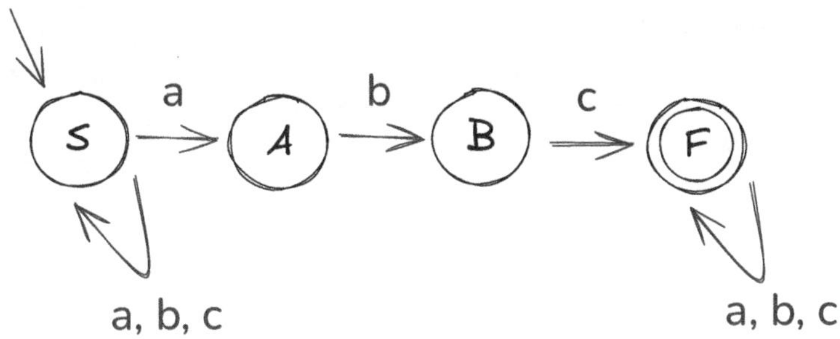

FIGURE 5.4: An FA recognizing the language $(\mathtt{a} \cup \mathtt{b} \cup \mathtt{c})^*\mathtt{abc}(\mathtt{a} \cup \mathtt{b} \cup \mathtt{c})^*$.

FA transition	Production rule
$(S, \mathtt{a}) \to S$	$S \to \mathtt{a}S$
$(S, \mathtt{b}) \to S$	$S \to \mathtt{b}S$
$(S, \mathtt{c}) \to S$	$S \to \mathtt{c}S$
$(S, \mathtt{a}) \to A$	$S \to \mathtt{a}A$
$(A, \mathtt{b}) \to B$	$A \to \mathtt{b}B$
$(B, \mathtt{c}) \to F$	$B \to \mathtt{c}F$
$(F, \mathtt{a}) \to F$	$F \to \mathtt{a}F$
$(F, \mathtt{b}) \to F$	$F \to \mathtt{b}F$
$(F, \mathtt{c}) \to F$	$F \to \mathtt{c}F$

The final rule $F \to \varepsilon$ completes the resulting grammar:

$$\begin{aligned}
S &\to \mathtt{a}S \mid \mathtt{b}S \mid \mathtt{c}S \mid \mathtt{a}A \\
A &\to \mathtt{b}B \\
B &\to \mathtt{c}F \\
F &\to \mathtt{a}F \mid \mathtt{b}F \mid \mathtt{c}F \mid \varepsilon
\end{aligned}$$

5.4.4 REGULAR GRAMMARS IN JFLAP

Grammar conversion functions are available in JFLAP. Let's use our previous examples to see how they work, but this time we will go the other way around: we will perform CFG-to-FA conversion for the language $(\mathtt{a} \cup \mathtt{b} \cup \mathtt{c})^*\mathtt{abc}(\mathtt{a} \cup \mathtt{b} \cup \mathtt{c})^*$ and the opposite conversion for the language $\mathtt{a}^*\mathtt{b}^*$.

To convert a finite state machine to a regular grammar, draw your machine as explained in Chapter 2, and use the menu **Convert, Convert to Grammar** to start the conversion. Click **Show All** to skip intermediate steps, and you will obtain the resulting right-linear grammar (Figure 5.5).

This grammar is a bit different from our handcrafted version, but ultimately it includes the same rules. Let's start with our original grammar for $\mathtt{a}^*\mathtt{b}^*$:

$$\begin{aligned}
S &\to \mathtt{a}S \mid \mathtt{b}B \mid \varepsilon \\
B &\to \mathtt{b}B \mid \varepsilon
\end{aligned}$$

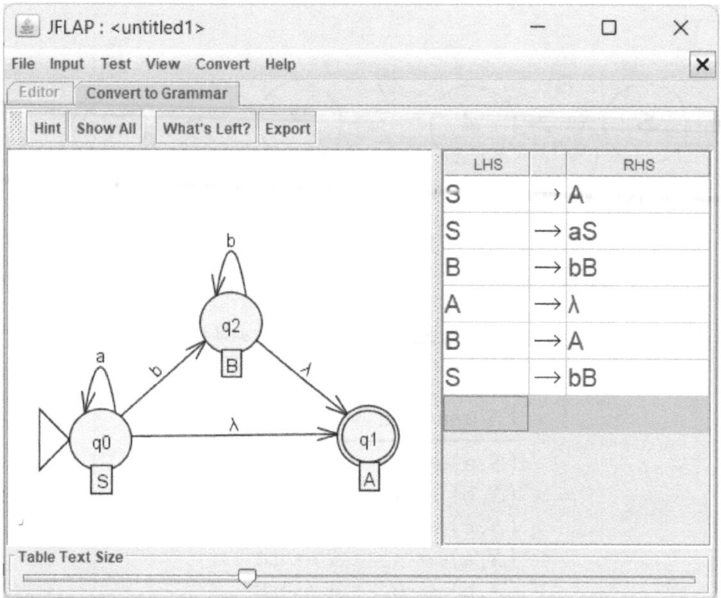

FIGURE 5.5: Converting an FA to a right-linear grammar in JFLAP.

JFLAP generates six rules in total. Three of them ($S \to \mathtt{a}S$, $S \to \mathtt{b}B$, and $B \to \mathtt{b}B$) are found in our grammar. The remaining rules simply represent a roundabout way to obtain ε (also known as λ) from S and B: $S \to A$, $B \to A$, $A \to \lambda$. In our grammar, this is done directly.

Conversion in the opposite direction is also quite easy. Use the **Grammar** option to open the grammar editor. The left-hand side of the very first rule is treated as the start symbol, so input $S \to \mathtt{a}S$ into the first line. Empty right-hand sides are treated as ε-strings. Combining rules with | is not possible, so you will have to enter the remaining rules line by line. Start the conversion using the menu **Convert, Convert Right-Linear Grammar to FA** and click **Show All** to complete this operation (Figure 5.6).

As expected, the resulting FA is almost the same as our version shown in Figure 5.4. It has a dedicated favorable state, accessible with a λ-transition from the original favorable state of our handcrafted FA.

5.5 TAKEAWAYS

1. Context-free languages represent a wider category of languages than regular languages. This category includes all regular and some nonregular languages. The existence of nonregular languages can be shown with the pumping lemma.

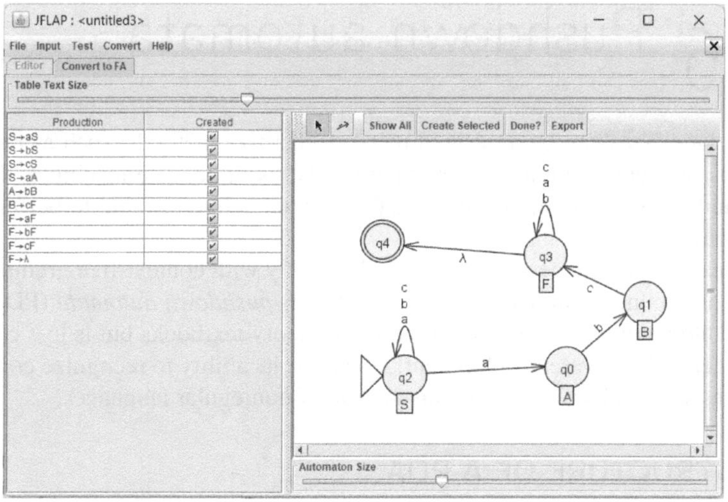

FIGURE 5.6: Converting a right-linear grammar to an FA in JFLAP.

2. Context-free languages can be described using context-free grammars. Just like regular expressions, context-free grammars are declarative: they do not offer any practical procedures for string validation.
3. By restricting the allowed production rules to a few selected kinds, we can turn a context-free grammar into a left-linear or right-linear regular grammar. Such grammars can only be used to describe regular languages.
4. Any given regular grammar can be converted to a finite automaton, and vice versa. These procedures bind together regular expressions, finite automata, and regular grammars.
5. Formal languages are equivalent to decision problems. Both languages and decision problems belong to certain complexity classes, characterized, most importantly, by the number of operations required to obtain a solution. For example, we have seen that the task of string validation for a regular language can be solved in "linear time," i.e., by performing a number of operations proportional to the length of the given string.

6 Pushdown automata

Regular languages can be described using declarative methods, such as regular expressions or regular grammars, or imperatively, as finite state machines. The latter form can be easily converted into actual computer programs able to perform string validation.

Context-free languages, described declaratively with context-free grammars, also have a corresponding imperative form, known as *pushdown automata* (PDAs). This type of automaton is a staple of computation theory textbooks but is less commonly seen in general software development. However, its ability to recognize context-free languages secures its place in any discussion of nonregular languages.

6.1 STRUCTURE OF A PDA

Informally speaking, a pushdown automaton is a finite state machine with *stack memory*. As a reminder, a stack is a kind of data storage that supports two operations (see Figure 6.1):

- **Push**: Place the given object on the top of the stack.
- **Pop**: Remove the top object from the stack and return it.

Normally, it is presumed that the stack is homogenous, i.e., all stored elements belong to the same data type. In the case of PDAs, the stack is presumed to be infinite and may store elements of a specified set Γ (called the *stack alphabet*). An attempt to perform the pop operation on an empty stack should be treated as an exceptional situation, similar to a missing transition rule. The most common option is to simply reject the input.

A pushdown automaton starts with an empty stack and operates according to transition rules, which are a bit more complex than the rules of a regular finite state machine. A rule $(A, c, s) \rightarrow (A', s')$ specifies that if the current PDA state is A, the current input symbol is c, and the symbol at the top of the stack is s, then 1) the device will switch into state A'; 2) s will be popped from the stack, and 3) the string s' will be pushed onto the top of the stack.

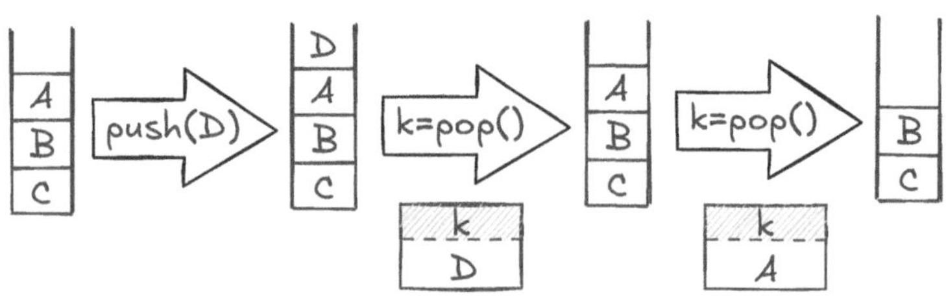

FIGURE 6.1: Stack operations.

DOI: 10.1201/9781032614991-6

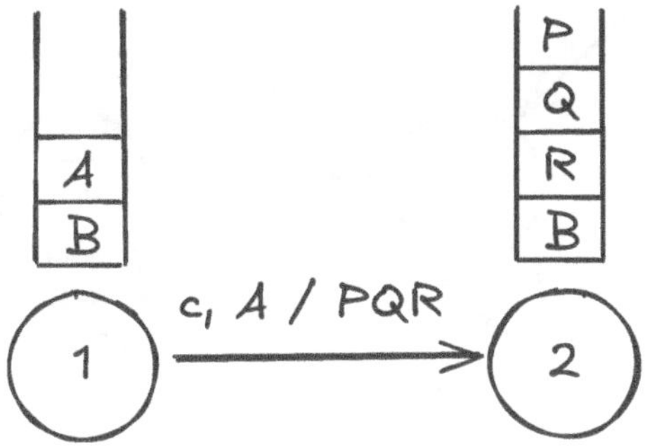

FIGURE 6.2: A stack update as a result of the transition $(1, c, A) \rightarrow (2, PQR)$.

A certain rule $(A, c) \rightarrow A'$ of a finite state machine can be applied if two conditions hold: the current state of the machine is A, and the current input symbol is c. In PDAs, there is a third condition: the current top of the stack must match the symbol s specified in the rule. Note that s in the left-hand side of a rule is a single stack symbol, while s' in the right-hand side is a string, meaning that it is possible to push several symbols onto the stack while performing a single transition. It is usually presumed that the symbols of s' are pushed in a right-to-left order, so the first symbol of s' will become the new top element of the stack (see Figure 6.2). A rule $(A, c, s) \rightarrow (A', s')$ is commonly labeled as $c, s/s'$ on a state diagram.[1]

By default, PDAs are considered to be nondeterministic machines. It is also allowed to use ε in stack operations. A rule like $(A, c, \varepsilon) \rightarrow (A', s')$ means that the current stack content is not important (it does *not* require the stack to be empty[2]) and that no symbols will be popped from the stack. In turn, a rule like $(A, c, s) \rightarrow (A', \varepsilon)$ means that s will be popped from the stack, but no new symbols will be pushed to replace it.

Just like regular FAs, PDAs may have designated favorable states indicating acceptance or rejection of the input. However, in the case of PDAs, there is an alternative established way to indicate the outcome: an input string can be considered accepted if the PDA finishes processing it with an empty stack. Both options, *acceptance by favorable state* and *acceptance by empty stack*, are equally valid, but it is important to choose one when designing a PDA. Any given PDA that accepts by favorable state can be converted to an equivalent PDA that accepts by empty stack, and vice versa [36, Sec. 6.2.3-6.2.4].

[1] Descriptions of pushdown automata vary from source to source. The version provided here can also be found, e.g., in Hopcroft et al. [36]. In contrast, Sipser [68] presumes it is only possible to push individual symbols onto the stack rather than strings of symbols and uses a slightly different notation for transition rules. However, these differences do not make PDAs more or less powerful.

[2] If you need a rule for the case of an empty stack, you can initialize the PDA by placing a special "sentinel" value Z on top of the stack and then use Z in rules as the empty-stack marker.

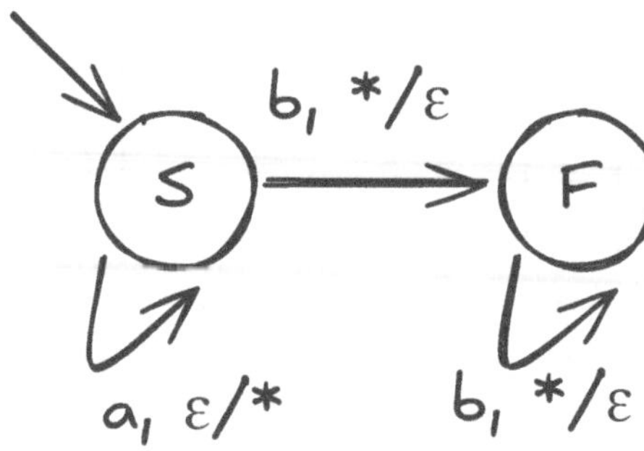

FIGURE 6.3: A PDA recognizing the nonregular language $L = \{a^n b^n\}$.

6.2 RECOGNIZING NONREGULAR LANGUAGES

As a simple example of a PDA's capabilities, let's again consider the nonregular language $L = \{a^n b^n\}$. It can be recognized by the PDA shown in Figure 6.3. Any string belonging to L leaves this device with an empty stack (thus, we use acceptance by empty stack here).

This PDA operates as follows. Suppose the input string consists of n as followed by n bs. Reading all the as will place n asterisk symbols on the stack. The subsequent n bs will pop all those asterisks, leaving the device with an empty stack. Any other combination of characters will either trigger a "missing transition" error or fail to empty the stack.

6.3 CONVERTING CONTEXT-FREE GRAMMARS TO PUSHDOWN AUTOMATA

Any context-free grammar can be converted into an equivalent PDA as follows:[3]

1. Create two PDA states: P and F. Mark P as the start state. Favorable states are not needed because the PDA will accept by empty stack.
2. Let the set of all terminal and nonterminal symbols of the source grammar be the stack alphabet.
3. Add the transition $(P, \varepsilon, \varepsilon) \to (F, S)$, where S is the start symbol of the grammar.
4. Add a transition $(F, c, c) \to (F, \varepsilon)$ for each terminal symbol c of the grammar.
5. For every grammar rule $A \to x$, add a transition $(F, \varepsilon, A) \to (F, x)$.

It might seem surprising that any context-free language can be recognized with a PDA having merely two states. To understand how such a device operates, let's once again return to the example of the language $L = \{a^n b^n\}$. We already know its CFG

[3] PDA-to-CFG conversion is also possible but is more complicated and less practically useful. For details, see, e.g., [36, Sec. 6.3.2].

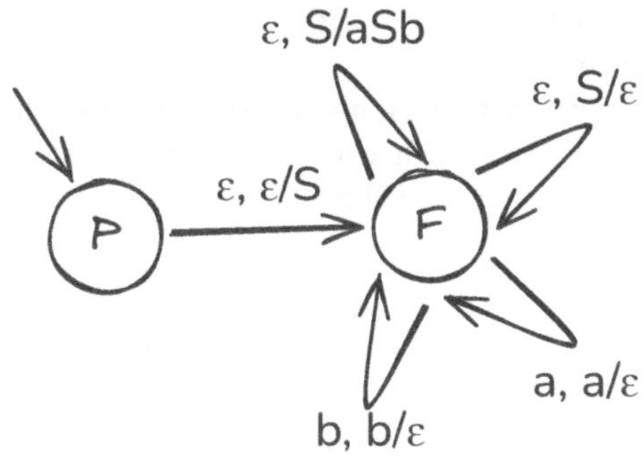

FIGURE 6.4: A PDA obtained from a context-free grammar.

definition from the previous chapter:

$$S \rightarrow \mathtt{a}S\mathtt{b} \mid \varepsilon$$

To convert this grammar into a PDA:

- We will first create states P and F, designate the set of symbols $\{\mathtt{a}, \mathtt{b}, S\}$ as the stack alphabet, and add the rule $(P, \varepsilon, \varepsilon) \rightarrow (F, S)$ (steps 1–3).
- We will add two new rules corresponding to the two terminal symbols of the grammar: $(F, \mathtt{a}, \mathtt{a}) \rightarrow (F, \varepsilon)$ and $(F, \mathtt{b}, \mathtt{b}) \rightarrow (F, \varepsilon)$ (step 4).
- Finally, we will translate the grammar rules $S \rightarrow \mathtt{a}S\mathtt{b}$ and $S \rightarrow \varepsilon$ into the transition rules $(F, \varepsilon, S) \rightarrow (F, \mathtt{a}S\mathtt{b})$ and $(F, \varepsilon, S) \rightarrow (F, \varepsilon)$.

The resulting PDA is shown in Figure 6.4.

This PDA looks simpler than the handcrafted version shown earlier (Figure 6.3). Nondeterminism certainly helps to keep the device concise; recall that NFAs also normally contain fewer states than their deterministic equivalents. Nondeterminism in PDAs works in the same way as in NFAs: any situation where it is possible to apply two or more different rules creates a "fork" in the multiverse. It is enough to find a single "happy path" to treat a given input string as accepted by the PDA.

Stack operations provide new options to disambiguate potentially conflicting rules. For example, the rules $(P, c, \mathtt{a}) \rightarrow (F, \mathtt{b})$ and $(P, c, \mathtt{b}) \rightarrow (F, \mathtt{k})$ do not conflict because they expect different top-of-stack symbols. In the same way, ε-transitions do not necessarily introduce nondeterminism. In NFAs, a rule like $(1, \varepsilon) \rightarrow 2$ is nondeterministic because it offers a choice: process the remaining input from state 1, or switch to state 2 and continue from there. In contrast, a PDA rule $(1, \varepsilon, \mathtt{x}) \rightarrow (2, \mathtt{y})$ offers a similar choice only if x is currently at the top of the stack.

A pushdown automaton constructed with the grammar conversion algorithm operates similarly to a grammar derivation. It starts by pushing S onto the stack and then processes the input as follows:

1. If the input string is fully consumed and the PDA stack is empty, accept the input string.

2. Pop the top-of-stack element s. If this is not possible (the stack is empty), reject the input string.
3. If s is a nonterminal symbol A, nondeterministically choose one of its production rules $A \rightarrow x$ and push x onto the stack.
4. If s is a terminal symbol c, read the next input symbol. If it is not c, reject the input string.

Technically, both cases of input rejection occur due to missing transition rules: the device either has to pop something from an empty stack, or it has to consume a mismatching input character.

Consider how our PDA (Figure 6.4) would process the string `aabb`:

Step	Tape	Stack	Action	Rule used
1	`aabb`	(empty)	Push S.	$(P, \varepsilon, \varepsilon) \rightarrow (F, S)$
2	`aabb`	S	Replace S with $\texttt{a}S\texttt{b}$ on the stack.	$(F, \varepsilon, S) \rightarrow (F, \texttt{a}S\texttt{b})$
3	`aabb`	$\texttt{a}S\texttt{b}$	Consume input, pop `a` from the stack.	$(F, \texttt{a}, \texttt{a}) \rightarrow (F, \varepsilon)$
4	`abb`	$S\texttt{b}$	Replace S with $\texttt{a}S\texttt{b}$ on the stack.	$(F, \varepsilon, S) \rightarrow (F, \texttt{a}S\texttt{b})$
5	`abb`	$\texttt{a}S\texttt{bb}$	Consume input, pop `a` from the stack.	$(F, \texttt{a}, \texttt{a}) \rightarrow (F, \varepsilon)$
6	`bb`	$S\texttt{bb}$	Replace S with ε on the stack.	$(F, \varepsilon, S) \rightarrow (F, \varepsilon)$
7	`bb`	`bb`	Consume input, pop `b` from the stack.	$(F, \texttt{b}, \texttt{b}) \rightarrow (F, \varepsilon)$
8	`b`	`b`	Consume input, pop `b` from the stack.	$(F, \texttt{b}, \texttt{b}) \rightarrow (F, \varepsilon)$
9	ε	(empty)	Accept.	

6.4 DETERMINISTIC PUSHDOWN AUTOMATA

Given our previous experience with finite state machines, it would be natural to take the same path toward the practical recognition of context-free languages: describe a certain language with a context-free grammar, build a corresponding PDA, convert it to a *deterministic PDA* (DPDA) and finally simulate it on a computer. Unfortunately, this path hits a wall: deterministic and nondeterministic pushdown automata have different expressive power.

Nondeterministic PDAs can recognize any context-free language. In contrast, DPDAs can recognize only *deterministic context-free languages* — a set of languages that includes all regular and *some* nonregular context-free languages. Furthermore, DPDAs that accept by favorable state recognize a wider class of languages than DPDAs that accept by empty stack. For this reason, acceptance by favorable state is normally used for DPDAs.

An obvious alternative to determinization would be the direct simulation of a non-deterministic PDA. In Chapter 2, we discussed how to simulate an NFA, so this approach is a familiar one. Unfortunately, PDAs are more challenging to simulate. The branching timelines of an NFA might be numerous, but the number of active configurations is always *finite*. In contrast, a PDA simulation may have to explore an *infinite* number of configurations.

Consider a grammar having a production rule $A \rightarrow A\mathtt{c}$. It will be transformed into the PDA rule $(F, \varepsilon, A) \rightarrow (F, A\mathtt{c})$. When the PDA uses this rule, the A at the top of the stack is replaced with two symbols: A and $\mathtt{c}$. This way, A is at the top of the stack again, and the PDA can again choose to use the same rule without consuming any input symbols.

An NFA simulator explores a space of pairs (*state*, *tape*). An NFA has a finite number of states, and its tape contains either the whole input string (which is finite) or a certain "tail" of it, still to be processed. A PDA simulator has to explore a space of triples (*state*, *tape*, *stack*), where the current stack content *stack* belongs to an infinite set. In the example above, the PDA may produce new triples indefinitely by repeatedly pushing $A\mathtt{c}$s onto the stack: $(F, tape, A)$, $(F, tape, A\mathtt{c})$, $(F, tape, A\mathtt{cc})$, and so on. Since no input tape symbols are consumed during this process, the simulator will not advance toward the end of any timeline.

Note that both PDAs and DPDAs are able to manipulate stack without consuming input, which means there is no easy way to say how much time a given pushdown machine would take to process a string of length N.

In practice, simulators work on real computers with limited memory, so the challenge is to simulate PDAs efficiently rather than to explore infinite branches. A straightforward solution is to set a maximum allowed stack size and to use *breadth-first search* rather than depth-first search. Our "breadcrumbs"-based NFA simulator explores paths in the same way an adventurer would explore a maze: once the end of a certain path is reached, the procedure takes a step back and examines the next path. In contrast, breadth-first search explores all neighbors of the starting location before examining their own neighbors. This way, it behaves more like molasses trickling from a broken bottle: it covers the maze gradually, from the starting location to nearby locations, and only then to more distant rooms. In the context of PDAs, such an algorithm would examine all possible configurations reachable in n steps before moving on to configurations reachable in $n + 1$ steps. Thus, if a certain string can be accepted in n steps, the simulator will find the "happy path" before exploring any longer routes.

In any case, the best practical approach to dealing with context-free languages is either to use a procedure *not* based on pushdown automata or be contend with deterministic languages that can be recognized with DPDAs. The class of deterministic languages is wide enough for most purposes. In particular, their power is sufficient to describe the syntax of a typical programming language.

A simple example of a context-free language that is not deterministic is the language of *palindromes*, i.e., sequences that read the same both ways, like `kayak`, `racecar`, or `rotator`.

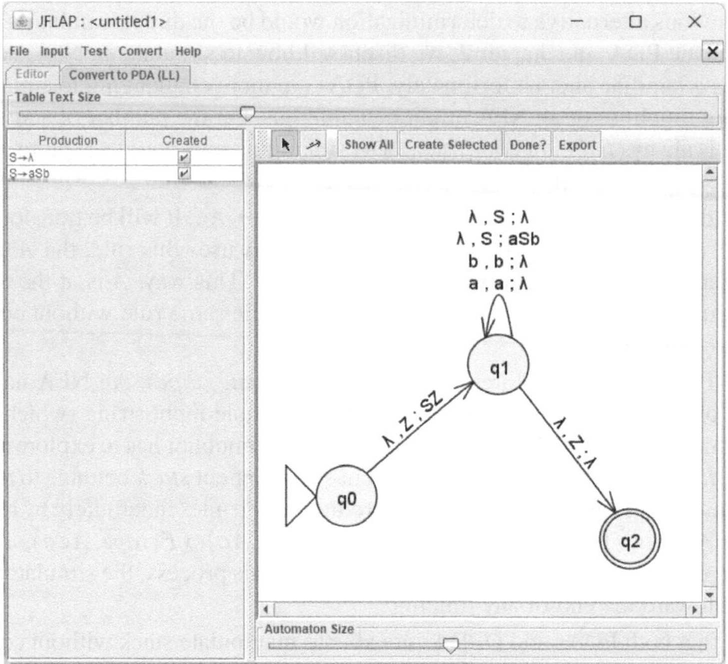

FIGURE 6.5: CFG-to-PDA conversion in JFLAP.

6.5 PUSHDOWN AUTOMATA IN JFLAP

JFLAP implements both CFG-to-PDA and PDA-to-CFG conversion routines, as well as a PDA simulator. Pushdown automata in JFLAP are slightly different from our version: they can both push and pop several stack elements within a single transition, and they come with a sentinel character z already placed on the stack.

Let's see how JFLAP converts our example grammar

$$S \to \mathtt{a}S\mathtt{b} \mid \varepsilon$$

to a pushdown automaton.

Run JFLAP and choose **Grammar** from the main menu. Next, enter both production rules in the editor window. Finally, choose **Convert, Convert CFG to PDA (LL)** or **Convert, Convert CFG to PDA (LR)** to start the conversion routine. The procedure discussed earlier in this chapter is the LL-algorithm, so choose this option to obtain a machine resembling the one shown in Figure 6.4. In the next window, press **Show All** to complete the conversion (see Figure 6.5).

Automata converted from CFGs in JFLAP always accept by favorable state. For this reason, apart from notational differences (rules are labeled as "c, s; s'" rather than "c, s/s'"), this PDA has a dedicated favorable state that can be reached when the stack is empty.

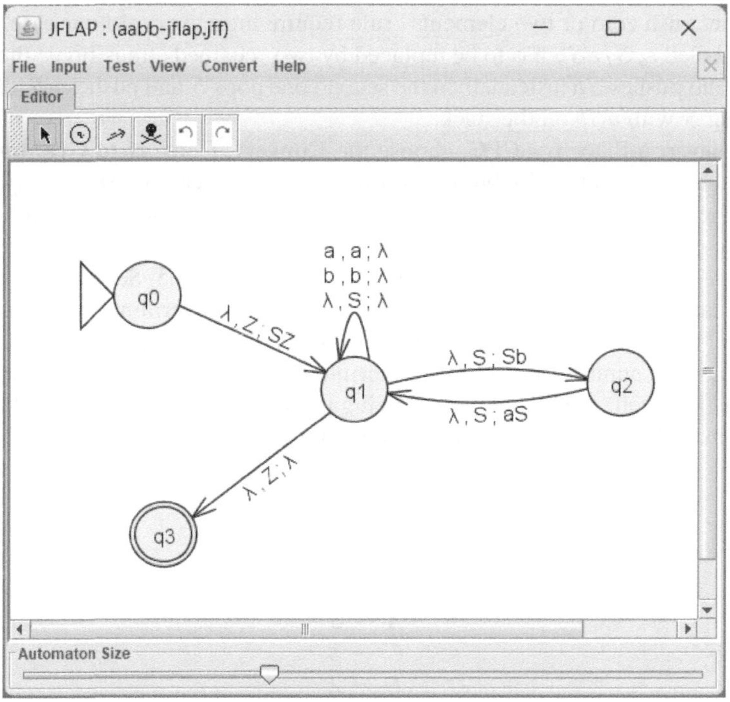

FIGURE 6.6: A PDA ready for conversion.

You can test the obtained PDA using the **Input, Fast Run** menu item.

The PDA-to-CFG conversion process is, unfortunately, more complicated. You can initiate it by selecting **Pushdown Automaton, Multiple Character Input** in the main menu and drawing the states and transitions of your PDA. This process is similar to designing a finite state machine, but here you'll have to specify three items for each transition label.

JFLAP requires that the PDA to be converted satisfy certain conditions:

1. It must have only one favorable state.
2. Transitions to this favorable state must pop only Z from the stack.
3. Each transition in the PDA must pop exactly one character from the stack.
4. Each transition in the PDA must push nothing (λ) or two characters onto the stack.

It is the user's responsibility to make sure the PDA is in the right format. For example, to make the PDA shown in Figure 6.4 convertible to a CFG, it has to be modified as shown in Figure 6.6.

Some changes are simple: the label of the "starting" transition $\varepsilon, \varepsilon / S$ becomes $\lambda, Z; SZ$ to take into account the sentinel value Z. Similarly, the transition to the favorable state must merely pop Z from the stack. Transitions that do not respect the "pop one, push zero or two elements" rule require more work. In our case, the transition labeled $\varepsilon, S/\mathtt{a}S\mathtt{b}$ has to be replaced by two "chained" transitions: the first one pops S and pushes Sb instead, then the second one pops S and pushes aS, effectively replacing S with aSb on the stack.

To convert a PDA to a CFG, choose the **Convert, Convert to Grammar** menu item and press the **Show All** button to complete the conversion. At this stage, JFLAP will use temporary names like `(q1Sq1)` or `(q3Sq0)` for the nonterminal symbols of the resulting grammar. Sadly, as the JFLAP developers admit, *"many useless productions will be generated in addition to the correct productions"* [65, Sec. 6.3].

You can try to remove redundant rules and rename nonterminal symbols into conventional uppercase Latin letters by pressing the **Export** button. This process will fail, however, if the number of resulting nonterminal symbols exceeds 26. In our case, the export works well, producing the following production rules (remember that JFLAP uses λ instead of ε to represent the empty string):

$$
\begin{aligned}
S &\rightarrow SD \\
C &\rightarrow EA \\
E &\rightarrow BC \\
B &\rightarrow \mathtt{a} \\
A &\rightarrow \mathtt{b} \\
C &\rightarrow \lambda \\
D &\rightarrow \lambda
\end{aligned}
$$

This grammar is not as simple and concise as our original version but works fine as an illustration.

6.6 TAKEAWAYS

1. Pushdown automata can recognize any context-free language but cannot handle languages that are not context-free.
2. The existence of CFG-to-PDA and PDA-to-CFG conversion algorithms proves the statement above.
3. In general, recognition of context-free languages requires a nondeterministic PDA, which is hard to simulate on a computer.
4. Deterministic PDAs (which are easy to simulate) recognize deterministic languages, a specific subset of context-free languages.
5. It remains to be discussed what kind of grammars describe deterministic languages and how to convert these grammars to DPDAs.

7 Parsing

Decision problems are formal languages, so any tool that is able to recognize wider classes of formal languages can also solve previously unsolvable decision problems and is thus a welcome addition to our growing collection of computational devices. Yet, given these new devices, it is harder and harder to be content with the ability to merely accept and reject input strings. Even our most restricted instrument, regular expressions, was adopted for a different task: pattern matching.

As discussed before, identified matches can be further dissected into meaningful fragments by using groups, a feature available in all practical regular expression engines. This feature turned out to be exceptionally useful even for relatively simple regular languages, so it is no surprise that a capability of a similar kind is a "must have" for devices able to recognize nonregular languages.

The problem of parsing, i.e., understanding what is what in a given input string, is related to language recognition but is still distinct enough to have its own theories and algorithms. Here we will barely scratch the surface of this topic, but it should be enough to gain confidence in processing context-free languages.[1] We will discuss some details that might seem a bit too technical for this book, but I think they are important for establishing a solid connection between parsing algorithms and pushdown automata.

To narrow down the scope of our work, we will focus on parsing context-free languages described with context-free grammars. Context-free grammars, in turn, represent the internal structure of strings in the form of *parse trees*, like the one shown in Figure 5.1. Therefore, the goal of a *parser*, in our case, will be to construct such trees.

7.1 UNAMBIGUOUS AND AMBIGUOUS GRAMMARS

Let's return to our very first example of a formal grammar:

$$
\begin{aligned}
&S \to A\_N \\
&A \to \texttt{brave} \mid \texttt{lazy} \mid \texttt{hungry} \\
&N \to \texttt{cat} \mid \texttt{dog} \mid \texttt{bear}
\end{aligned}
$$

How do we show that the string `lazy_cat` belongs to the language described by this grammar? For example, we can reason in the following way. Any string derived from S is of the form A_N. One possible option for A is `lazy`, so S can be derived into `lazy_`N. In the same way, one of the possible options for N is `cat`, so S can indeed become `lazy_cat`:

$$S \to A\_N \to \texttt{lazy\_}N \to \texttt{lazy\_cat}$$

[1]If you do not feel this way after reading this chapter, try Grune and Jacobs [32], which is both an extensive and accessible overview of the subject.

DOI: 10.1201/9781032614991-7

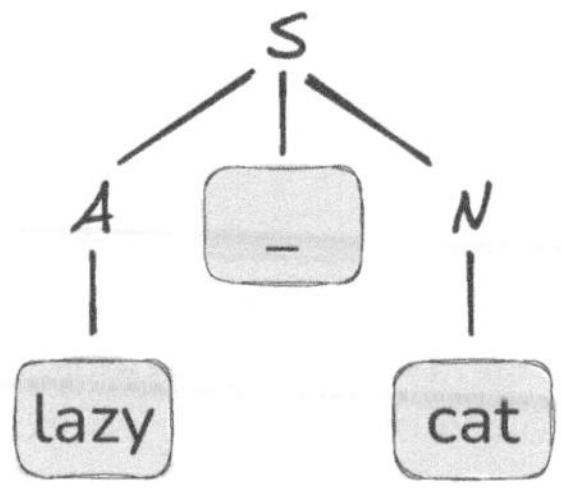

FIGURE 7.1: Parse tree of the string `lazy cat`.

The parse tree of this derivation is shown in Figure 7.1.

Each node of the parse tree labeled with a nonterminal symbol has a certain number of descendants, revealing the rule that was applied. For instance, the three children of S show that S was replaced with a sequence A_N. Similarly, a parent-child relationship between A and `lazy` points to the rule $A \rightarrow \mathtt{lazy}$.

In the course of deriving `lazy_cat`, we had to decide which nonterminal symbol of the string A_N to replace first: A or N. Our choice was the leftmost symbol (A), but we could have equally well started with N, obtaining a slightly different chain of operations: $S \rightarrow A\_N \rightarrow A\_\mathtt{cat} \rightarrow \mathtt{lazy\_cat}$.

This choice has no effect on the resulting parse tree, which is going to be the same as in Figure 7.1. However, such independence of the final result from the selected sequence of operations is not universal. Let's consider a somewhat cumbersome way to describe the language $\mathtt{a}^*\mathtt{b}^*$:

$$
\begin{aligned}
&S \rightarrow ANB \\
&A \rightarrow \mathtt{a}A \mid \varepsilon \\
&B \rightarrow \mathtt{b}B \mid \varepsilon \\
&N \rightarrow \mathtt{a}N\mathtt{b} \mid \varepsilon
\end{aligned}
$$

Now, let's try proving that the string `aab` belongs to this language. This can be done by applying production rules as follows (downward arrows indicate the next rule to be applied):

$$
\begin{array}{ccccccccccccccc}
S & \rightarrow & ANB & \rightarrow & \mathtt{a}ANB & \rightarrow & \mathtt{aa}ANB & \rightarrow & \mathtt{aa}NB & \rightarrow & \mathtt{aa}B & \rightarrow & \mathtt{aab}B & \rightarrow & \mathtt{aab} \\
 & & \downarrow & & \downarrow & & \downarrow & & \downarrow & & \downarrow & & \downarrow & & \\
 & & \mathtt{a}A & & \mathtt{a}A & & \varepsilon & & \varepsilon & & \mathtt{b}B & & \varepsilon & &
\end{array}
$$

Alternatively,

$$
\begin{array}{ccccccccccccc}
S & \rightarrow & ANB & \rightarrow & \mathtt{a}ANB & \rightarrow & \mathtt{a}NB & \rightarrow & \mathtt{aa}N\mathtt{b}B & \rightarrow & \mathtt{aab}B & \rightarrow & \mathtt{aab} \\
 & & \downarrow & & \downarrow & & \downarrow & & \downarrow & & \downarrow & & \\
 & & \mathtt{a}A & & \varepsilon & & \mathtt{a}N\mathtt{b} & & \varepsilon & & \varepsilon & &
\end{array}
$$

These chains of operations yield different parse trees (see Figure 7.2).

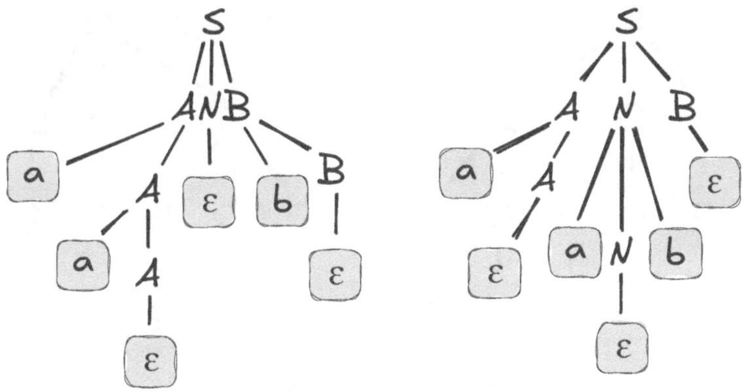

FIGURE 7.2: Different parse trees of the string `aab`.

Thus, the string `aab` is *ambiguous*: in particular, we do not know whether the trailing `b` is obtained from N or from B. Ambiguity becomes an issue if the difference between N and B is meaningful. For example, imagine that the grammar of a certain programming language includes the following rule:

$$\text{PHRASE} \rightarrow \text{OPERATION} \mid \text{COMMENT} \mid \text{KEYWORD}$$

Suppose a certain code fragment can be parsed either as OPERATION or as COMMENT. This would mean that the language parser will not be able to identify the meaning of the fragment. Programming language designers are well aware of this problem and strive to produce unambiguous syntax. Yet, sometimes things happen. Here is a classical example from the C programming language. In C,

- a forward slash denotes division: `a/10`;
- comments start with `/*` and end with `*/`: `/* this is a comment */`;
- a star before a variable name is the "dereference operator" that retrieves a value from the memory address specified by the given pointer variable: `*p`.

Imagine a C compiler faces the following fragment: `R = total/*p`. Is it division (`total` divided by the value taken from the memory location `p`) or `total` followed by the beginning of a comment section? In this particular case, there is a rule saying that the sequence `/*` is always treated as the beginning of a comment. The C preprocessor detects and removes comments before parsing, leaving no room for confusion.

The effects of ambiguity can be more subtle. Consider the following ambiguous grammar describing simple arithmetic expressions:

$$E \rightarrow EOE \mid \texttt{0} \mid \texttt{1} \mid \ldots \mid \texttt{9}$$
$$O \rightarrow \texttt{+} \mid \texttt{-} \mid \texttt{*} \mid \texttt{/} \mid \texttt{=}$$

An expression (E) is an ⟨expr⟩⟨operation⟩⟨expr⟩ (EOE) or a single digit. An operation (O) is an equality symbol or one of the four arithmetic operations. Suppose

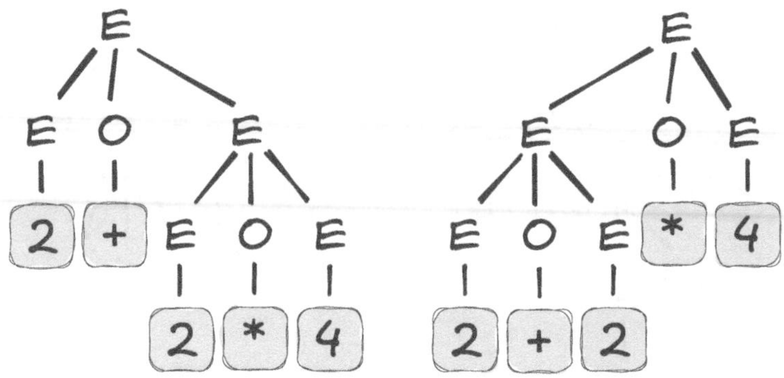

FIGURE 7.3: Parse trees of the string `2+2*4`.

our task is to make sure the string `2+2*4` belongs to the language described by this grammar. It can be done with the following chain of derivations:

$$E \to EOE \to 2OE \to 2{+}E \to 2{+}EOE \to 2{+}2OE \to 2{+}2{*}E \to 2{+}2{*}4$$

The same objective can be accomplished with another chain:

$$E \to EOE \to EOEOE \to 2OEOE \to 2{+}EOE \to 2{+}2OE \to 2{+}2{*}E \to 2{+}2{*}4$$

These chains yield the parse trees shown in Figure 7.3. Here, all digits and operations are obtained from the nonterminals E and O, respectively. However, the different structures of the parse trees suggest different interpretations of the input. The left tree says that the expression `2` is added to the expression `2*4`, while the right tree identifies the expression `2+2` multiplied by the expression `4`.

More often than not, ambiguity is a property of a grammar rather than of a language. Our grammar for $\mathtt{a}^*\mathtt{b}^*$ is ambiguous because it produces alternative parse trees for certain strings, but it is also possible to describe the same language with an unambiguous grammar:

$$\begin{aligned} S &\to \mathtt{a}S \mid \mathtt{b}A \mid \varepsilon \\ A &\to \mathtt{b}A \mid \varepsilon \end{aligned}$$

Some languages, however, are ambiguous by nature. A classic example is a language consisting of strings of two types: $\mathtt{a}^n\mathtt{b}^n\mathtt{c}^m\mathtt{d}^m$ and $\mathtt{a}^n\mathtt{b}^m\mathtt{c}^m\mathtt{d}^n$. This language can be described, for instance, with the following context-free grammar:

$$\begin{aligned} S &\to AB \mid C \\ A &\to \mathtt{a}A\mathtt{b} \mid \mathtt{ab} \\ B &\to \mathtt{c}B\mathtt{d} \mid \mathtt{cd} \\ C &\to \mathtt{a}C\mathtt{d} \mid \mathtt{a}D\mathtt{d} \\ D &\to \mathtt{b}D\mathtt{c} \mid \mathtt{bc} \end{aligned}$$

Consider the string `aabbccdd`. Regardless of the grammar used, it is not possible to tell whether it belongs to the type $\mathtt{a}^n\mathtt{b}^n\mathtt{c}^m\mathtt{d}^m$ or $\mathtt{a}^n\mathtt{b}^m\mathtt{c}^m\mathtt{d}^n$ (where $n = m = 2$).

Languages that cannot be described with an unambiguous grammar are called *inherently ambiguous*. Unfortunately, there is no general algorithm that can find out whether a given language is inherently ambiguous or not [30]. It is also not possible to determine whether a given context-free grammar is ambiguous [10, p. 154] (although it might be possible for certain specific grammars). Even if a certain language described with an ambiguous grammar is believed not to be inherently ambiguous, there is no general routine to derive an unambiguous grammar for it. There are only several "rules of thumb" for eliminating certain kinds of ambiguity [2, Sec. 4.3.4].

The practical way to deal with the ambiguity of grammars is to impose further restrictions on the types of allowed production rules and on certain principles that direct the parsing algorithm. These limitations further narrow down the kinds of languages that can be described, but this is a small price to pay for the absence of ambiguity as well as for the simplicity and efficiency of parsing.

7.2 LEFTMOST DERIVATION AND RIGHTMOST DERIVATION

Look again at the left side of Figure 7.3. This tree was obtained by applying production rules as follows:

$$E \rightarrow EOE \rightarrow 2OE \rightarrow 2{+}E \rightarrow 2{+}EOE \rightarrow 2{+}2OE \rightarrow 2{+}2{*}E \rightarrow 2{+}2{*}4$$

Such a sequence of operations is called a *leftmost derivation* because the leftmost nonterminal symbol of the current string is replaced at every step. The same tree can be produced by a series of replacements of the rightmost nonterminal symbol (a *rightmost derivation*):

$$E \rightarrow EOE \rightarrow EO4 \rightarrow E{*}4 \rightarrow EOE{*}4 \rightarrow EO2{*}4 \rightarrow E{+}2{*}4 \rightarrow 2{+}2{*}4$$

It is also possible to replace nonterminals in an arbitrary order:

$$E \rightarrow EOE \rightarrow E{+}E \rightarrow E{+}EOE \rightarrow E{+}E{*}E \rightarrow 2{+}E{*}E \rightarrow 2{+}E{*}4 \rightarrow 2{+}2{*}4$$

Most common parsing methods implement either leftmost or rightmost derivation procedures. It might seem that the practical difference between them is as insignificant as that between the heads and tails of a coin, but such an intuition would be wildly inaccurate. Parsers that follow different derivations can parse different classes of languages and are not similar in their internal design.

7.3 DIRECTIONALITY AND LOOKAHEAD

The procedure of choosing the kind of derivation chain to follow is one of the principal attributes of a parser. Another important attribute is *directionality*, which specifies whether the parser processes input sequentially or in an arbitrary order. We'll focus on the more common *directional parsers*, which process symbols sequentially, from left to right. The words "left" and "right" here refer to the beginning and the end of the input string rather than to literal left-hand-side and right-hand-side symbols. Conceptually, a directional parser can be imagined as a tape-reading device, just like a finite state machine. The parser can access symbols in the middle of the tape only after reading its beginning ("leftmost" symbols). In contrast, non-directional methods assume that all the symbols constituting the input string are freely accessible.

Unlike FSMs, parsers are normally presumed to have access to k consecutive characters of the tape. This capability is called *lookahead*: while FSMs have to choose the next state on the basis of a single-symbol input, a parser can make a more informed decision.

Combining the choice between the leftmost and rightmost derivation with directional parsing and the possibility of lookahead, we obtain two classes of parsers to consider: LL(k) (**L**eft-to-right, **L**eftmost derivation, k symbols of lookahead) and LR(k) (**L**eft-to-right, **R**ightmost derivation, k symbols of lookahead). The languages recognized by these kinds of parsers are called LL(k) and LR(k) languages, respectively.

7.4 PROPERTIES OF LL(K) AND LR(K) GRAMMARS

Our next major goal will be to discuss several practical parsing algorithms. Before we move on, let's clarify some facts about the expressive power of the grammars we have considered so far.

There are two related yet distinct concepts: LL(k)/LR(k) *languages* and LL(k)/LR(k) *grammars*. As stated above, LL(k)/LR(k) languages are languages that can be recognized using left-to-right parsers with leftmost or rightmost derivation and k symbols of lookahead. In turn, LL(k)/LR(k) grammars are context-free grammars with certain restrictions on their production rules that make it possible to build LL(k)/LR(k) parsers for them. Therefore, we can alternatively define LL(k)/LR(k) languages as languages that can be described with corresponding LL(k)/LR(k) grammars.

A language, however, can also be described with a more powerful grammar than necessary, such as a general context-free grammar with no LL/LR-specific restrictions. For example, it is easy to imagine a certain LL(1) language being described with an LL(2) grammar, meaning that whoever designed the grammar found it easier to employ a two-symbol lookahead rather than to take on the challenge of reducing the number of lookahead symbols, even if it is known to be theoretically possible.

Knuth [41, Sec. V] established that LR(k) grammars correspond to deterministic languages: any deterministic language can be described with a certain LR(k) grammar, and the expressive power of LR(k) grammars is limited to deterministic languages. This statement holds for any $k \geq 1$, so even a one-symbol lookahead is enough for an LR-parser to recognize all deterministic languages. This also means that it is not possible to make LR grammars more powerful by increasing the lookahead value.

LL(k) grammars work differently. Each additional lookahead symbol increases the expressive power of an LL(k) grammar, but no finite k is sufficient to describe all possible deterministic languages [66, p. 246].

In the previous chapter, we discussed how certain restrictions in production rules turned context-free grammars into regular grammars that describe regular languages. Unfortunately, no simple method of this kind can be used to obtain LL(k) or LR(k) grammars. There are, however, standard algorithms for building LL(k) and LR(k) parsers. If such an algorithm fails, it means that the input grammar does not belong to the required type and has to be modified.

The usual issue is ambiguity. For example, it is not possible to construct an LL(1) parser for the following grammar:

$$
\begin{aligned}
S &\rightarrow DM \mid DP \\
D &\rightarrow \mathtt{a} \mid \mathtt{b} \\
M &\rightarrow *D \\
P &\rightarrow **D
\end{aligned}
$$

This grammar describes two kinds of expressions: multiplication (e.g., `a*b`) and exponentiation (e.g., `b**a`). A one-symbol lookahead is not sufficient to decide which rules to apply: after seeing an input like `a*...`, the parser knows that `a` can be derived from D, but the next character `*` might mean either M or P.

An obvious solution in this case is to resort to a two-symbol lookahead, thus building an LL(2) parser. Alternatively, it might be possible to modify the language described by the given grammar (for example, if you are designing your own language, you can tinker with its syntax freely). If it is possible to use `^` instead of `**` for exponentiation, the ambiguity disappears.

Yet another option is to modify the grammar:

$$
\begin{aligned}
S &\rightarrow DOT \\
T &\rightarrow D \mid OD \\
D &\rightarrow \mathtt{a} \mid \mathtt{b} \\
O &\rightarrow *
\end{aligned}
$$

The input string `a*b` is parsed as DOT, where T expands to D. In turn, `b**a` is parsed as DOT, where T expands to OD. In either case, `*` is always derived from O, which makes a one-symbol lookahead sufficient. However, this solution works by passing additional responsibilities to subsequent stages of text analysis. The LL(2) grammar could clearly distinguish multiplication from exponentiation (M from P), while our new LL(1) grammar merely identifies one or two nonterminals O. Making sense of the difference between O and OO will be the job of post-parsing procedures.

Detecting ambiguity while crafting a parser is easy. LL(k) and LR(k) parsers are state machines. Grammar rules that violate LL(k)/LR(k) requirements produce conflicting (nondeterministic) transitions that can be reported immediately. At this stage, one may employ an additional method of overcoming ambiguity by deciding which of the conflicting transitions should take precedence.

The remainder of this chapter will be dedicated to three parsing algorithms, able to process LR(1), LL(1), and arbitrary context-free grammars, respectively. The rationale for this selection is simple. LR(1) grammars can be used to describe any deterministic language, so an LR(1) parser can be employed in a large variety of practical tasks. The class of LL(1) languages is quite restricted, but an LL(1) parser is easy to code and can be modified for larger lookahead values, so if the power of LL(k) grammars happens to be sufficient for the task, the LL parser is a reasonable choice. Finally, a universal parsing algorithm for context-free grammars shows how to parse any (not necessarily deterministic) context-free language. However, this algorithm achieves universality at the expense of speed. Specialized LL(k) and LR(k) parsers can parse input faster (in linear time) thanks to the properties of the corresponding grammars.

7.5 PARSING LR(1) GRAMMARS

The LR(1) parser is especially interesting for us because it is based on the pushdown automaton model, supplying the missing link between declarative LR(1) grammars, which are able to describe any deterministic language, and imperative deterministic devices, which are able to recognize them in practice. At the same time, the LR(1) parser building algorithm is by far the most complex part of this book, so please proceed with patience.[2]

7.5.1 PRELIMINARY NOTES

We will create a standard type of LR(1) parser known as a *shift-reduce parser*. It implements *bottom-up parsing*, which gradually builds a parse tree from the terminal symbols of the input string all the way up to the start symbol, which forms the root node. In practice, the complete tree is rarely needed: typically, it is sufficient to output the identified production rules in a certain well-defined order, allowing for the reconstruction of the tree if necessary.

Conceptually, our program will consist of two independent procedures. The first procedure will create the states and transitions that form the pushdown automaton core of the parser. Since creating the automaton for a given grammar is not the same task as parsing input strings, this is normally the job of a separate instrument known as a *parser generator*. The second procedure will parse any given input string by actually simulating the work of the pushdown machine.

We will store the production rules of the given grammar in a Python `set` object. Shorthand notation will not be supported: each rule is going to be represented explicitly as a pair (N, s), where N is a nonterminal symbol, and s is an empty string or a string of terminal and nonterminal symbols. All uppercase Latin letters will be treated as nonterminals, and all other symbols will be considered terminals. We will reserve the letter S for the start symbol of the grammar.

For example, the grammar

$$S \rightarrow \mathtt{a}S\mathtt{b} \mid \varepsilon$$

will be represented as:

[2] For a much more in-depth discussion of LR(1) parsing, see Sec. 4.7 of the "Dragon Book" [2].

```
g = {("S", "aSb"), ("S", "")}
```

7.5.2 REMOVING ε-RULES

While production rules like $N \rightarrow \varepsilon$ are often convenient, they are not essential for declaring context-free languages. Since the process of parser generation is simpler for grammars without ε-rules, we will remove them by using the following observation. A rule $A \rightarrow \varepsilon$ can be removed if we generate an additional rule $X \rightarrow \alpha\beta$ for any existing rule $X \rightarrow \alpha A \beta$, where α and β are arbitrary (possibly empty) strings. This process is not as straightforward as it may seem because any occurrences of A can be replaced with empty strings, meaning that all possibilities must be covered. For example, if we have a rule $X \rightarrow \alpha A \beta A \gamma$, then three additional rules have to be generated:

$$X \rightarrow \alpha\beta A\gamma$$
$$X \rightarrow \alpha A\beta\gamma$$
$$X \rightarrow \alpha\beta\gamma$$

Furthermore, the removal of certain ε-rules may trigger the generation of new ε-rules. To exclude a rule $A \rightarrow \varepsilon$ from a grammar having a rule like $X \rightarrow A$, we'll have to generate the new rule $X \rightarrow \varepsilon$. Such new rules will have to be excluded using the same procedure.

This algorithm presumes that each *nullable nonterminal* (i.e., a symbol that can be replaced with an empty string) must appear elsewhere in the right-hand side of production rules. This logic does not work for the start symbol S, so by removing the rule $S \rightarrow \varepsilon$, we would make empty strings unrecognizable by the parser. This error is easy to fix: we will have a dedicated "empty strings are accepted" marker that will be set when the rule $S \rightarrow \varepsilon$ is removed from the given grammar.

Let's now create the initial version of our LR parser class:

```
from dataclasses import dataclass


@dataclass
class LRParser:
    grammar: set

    def preprocess_grammar(self): # remove epsilon-rules
        pass


parser = LRParser({("S", "aSb"), ("S", "")})
parser.preprocess_grammar()
```

The actual procedure of ε-rule removal is straightforward: we identify the next ε-rule, remove it from the grammar, and add a list of new rules obtained by removing nullable nonterminals. The process of generating new rules is similar to creating NFA states: each rule with N nullable nonterminal symbols on the right-hand side yields $2^N - 1$ new rules, reflecting all possible ways of removing some of these nonterminals.

Excluded rules might reappear later, so before adding a certain rule, it is important to make sure it was not handled previously. For example, suppose we have $A \to B$, $A \to \varepsilon$, and $B \to A$. When the algorithm removes $A \to \varepsilon$, it has to add a new rule $B \to \varepsilon$. Then it needs to remove $B \to \varepsilon$, which means it has to add $A \to \varepsilon$ again.

The removal of ε-rules will be performed inside `preprocess_grammar()`:

```
@dataclass
class LRParser:
    grammar: set
    accept_empty: bool = False

    def gen_rules(self, lhs, x, rules, prefix, suffix):
        if x not in suffix:
            rules.add((lhs, prefix + suffix))  # new rule is ready
        else:
            i = suffix.index(x)  # process remaining entries of x
            self.gen_rules(lhs, x, rules, prefix + suffix[:i], suffix[i + 1 :])
            self.gen_rules(lhs, x, rules, prefix + suffix[: i + 1],
            suffix[i + 1 :])

    # return all rules generated to exclude x -> epsilon
    def all_gen_rules(self, lhs, rhs, x):
        rules = set()
        self.gen_rules(lhs, x, rules, "", rhs)
        return rules

    # return the first rule with an empty right-hand side
    def first_e_rule(self):
        e_rules = {(lhs, rhs) for (lhs, rhs) in self.grammar if rhs == ""}
        return e_rules.pop() if e_rules else None

    def preprocess_grammar(self):
        excluded = set()

        while e_rule := self.first_e_rule():
            x, _ = e_rule

            # set "empty strings are accepted" marker
            if x == "S":
                self.accept_empty = True

            excluded.add(e_rule)
            self.grammar.remove(e_rule)

            # add new generated rules except previously excluded
            rules_with_x = {(lhs, rhs) for lhs, rhs in self.grammar if x
             in rhs}

            for lhs, rhs in rules_with_x:
                self.grammar.update(self.all_gen_rules(lhs, rhs, x) - excluded)
```

7.5.3 PARSING PROCEDURE

To process input strings, our parser will need access to the pushdown automaton configuration tables ACTION and GOTO, prepared by the parser generator. This is quite a complicated task that would distract us from parsing, our primary goal. For this reason, let's pretend that the configuration tables are already available and focus on the parsing algorithm. We'll discuss how to create the tables a bit later.

The `GOTO` table is a dictionary where the keys are pairs (*state*, *nonterminal*) and the values are states:

```
GOTO[stateA, symbol] = stateB
```

The `ACTION` table is a dictionary where the keys are pairs (*state*, *terminal*) and the values are "actions" of three kinds:

- `shift(s)`: Place state `s` on the stack, then proceed to the next input character.
- `reduce(A → x)`: Remove `len(x)` symbols from the stack; switch to the state `s` stored on the top of the stack; place state `GOTO[s, A]` on the stack.
- `accept`: Accept the input string immediately.

The parsing procedure first places the start state on the stack and then performs a simple loop:

```
LOOP
    s = value on top of the stack
    a = next input character
    execute ACTION[s, a]
END LOOP
```

If this algorithm ever requests an action for a non-existent key value, the input string is rejected.

The complete parsing routine must also take care of the following points:

- Empty strings should be accepted or rejected in accordance with the value of `accept_empty`.
- The input string needs a dedicated *end-of-string marker* character (we'll use `$`).
- The start symbol of the grammar must not appear in the right-hand side of production rules. This can be ensured by creating an *augmented grammar* with a new start symbol $>$ and adding the rule $> \rightarrow S$.

Therefore, the resulting Python code becomes:

```
@dataclass
class LRParser:
    ...
    stack: list = None
    action_table: dict = None
    goto_table: dict = None
    input: str = None

    class AcceptException(BaseException):
        pass

    class GrammarException(BaseException):
```

```
        pass

    def preprocess_grammar(self):
        ...
        self.grammar.add((">", "S"))

    def shift(self, v):
        self.stack_push(v)
        self.input = self.input[1:]

    def reduce(self, rule):
        lhs, rhs = rule
        self.stack_pop(len(rhs))
        state = self.stack_top()
        self.stack_push(self.goto_table[state, lhs])
        print(rule)

    def accept(self, _):
        raise LRParser.AcceptException()

    def stack_push(self, v):
        self.stack.append(v)

    def stack_pop(self, count):
        self.stack = self.stack[:-count]

    def stack_top(self):
        return self.stack[-1]

    def parse(self, tape):
        if not tape:
            return self.accept_empty

        try:
            self.input = tape + "$"
            self.stack = [0]

            while True:
                s = self.stack_top()
                a = self.input[0]
                action, arg = self.action_table[s, a]
                action(arg)
        except LRParser.AcceptException:
            return True
        except KeyError:
            return False
```

The function `parse()` tells whether the input string is accepted or rejected and prints production rules in the order they are discovered.

Consider our first attempt to construct a grammar for multiplication and exponentiation. Its Python version takes a bit more space:

```
parser = LRParser(
    {
        ("S", "DM"),
        ("S", "DP"),
```

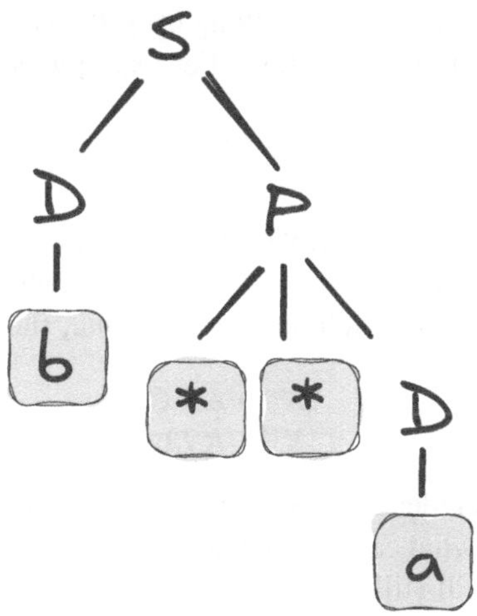

FIGURE 7.4: Parse tree of the string `b**a`.

```
        ("D", "a"),
        ("D", "b"),
        ("M", "*D"),
        ("P", "**D"),
    }
)
```

For the input string `b**a`, the parser (when it is fully implemented) would produce the following output:

```
('D', 'b')
('D', 'a')
('P', '**D')
('S', 'DP')
```

This corresponds to the parse tree shown in Figure 7.4.

In the output of the bottom-up LR parser, each parent node is preceded by its children, listed in left-to-right order [32, Sec. 3.1.3]. Thus, *S* is preceded by *D* and *P*, while *P* is preceded by its own child node *D*. Knowing this principle, it is possible to reconstruct the complete parse tree if needed. In practice, it is more common to execute a certain action when a particular production rule is identified.

7.5.4 *FIRST* SETS

The best way to understand the inner workings of an LR(1) parser is to examine how its configuration tables are created. This work starts with the generation of *FIRST* sets.

For any terminal or nonterminal symbol s, *FIRST(s)* is the set of terminals that can start strings derivable from s using production rules. If s is a terminal symbol,

FIRST(s) is a set that contains only one element, *s*. If *s* is a nonterminal symbol, we'll have to trace its possible transformations. For example, suppose our input grammar is:

$$S \rightarrow \mathtt{a}A$$
$$A \rightarrow \mathtt{cb} \mid \mathtt{d}$$

Here, $FIRST(S) = \{\mathtt{a}\}$, and $FIRST(A) = \{\mathtt{c}, \mathtt{d}\}$.

Computation of $FIRST$ sets is one of those tasks where ε-rules complicate matters. Consider a grammar that includes, in particular, the following two production rules:

$$X \rightarrow \mathtt{a}NC$$
$$Y \rightarrow KT\mathtt{b}$$

Clearly, $FIRST(X)$ includes a, because $\mathtt{a}NC$ is derived from X. It is also clear that we do not need to know what can be obtained from N or C: the first character of any string derived from X will still be a. Computing $FIRST(Y)$ is harder: it includes b only if both K and T are nullable. Thus, by excluding ε-rules, we can make the computation of $FIRST$ sets much simpler:

```
@dataclass
class LRParser:
    ...
    first: dict = None

    def extend_first_sets(self):
        for lhs, rhs in self.grammar:
            for a in self.terminals():
                if a in self.first[rhs[0]] - self.first[lhs]:
                    self.first[lhs].add(a)
                    return True
        return False

    def gen_first_sets(self):
        self.first = {k: set() for k in self.nonterminals()}  # FIRST[X] = {}
        self.first.update({k: {k} for k in self.terminals()})  # FIRST[c] = {c}

        while self.extend_first_sets():
            pass
```

We start by setting `FIRST[c]` to `{}` if `c` is a nonterminal and to `{c}` if `c` is a terminal symbol. Next, we examine whether there is a grammar rule `lhs` → `rhs` and a terminal symbol `a` such that `a` is in `FIRST[rhs[0]]` but not yet in `FIRST[lhs]`. If so, we add `a` to `FIRST[lhs]`. This process is repeated until no further changes can be made.

7.5.5 SET OF ITEMS AND ITS CLOSURE

The next concept we need is called an *LR(1) item* (or simply an *item*). It characterizes a "snapshot" of a process that matches a certain production rule with the input string. An item is a production rule with a dot marker separating already-recognized symbols from the symbols yet to be processed, paired with the next expected terminal. For example, our starting rule will always be $> \rightarrow S$. Thus, the starting point of string recognition can be described with the item ($>\rightarrow \bullet S$, \$). The parser is about to recognize the symbol S, and after that, it expects to face the end-of-input marker \$. The "snapshot" of the parser after the successful processing of S will be ($>\rightarrow S\bullet$, \$).

We will only deal with sets of items and their *closures*. A closure of a certain set of items is formed by the elements of this set and all items accessible from them using production rules. Calculation of the closure is where we will need *FIRST* sets.

Imagine our set of items contains an item $(A \rightarrow \alpha \bullet B\beta, a)$, where α and β are arbitrary (possibly empty) strings. Suppose there is a production rule $B \rightarrow \gamma$. When the parser starts processing B, it gets into a state described by the item $(B \rightarrow \bullet\gamma, b)$, where b belongs to *FIRST(first symbol of βa)*. In other words, after processing γ, the parser expects a certain terminal symbol b that starts a string derivable from the first character of βa.

We will represent a single LR(1) item $(A \rightarrow \alpha \bullet \gamma, a)$ in our Python code as a four-element tuple (A, α, γ, a).

Thus, a set of items will be represented by a set of such tuples. To compute the closure of a given set of items, we'll keep updating its copy until no further changes can be made:

```
@dataclass
class LRParser:
    ...

    def update_closure(self, r):
        B_items = [
            (Bb[0], Bb[1:], a)
            for _, _, Bb, a in r
            if Bb and Bb[0] in self.nonterminals()
        ]

        r_count = len(r)

        for B, beta, a in B_items:
            for gamma in (gamma for X, gamma in self.grammar if X == B):
                for b in self.first[(beta + a)[0]]:
                    item = (B, "", gamma, b)
                    r.add(item)

        return r_count != len(r)

    def closure(self, items):
        r = set(items)  # clone items

        while self.update_closure(r):
            pass

        return r
```

The function `update_closure()` works as follows. It starts by identifying items of the form $(A \rightarrow \alpha \bullet B\beta, a)$, where B is a nonterminal symbol. Next, for each such B, a rule of the kind $B \rightarrow \gamma$ is retrieved. Finally, the closure is extended with items of the form $(B \rightarrow \bullet\gamma, b)$ for each b in *FIRST(first symbol of βa)*.

7.5.6 COLLECTION OF SETS OF LR(1) ITEMS

The final step before the actual construction of the ACTION and GOTO configuration tables is the building of a sequence (usually called a "collection") of sets of LR(1) items. The individual elements of this sequence will represent the states of the pushdown automaton we are developing.

This step needs a simple helper function `goto()` (distinct from the GOTO table), defined as follows:

```
@dataclass
class LRParser:
    ...
    def goto(self, s, X):
        return self.closure(
            {(A, alpha + X, Bb[1:], a) for A, alpha, Bb, a in s if
             Bb.startswith(X)}
        )
```

This function takes a set of items `s` and a symbol `X` and returns the closure of a new set of items obtained from `s` by "stepping over" `X`. For each original item $(A \rightarrow \alpha \bullet X\beta, a)$, we add $(A \rightarrow \alpha X \bullet \beta, a)$ to this new set.

The collection of sets of LR(1) items is generated with the following code:

```
@dataclass
class LRParser:
    ...

    def next_collection_elem(self, c):
        for x in self.terminals() | self.nonterminals():
            for elem in c:
                next_elem = self.goto(elem, x)
                if next_elem and next_elem not in c:
                    return next_elem
        return None

    def lr_collection(self):
        c = [self.closure({(">", "", "S", "$")})]
        while elem := self.next_collection_elem(c):
            c.append(elem)

        return c
```

The first element of the collection is the closure of the start item ($> \rightarrow \bullet S$, $). Subsequent elements are obtained by calling `goto()` with all possible combinations of grammar symbols and existing collection elements.

Consider again the grammar:

$$
\begin{aligned}
S &\rightarrow DM \mid DP \\
D &\rightarrow \mathsf{a} \mid \mathsf{b} \\
M &\rightarrow *D \\
P &\rightarrow **D
\end{aligned}
$$

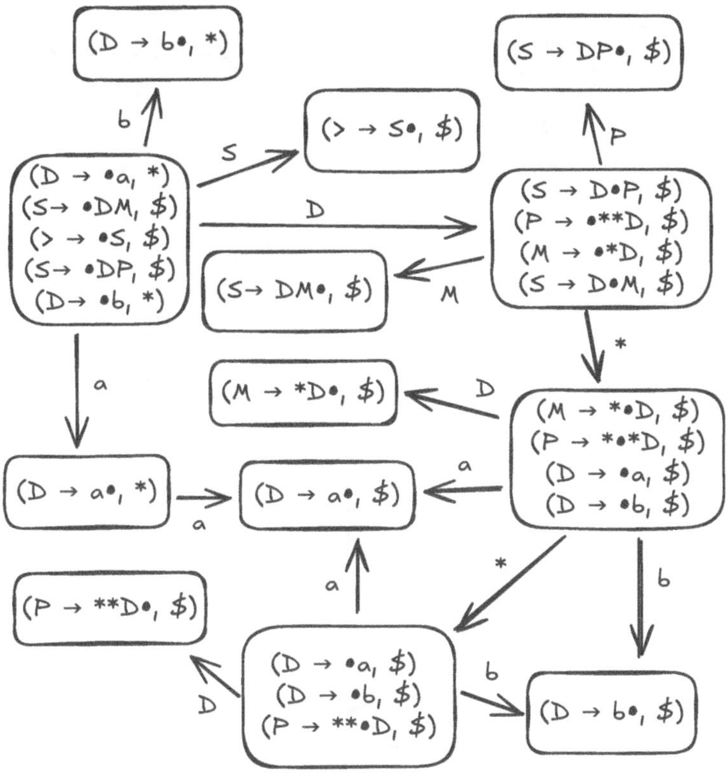

FIGURE 7.5: The goto graph for the example grammar.

Its collection of sets of LR(1) elements is shown in Figure 7.5 as a graph. The graph vertices are the collection elements, and the graph edges are obtained by calling `goto()`: an edge from *A* to *B* is labeled *c* if `goto(A, c)` returns *B*.

Each set in the collection (representing a state of a pushdown automaton) represents the LR(1) items that may describe the current "snapshot" of the parsing process. The edges point to states that will become current as a result of processing certain terminal or nonterminal symbols. This graph is still an intermediate data structure rather than the target state machine, but it already shows what is going on inside the LR(1) parser. Figure 7.6 visualizes the order of operations that take place when the parser recognizes the input string `b**a`. Each visited state is labeled with the corresponding step number.

The logic of this process is easier to understand by tracing its steps backward. The last visited state is 9, where *S* has already been processed and the parser expects the end-of-input marker `$`. In turn, *S* was recognized as a result of processing its children *D* and *P* in state 8. In the same way, *P* was derived from $**D$ in state 7, and *D* was derived from `a` in state 6. Deriving *P* from $**D$ takes more effort: state 5 recognizes *D*, while states 4 and 3 read the asterisks. Finally, state 2 recognizes the only missing

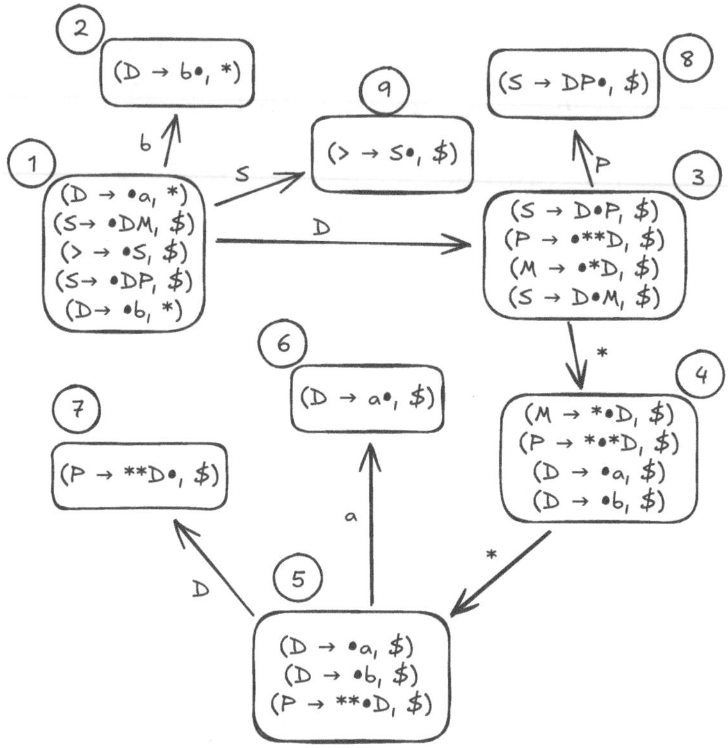

FIGURE 7.6: States visited during the recognition of the string `b**a`.

child node, D, in ($S \rightarrow \bullet DP$, $), which brings us to state 1. Thus, child nodes are processed before their parent nodes, as expected in LR parsing.

The parser is able to recognize strings like `b**a` even with a one-symbol lookahead because it defers decisions until no ambiguity is left. When the beginning of the string `b*` is recognized, the parser is in state 4, which corresponds to items covering both multiplication and exponentiation: ($M \rightarrow * \bullet D$, $) and ($P \rightarrow * \bullet *D$, $). A similar approach is used in the NFA determinization algorithm, which produces a DFA able to keep track of possibilities across timelines. Like determinization, the basic LR(1) parser generation algorithm may produce a considerable number of states (but various memory-saving optimizations are possible [70]).

7.5.7 CREATING ACTION AND GOTO TABLES

We are approaching the last stages of LR parser development. Having the collection of sets of LR(1) items, it is finally possible to generate the ACTION and GOTO tables.

The individual elements of our collection are sets that represent the states of the target pushdown automaton. The GOTO table provides the same functionality as the goto() function but represents states as integers, which is more convenient. This table can be constructed as follows:

```
@dataclass
class LRParser:
    ...
    goto_table: dict = None

    def create_goto_table(self, c):
        self.goto_table = {}

        for A in self.nonterminals():
            for i, elem in enumerate(c):
                if (s := self.goto(elem, A)) in c:
                    self.goto_table[i, A] = c.index(s)
```

This code simply replaces the elements of the collection c with their indices and stores the values returned by goto() in the resulting table.

Constructing the ACTION table is a bit more complicated:

```
@dataclass
class LRParser:
    ...
    action_table: dict = None

    def write_action(self, key, action):
        if key in self.action_table and self.action_table[key] != action:
            raise LRParser.GrammarException()
        self.action_table[key] = action

    def create_action_table(self, c):
        self.action_table = {}

        for i, elem in enumerate(c):
            for A, alpha, Bb, b in elem:  # single item
                if not Bb and A != ">":
                    self.write_action((i, b), (self.reduce, (A, alpha)))

                elif (A, alpha, Bb, b) == (">", "S", "", "$"):
                    self.write_action((i, "$"), (self.accept, None))

                else:
                    a = Bb[0]
                    s = self.goto(elem, a)

                    if a in self.terminals() and s in c:
                        self.write_action((i, a), (self.shift, c.index(s)))
```

For each LR(1) item found in the collection, we have to generate a certain action:

- If the item is $(A \to \alpha\bullet, b)$ and A is not >, we generate reduce($A \to \alpha$).
- Otherwise, if the item is $(> \to S\bullet,$ $), we generate accept.
- Otherwise, if the item is $(A \to \alpha \bullet a\gamma, b)$, where a is a terminal symbol, we generate shift. It takes the state obtained by calling goto(elem, a), where elem is the current collection element.

The small utility function `write_action` checks whether the given element of the ACTION table has been already generated. This situation means there are conflicting rules, so the whole process has to be interrupted with an exception.

7.5.8 TESTING THE PARSER

Now we can test the whole pipeline by parsing, for example, the same string `b**a`:

```
...

parser = LRParser(
    {
        ("S", "DM"),
        ("S", "DP"),
        ("D", "a"),
        ("D", "b"),
        ("M", "*D"),
        ("P", "**D"),
    }
)

parser.preprocess_grammar()
parser.gen_first_sets()
c = parser.lr_collection()

try:
    parser.create_action_table(c)
    parser.create_goto_table(c)

    print(parser.parse("b**a"))
except LRParser.GrammarException:
    print("non-LR(1) grammar")
```

We already know what this code prints:

```
('D', 'b')
('D', 'a')
('P', '**D')
('S', 'DP')
```

Now let's revisit Figure 7.6 to see which operation is executed in every state:

```
state 1: shift
state 2: reduce D → b
state 3: shift
state 4: shift
state 5: shift
state 6: reduce D → a
state 7: reduce P → **D
state 8: reduce S → DP
state 9: accept
```

In a nutshell, the `shift` operation moves from parent nodes to child nodes, consuming one input character, and the `reduce` operation completes the processing of the currently identified production rule.

We have already considered some examples of ambiguous grammars. Our algorithm cannot handle them. For example, a simple grammar

```
parser = LRParser(
    {
        ("S", "E"),
        ("E", "EOE"),
        ("E", "a"),
        ("O", "+"),
    }
)
```

causes `LRParser.GrammarException` inside `create_action_table()`.

As a more advanced example of a proper LR(1) grammar, consider the following way of describing arithmetic expressions [2, Sec. 4.1.2]:

$$\begin{aligned} S &\to E \\ E &\to E\text{+}T \mid E\text{-}T \mid T \\ T &\to T*F \mid F \\ F &\to (E) \mid \mathtt{a} \mid \mathtt{b} \mid \mathtt{c} \end{aligned}$$

This grammar causes no trouble for our parser:

```
parser = LRParser(
    {
        ("S", "E"),
        ("E", "E+T"),
        ("E", "E-T"),
        ("E", "T"),
        ("T", "T*F"),
        ("T", "F"),
        ("F", "(E)"),
        ("F", "a"),
        ("F", "b"),
        ("F", "c"),
    }
)

parser.preprocess_grammar()
parser.gen_first_sets()
c = parser.lr_collection()

try:
    parser.create_action_table(c)
    parser.create_goto_table(c)
    print(parser.parse("c-a-b-c*(a+b)"))
except LRParser.GrammarException:
    print("non-LR(1) grammar")
```

The string `c-a-b-c*(a+b)` is parsed as follows:

```
('F', 'c')
('T', 'F')
('E', 'T')
```

```
('F', 'a')
('T', 'F')
('E', 'E-T')
('F', 'b')
('T', 'F')
('E', 'E-T')
('F', 'c')
('T', 'F')
('F', 'a')
('T', 'F')
('E', 'T')
('F', 'b')
('T', 'F')
('E', 'E+T')
('F', '(E)')
('T', 'T*F')
('E', 'E-T')
('S', 'E')
```

Now let's reconstruct the parse tree by tracing the productions from the very last one all the way back. S is E. In turn, that E is E-T. The children are listed in left-to-right order, but since we are moving backward, the next line in the output shows that the rightmost nonterminal T is $T*F$. In turn, that F is (E), and that E is E+T, where T is F. The next production ($F \rightarrow$ b) has no children, so the subsequent production to consider ($E \rightarrow T$) defines the E that is a sibling of T in $E \rightarrow E$+T. By proceeding in this manner, we can obtain the complete tree (see Figure 7.7).

A context-free grammar only describes the syntax of a formal language. In our case, its job is to distinguish between valid strings like `a+b*c` and invalid strings like `a--b`. However, it does not attach any meaning to the resulting trees: treating symbols like `+` and `*` as addition and multiplication of sibling nodes is beyond the scope of parsing. However, a grammar is able to represent concepts like associativity and precedence: it is not a coincidence that `c-a-b-c*(a+b)` is parsed as `((c-a)-b)-c*(a+b)`. The grammar states that `c-a-b` must be computed as `(c-a)-b` rather than `c-(a-b)` and that multiplication must be done before addition and subtraction.

7.5.9 THE LR(1) PARSER AS A PUSHDOWN AUTOMATON

Clearly, our code operates like a pushdown automaton, but at the same time, it is slightly different from the state machine described in Chapter 5. It is, however, possible to show that the LR(1) parser is indeed equivalent to a DPDA. A complete proof is beyond the scope of this book, but we will discuss some relevant ideas (for more details, see [35, Sec. 10.8]).

Our parser has certain features not found in DPDAs, but they are either irrelevant or can be simulated with DPDA transitions.

1. States and transitions are generated "on the fly" and stored in `ACTION` and `GOTO` tables.

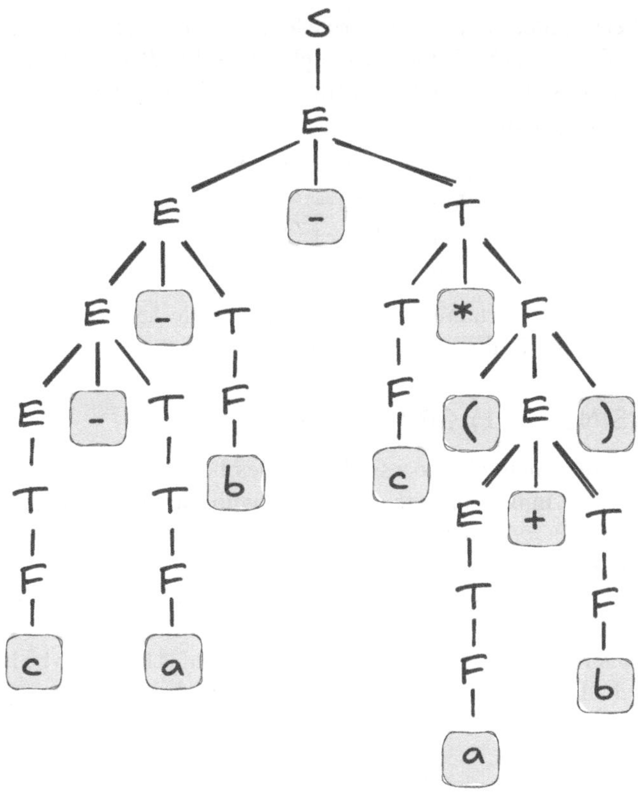

FIGURE 7.7: The parse tree of the expression `c-a-b-c*(a+b)`, constructed bottom-up.

While our code does indeed generate `ACTION` and `GOTO` on the fly, this task is the responsibility of a parser generator, not the parser. The parser relies on precomputed tables.

2. A PDA can read the current symbol on the tape and move to the next symbol. It cannot do a lookahead without actually consuming the input. Similarly, a PDA reads and removes stack values. It cannot read the top of the stack and keep it intact.

   Keeping the top of the stack intact is easy: it is enough to place the read element back, as in a rule $(S, a, p) \to (S', p)$. Input symbols cannot be written back in the same way, but a PDA can store the lookahead symbol on the stack. A rule like $(P, a, \varepsilon) \to (S, a)$ places the next input symbol a on the stack, where it can be read as many times as necessary.
3. The operation `reduce(`$A \to x$`)` removes `len(x)` stack elements. This is not possible in a PDA.

   The length of x is known in advance, so the actual task is to remove a certain constant number of symbols from the stack. Next, since the stack alphabet is finite, we can create a rule for every possible string of the required length. For example, if the stack alphabet is $\{A, B, C\}$, and our task is to switch from state X to state Y while removing three characters, we can add the following eight rules:

$$(X, \varepsilon, AAA) \to (Y, \varepsilon)$$
$$(X, \varepsilon, AAB) \to (Y, \varepsilon)$$
$$(X, \varepsilon, ABA) \to (Y, \varepsilon)$$
... and so on for all 8 combinations.

This method is certainly inefficient, but its role here is only to show the theoretical possibility of such a simulation.

7.6 PARSING LL(1) GRAMMARS

Bottom-up parsing methods process child nodes before their parents. It is possible to perform parsing in the opposite order: start with the topmost grammar symbol S and apply rules in a *top-down* fashion until all nonterminal symbols are turned into terminals or empty strings.

LL(k) parsers operate in such a top-down way. Since their power depends on the lookahead value k, the LL(1) parser is the most restricted of them but is also the easiest to implement. Even if the language to be parsed is known to be LL(1), it might be a bit of a challenge to describe it with an LL(1) grammar. For example, arithmetic expressions can be parsed with an LL(1) parser, but the grammar we used earlier

$$S \to E$$
$$E \to E\texttt{+}T \mid E\texttt{-}T \mid T$$
$$T \to T\texttt{*}F \mid F$$
$$F \to \texttt{(}E\texttt{)} \mid \texttt{a} \mid \texttt{b} \mid \texttt{c}$$

is not an LL(1) grammar.

Suppose the input string consists of a single character `c`. When the parser sees the first input character (`c`), it should be able to produce the whole sequence of rules from the very top of the tree ($S \to E$) to the very bottom ($F \to \texttt{c}$), showing how to obtain `c` from S. The parser can start with $S \to E$, but it does not know whether to proceed with $E \to E\texttt{+}T$, $E \to E\texttt{-}T$, or $E \to T$.

Fortunately, in this particular case, it is possible to provide an alternative grammar that has an LL(1) form [2, Sec. 4.1.2]:

$$S \to E$$
$$E \to TG$$
$$G \to \texttt{+}TG \mid \texttt{-}TG \mid \varepsilon$$
$$T \to FH$$
$$H \to \texttt{*}FH \mid \varepsilon$$
$$F \to \texttt{(}E\texttt{)} \mid \texttt{a} \mid \texttt{b} \mid \texttt{c}$$

Now the parser can recognize `c` as follows. Naturally, it chooses $S \to E$, $E \to TG$, and $T \to FH$, because there are no other options. Next, it chooses $F \to \texttt{c}$ because `c` is the next input character (which is consumed here). The next input character is the end-of-string marker, which is not $*$, so the parser picks $H \to \varepsilon$, and, for the same reason, $G \to \varepsilon$.

7.6.1 RECURSIVE DESCENT PARSER

Now we will consider a very simple kind of LL(1) parser called a *recursive descent parser*. For each nonterminal symbol A of the given grammar, the parser has a function `A()` that operates as follows:

1. If there are several production rules having A on the left-hand side, use the next input character to decide which rule to apply.
2. If there is a rule $A \to \varepsilon$ and no suitable match is found, apply it; otherwise, reject the input string.
3. Print out the chosen rule.
4. Process the right-hand side of the rule in left-to-right order. If the next symbol is a nonterminal X, call `X()`. If the next symbol is a terminal `c`, check that the next input character is `c` and then consume it. If there is a mismatch, reject the input string.

The main parsing procedure has to call `S()` and check that the whole input string has been consumed.

Let's see how this algorithm translates into Python by creating a recursive descent parser for the grammar of arithmetic expressions shown above. In principle, this is the job of a parser generator, but it is not hard to code everything manually in our case:

```
from dataclasses import dataclass


@dataclass
class LLParser:
    grammar: set
    input: str = None

    class RejectException(BaseException):
        pass

    def next_char(self):
        return self.input[0]

    def consume(self, c):
        if self.input[0] != c:
            raise LLParser.RejectException()
        self.input = self.input[1:]

    def S(self):
        print("S -> E")
        self.E()

    def E(self):
```

```
        print("E -> TG")
        self.T()
        self.G()

    def G(self):
        if self.next_char() in "+-":
            print(f"G -> {self.next_char()}TG")
            self.consume(self.next_char())
            self.T()
            self.G()
        else:
            print("G -> epsilon")

    def T(self):
        print("T -> FH")
        self.F()
        self.H()

    def H(self):
        if self.next_char() == "*":
            print("H -> *FH")
            self.consume("*")
            self.F()
            self.H()
        else:
            print("H -> epsilon")

    def F(self):
        if self.next_char() == "(":
            print("F -> (E)")
            self.consume("(")
            self.E()
            self.consume(")")
        elif self.next_char() in "abc":
            print(f"F -> {self.next_char()}")
            self.consume(self.next_char())
        else:
            raise LLParser.RejectException()

    def parse(self, tape):
        try:
            self.input = tape + "$"
            self.S()
            if self.input != "$":
                raise LLParser.RejectException()

        except LLParser.RejectException:
            return False

        return True


parser = LLParser(
    {
        ("S", "E"),
        ("E", "TG"),
        ("G", "+TG"),
```

```
        ("G", "-TG"),
        ("G", ""),
        ("T", "FH"),
        ("H", "*FH"),
        ("H", ""),
        ("F", "(E)"),
        ("F", "a"),
        ("F", "b"),
        ("F", "c"),
    }
)

print(parser.parse("c-a-b-c*(a+b)"))
```

The complete list of derivations will be longer this time:

```
S -> E
E -> TG
T -> FH
F -> c
H -> epsilon
G -> -TG
T -> FH
F -> a
H -> epsilon
G -> -TG
T -> FH
F -> b
H -> epsilon
G -> -TG
T -> FH
F -> c
H -> *FH
F -> (E)
E -> TG
T -> FH
F -> a
H -> epsilon
G -> +TG
T -> FH
F -> b
H -> epsilon
G -> epsilon
H -> epsilon
G -> epsilon
```

This corresponds to the parse tree shown in Figure 7.8.

Reconstructing a tree from a list of production rules is easy for LL(1) parsing. The rules are printed in the order of a depth-first tree traversal. The parser begins with the start symbol S, expanding it into E. Then it proceeds to E, which becomes TG. Sibling nonterminals are processed in left-to-right order, and the children of any node are fully explored before its right-hand-side siblings. Therefore, the next lines of the output explore T ($T \rightarrow FH$) and its children ($F \rightarrow$ c, $H \rightarrow \varepsilon$).

Unfortunately, some features of the original LR(1) grammar are lost in translation. The new grammar asserts that an expression (E) consists of a left-hand-side element

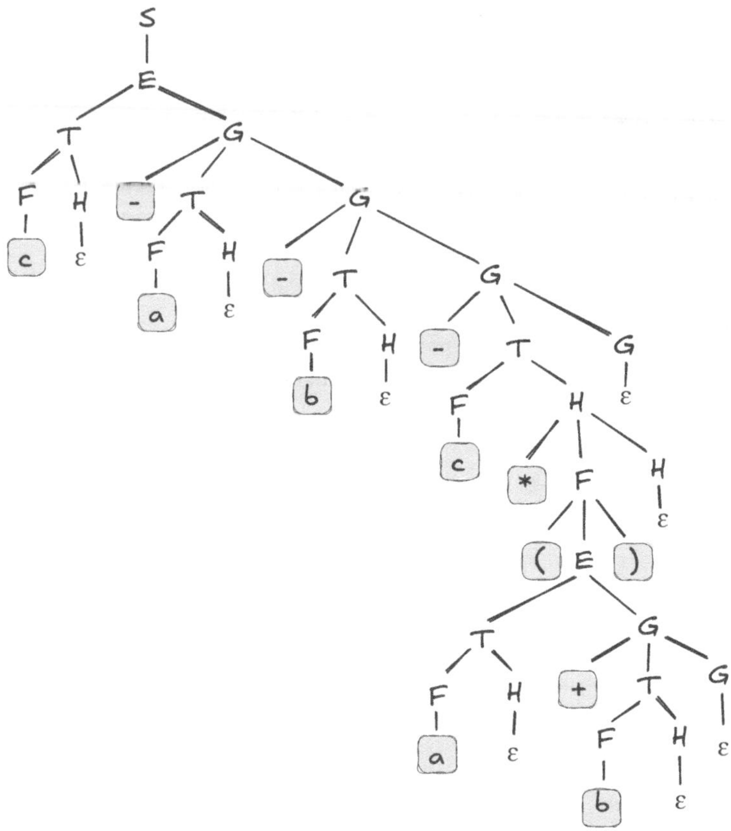

FIGURE 7.8: The parse tree of the expression `c-a-b-c*(a+b)`, constructed top-down.

T and a right-hand-side element G. To compute E, we'll have to compute both T and G and apply the operation taken from G. For our tree, this procedure would correctly handle precedence by starting with multiplication. However, associativity is not correct anymore: `c-a-b-c*(a+b)` will be computed as `c-(a-(b-c*(a+b)))`.

Such issues are well outside the scope of this book, but they can be fixed by using Dijkstra's shunting-yard algorithm or by modifying the basic recursive descent parsing procedure [53].

7.6.2 CONVERTING GRAMMARS TO LL(1) FORM

While writing a recursive descent parser is easy, it can be quite a challenge to make sure the input grammar has an LL(1) form.

One obvious type of LL(1) form violation is *left recursion*, seen in production rules like $E \to EA$. This rule is supposed to be handled by `E()` as follows:

```
def E(self):
    self.E()
    self.A()
```

Unfortunately, here `E()` calls `E()` infinitely without doing any useful work.

While *immediate* left recursion (as in $E \to EA$) is easy to spot, indirect cases, such as in the rules $E \to AK$, $A \to CD$, $C \to EF$, where `E()` still eventually calls `E()`, can be harder to trace.

Immediate left recursion of the form $A \to A\beta \mid \alpha$ can be removed by introducing a new nonterminal B as follows [2, Sec. 5.4.4]:

$$
\begin{aligned}
A &\to \alpha B \\
B &\to \beta B \mid \varepsilon
\end{aligned}
$$

For rules like $A \to A\beta \mid \alpha_1 \mid \alpha_2 \mid \ldots \mid \alpha_n$, this procedure has to be performed for each α_i, resulting in a list of rules:

$$
\begin{aligned}
A &\to \alpha_1 B \mid \alpha_2 B \mid \ldots \mid \alpha_n B \\
B &\to \beta B \mid \varepsilon
\end{aligned}
$$

Recursion elimination is necessary for a nonempty β in $A \to A\beta \mid \alpha$. If β is empty, we have a rule $A \to A$, which can be simply excluded from the grammar.

Another obvious type of LL(1) form violation is the need to choose between two right-hand sides with the same prefix:

$$A \to \alpha\beta \mid \alpha\gamma, \text{ where } \alpha \text{ is not empty, and } \beta \neq \gamma$$

Such a violation can be fixed with *left-factoring*. [32, Sec. 8.2.5.2]. We'll need to introduce a new nonterminal B, defined as $B \to \beta \mid \gamma$. Now the original rule can be rewritten as $A \to \alpha B$.

In the general case, checking whether a given grammar belongs to the LL(1) class is a relatively complex procedure that identifies conflicts in a state machine-based parser [2, Sec. 4.4.3]. We used a similar approach to identify conflicts in LR(1) grammars.

7.7 PARSING ARBITRARY CONTEXT-FREE GRAMMARS

A discussion of context-free grammars would be incomplete without a brief look at a general algorithm able to parse any given context-free grammar. We will discuss one of the most commonly mentioned approaches, known as the *Cocke-Younger-Kasami algorithm* (or *CYK algorithm*).

As a reminder, context-free grammars consist of production rules of the kind $A \to (\Sigma \cup V)^*$, describing how a nonterminal symbol A can be transformed into a string of terminal and nonterminal symbols. However, the CYK algorithm presumes that the input grammar is represented in *Chomsky normal form* (CNF).

7.7.1 OBTAINING CHOMSKY NORMAL FORM

A context-free grammar in Chomsky normal form includes only two kinds of production rules: $A \rightarrow BC$, where B and C are non-start nonterminals, and $A \rightarrow a$, where a is a terminal. Any context-free grammar can be converted into Chomsky normal form in several steps [32, Sec. 4.2.3]:

1. Make sure the start symbol S is not present in the right-hand side of production rules by introducing a new start symbol $>$ and adding the rule $> \rightarrow S$.
2. Remove productions of the kind $A \rightarrow \varepsilon$.
3. Remove productions of the kind $A \rightarrow B$.
4. Transform productions of the kind $A \rightarrow \alpha$, where len(α) ≥ 2, into CNF.

We have already discussed the first two steps while dealing with LR(1) parsing. Removing productions of the kind $A \rightarrow B$ is somewhat similar:

```
@dataclass
class CYK:
    grammar: set
    accept_empty: bool = False

    # same as in LRParser
    def all_symbols(self):
        rules_str = {lhs + rhs for lhs, rhs in self.grammar}
        return set("".join(rules_str))

    def terminals(self):
        return self.all_symbols() - self.nonterminals() | {"$"}

    def nonterminals(self):
        return set(s for s in self.all_symbols() if s.isupper()) | {">"}

    # remove epsilon-rules and add > -> S
    def preprocess_grammar(self):
        ...

    # new code
    def first_ab_rule(self):
        a_to_b = {(A, B) for (A, B) in self.grammar if B in self.nonterminals()}
        return a_to_b.pop() if a_to_b else None

    def remove_a_to_b(self):
        excluded = set()

        while ab_rule := self.first_ab_rule():
            excluded.add(ab_rule)
            self.grammar.remove(ab_rule)

            A, B = ab_rule
            new_rules = {(A, rhs) for lhs, rhs in self.grammar if lhs == B}
            self.grammar.update(new_rules - excluded)
```

The procedure finds the next rule $A \rightarrow B$ to exclude and removes it from the grammar. If B can be derived from A, then any string α derivable from B can also be derived from A. Therefore, we should add a rule $A \to \alpha$ for any existing rule $B \to \alpha$ to preserve the grammar. This method can generate new rules of the kind $A \to B$, so we have to keep track of removed rules and not add them again. Note that rules like $A \to A$ will also be removed as a result.

The next step is tedious but conceptually simple. Suppose we have a rule $A \to B_0 B_1 \ldots B_k$, where each B_i is either a terminal or a nonterminal symbol. It can be excluded from the grammar if we add the following productions:

$$
\begin{aligned}
&A \to X_{B_0} X_{B_1 \ldots B_k} \\
&X_{B_1 \ldots B_k} \to X_{B_1} X_{B_2 \ldots B_k} \\
&X_{B_2 \ldots B_k} \to X_{B_2} X_{B_3 \ldots B_k} \\
&\ldots \\
&X_{B_{k-1} B_k} \to X_{B_{k-1}} X_{B_k}
\end{aligned}
$$

Here, any X symbol with a subscript is a certain nonterminal symbol. If B_i is a nonterminal, then X_{B_i} is simply B_i. If B_i is a terminal, we must create a new nonterminal symbol X_{B_i} and add a rule $X_{B_i} \to B_i$. All other $X_{\text{something}}$ nonterminal symbols also have to be created.

Essentially, this algorithm splits a long right-hand side α of any rule $A \to \alpha$ into a one-symbol "head" and a "tail" comprising the remaining symbols. Next, it ensures that both the head and the tail are nonterminals, thus obtaining a rule allowed in CNF: $A \to \langle \text{HEAD} \rangle \langle \text{TAIL} \rangle$.

Let's examine how this process works for a production rule $S \to F\mathtt{ab}DFG$:

$$
\begin{aligned}
&S \to F X_{abDFG} \\
&X_{abDFG} \to X_a X_{bDFG} \\
&X_{bDFG} \to X_b X_{DFG} \\
&X_{DFG} \to D X_{FG} \\
&X_{FG} \to FG \\
&X_a \to a \\
&X_b \to b
\end{aligned}
$$

Our existing Python functions presume that nonterminal symbols are uppercase Latin letters, so we will not be able to use names like X_{abDFG}. Instead, we will simply take the next available letter when a new nonterminal is required. The total count of possible nonterminal names will still be limited to 26, which should be sufficient for our purposes. The Python version of this algorithm is straightforward:

```
@dataclass
class CYK:
    ...

    def next_free_nt(self):
        all_nonterminals = {chr(c) for c in range(ord("A"), ord("Z") + 1)}
        free_nonterminals = all_nonterminals - self.nonterminals()
        return free_nonterminals.pop()

    def is_cnf(self, rhs):
```

```
        return len(rhs) == 1 or (
            len(rhs) == 2
            and rhs[0] in self.nonterminals()
            and rhs[1] in self.nonterminals()
        )

    def first_non_cnf_rule(self):
        r = {(A, x) for (A, x) in self.grammar if not self.is_cnf(x)}
        return r.pop() if r else None

    # if s is a nonterminal, return it; otherwise generate X -> s and return X
    def gen_nonterminal(self, s):
        if s in self.nonterminals():
            return s

        X = self.next_free_nt()
        self.grammar.add((X, s))
        return X

    def convert_to_cnf(self):
        while rule := self.first_non_cnf_rule():
            L, alpha = rule
            self.grammar.remove(rule)

            while len(alpha) > 2:
                # transform L -> alpha into L -> XY
                X = self.gen_nonterminal(alpha[0])
                Y = self.next_free_nt()
                self.grammar.add((L, X + Y))
                L, alpha = Y, alpha[1:]

            # handle the last rule L -> XY
            X = self.gen_nonterminal(alpha[0])
            Y = self.gen_nonterminal(alpha[1])
            self.grammar.add((L, X + Y))
```

7.7.2 COCKE-YOUNGER-KASAMI ALGORITHM

Having our grammar converted to CNF, it is easy to implement the CYK parser. Let's look at the following Python code and discuss how it works:

```
@dataclass
class CYK:
    ...

    def has_bc_rule(self, A, v1, v2):
        for X, rhs in self.grammar:
            if A == X and len(rhs) == 2 and rhs[0] in v1 and rhs[1] in v2:
                return True
        return False

    def parse(self, tape):
        if not tape:
            return self.accept_empty
```

```
        v = {}
        n = len(tape)

        for i in range(1, n + 1):
            v[i, 1] = {A for A, x in self.grammar if x == tape[i - 1]}

        for j in range(2, n + 1):
            for i in range(1, n - j + 2):
                v[i, j] = set()
                for k in range(1, j):
                    v[i, j] |= {
                        A
                        for A in self.nonterminals()
                        if self.has_bc_rule(A, v[i, k], v[i + k, j - k])
                    }

        return ">" in v[1, n]


# example use
parser = CYK({("S", "aS"), ("S", "bN"), ("S", ""), ("N", "bN"), ("N", "")})

parser.preprocess_grammar()
parser.remove_a_to_b()
parser.convert_to_cnf()

print(parser.parse("aabbb"))
```

Suppose our task is to parse input strings of the language $\mathtt{a}^*\mathtt{b}^*$, represented with a context-free grammar:

$$S \to \mathtt{a}S \mid \mathtt{b}N \mid \varepsilon$$
$$N \to \mathtt{b}N \mid \varepsilon$$

Our CNF conversion routine yields the following CNF-compliant rules for this grammar:

$$> \to IS \mid CN \mid \mathtt{a} \mid \mathtt{b}$$
$$S \to AS \mid BN \mid \mathtt{a} \mid \mathtt{b}$$
$$N \to DN \mid \mathtt{b}$$
$$A \to \mathtt{a}$$
$$B \to \mathtt{b}$$
$$C \to \mathtt{b}$$
$$D \to \mathtt{b}$$
$$I \to \mathtt{a}$$

Now, consider how the CYK algorithm parses the input string `aabb`:

It starts by building the first column of the table v (see Figure 7.9). Its i-th element contains the set of nonterminals that can be used to produce the i-th symbol of the input string. In other words, if the i-th input symbol is c, then $v[i, 1]$ contains every nonterminal X for which there is a production rule $X \to c$. Following the usual mathematical conventions, the column and row indices of v start with 1, so in our case, the element `v[i, 1]` corresponds to `tape[i - 1]`.

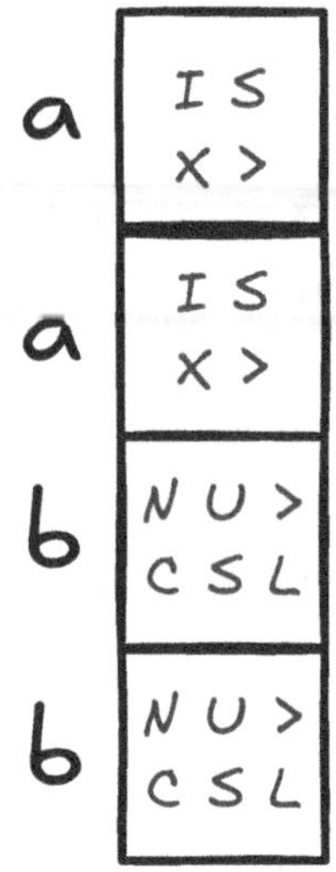

FIGURE 7.9: Computing the first column of v.

The individual symbols of the input string can also be viewed as its one-symbol substrings. Thus, the string `aabb` has four substrings of length 1: `a`, `a`, `b`, `b`. The next column of v will contain the nonterminals that can produce the two-symbol substrings `aa`, `ab`, and `bb`. Since the only CNF-compliant production rule type that combines strings is $A \rightarrow BC$, the algorithm collects all such rules that can be used to obtain two-symbol substrings of `aabb` (see Figure 7.10).

Proceeding in the same way, the algorithm can find the nonterminals that produce three-symbol substrings and, finally, the whole four-symbol input string (see Figure 7.11).

Finding production rules for substrings longer than two symbols requires more work. There is only one way to form a two-symbol string, such as `ab`: $A \rightarrow BC$, $B \rightarrow$ a, $C \rightarrow$ b. A three-symbol string can be obtained from two possible combinations: `aab` is either `a` + `ab` or `aa` + `b`. There are more "split-point" options for longer strings, and the CYK algorithm checks all of them in the inner `for k` loop.

If the complete input string can be derived from the start symbol > (i.e., `v[1, n]` contains >), it is accepted by the parser. Note that the basic CYK version we discussed does not produce parse trees, but it can be extended to provide this functionality [32, Sec. 4.2.8]. Since general context-free grammars can be ambiguous, such an extended CYK parser generates a "parse forest," representing a collection of possible parse trees.

The CYK algorithm has three nested loops, each performing a number of iterations proportional to the length of the input string, n. Therefore, the total number of operations required for parsing is proportional to n^3. Such *cubic* complexity is considered efficient, given that CYK is able to deal with arbitrary context-free grammars.

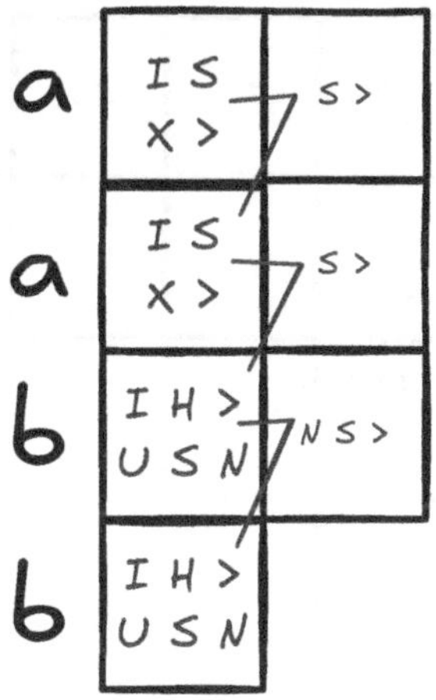

FIGURE 7.10: Computing the second column of v.

While somewhat more efficient parsing algorithms for context-free languages do exist, they cannot compete with linear-time LL or LR parsers in terms of efficiency. Thus, artificial formal languages (such as programming languages) are normally described with LL or LR grammars. Since an LR(1) parser needs a lot of space for its ACTION and GOTO tables, a more space-efficient variation known as an *Lookahead LR (LALR) parser* is normally employed instead.[3] The class of LALR languages, recognizable by this parser, is a good practical trade-off: it is somewhat narrower than LR(1) but still sufficient for typical purposes.

7.8 TAKEAWAYS

1. The goal of parsing is to decide whether a certain string belongs to a given language and, if it does, to construct its parse tree. Thus, the task of language recognition is a subtask of parsing.
2. Any context-free language can be parsed. In the world of automata, this requires the power of a nondeterministic pushdown machine. A conventional computer can parse context-free languages using, for example, the CYK algorithm.
3. Deterministic pushdown automata can only recognize deterministic context-free languages, which is the same class as LR(1) languages. They can be recognized with an LR(1) parser that simulates a deterministic pushdown machine.
4. LL(1) languages are more restricted than deterministic context-free languages, but the LL(1) parser is very easy to code, which makes it a viable

[3] "LALR is the method of choice in most situations" [2, Sec. 4.7].

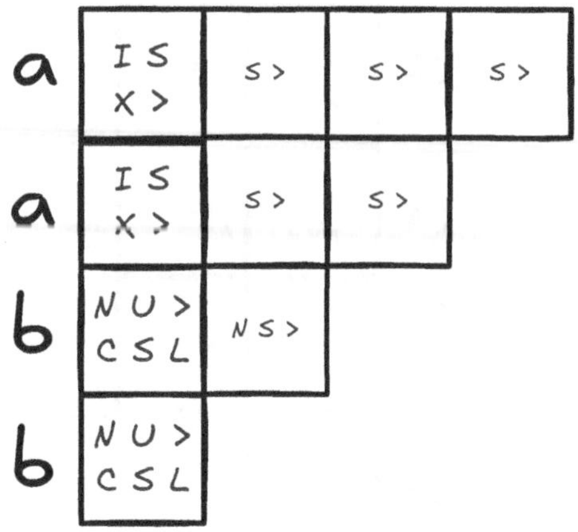

FIGURE 7.11: Computing the whole table v.

alternative to more complex parsing methods when the input language happens to be LL(1).

5. Both LL(1) and LR(1) parsing can be accomplished in linear time.
6. The Cocke-Younger-Kasami (CYK) algorithm is able to parse any context-free language but requires on the order of n^3 operations to process an input string of n symbols.

8 Building compilers

Parsing is an integral stage of processing *semi-structured data*, such as text-based JSON, XML, or YAML data files. A parser that converts its input string into JSON arrays and objects achieves a well-defined goal: it turns a stored sequence of bytes into an in-memory data structure that can be easily examined or modified.

Another common role of a parser is to be a part of a programming language translation pipeline. In this case, a parser belongs to a larger mechanism designed to execute human-readable programs.

In this chapter, we will take a glimpse into the inner workings of this pipeline. Admittedly, the tasks of designing programming languages and generating executable code are even further away from the core themes of the book than parsing, but I think our study would be incomplete without a quick discussion of what happens before and after parsing.

Making your own programming language is a great exercise that I wholeheartedly recommend. However, doing so for practical purposes is rarely warranted in our age of widespread data representation languages like JSON and embeddable scripting languages like Lua. Hunt and Thomas suggested designing your own "mini-language" in certain cases in the first edition of their must-read book "The Pragmatic Programmer" [39, Topic 12]. Twenty years later, they advise to "use off-the-shelf external languages," and if that is not possible, "look at internal languages" (i.e., languages that seamlessly extend the capabilities of the primary "host" language, such as custom decorators for Python). Doing everything on your own is for the "stout of heart" now [72, Topic 14].

8.1 TRANSLATORS, COMPILERS, INTERPRETERS

In this chapter, we will use a third-party *compiler generator* (or *compiler-compiler*) tool, Coco/R.[1] As the name implies, the output produced by Coco/R must be a compiler. This term is not very strictly defined, so let's begin by discussing some terminology.

1. A *translator* is a program that transforms code written in a certain computer language into code in another language, e.g., a program in Pascal into a program in C or a program in C into assembly language. "Translator" is a generic term applicable to a wide variety of code-converting systems.
2. A *transpiler* is a translator that converts source code written in a certain computer language into the source code of another language that operates at a comparable level of abstraction. This term grew in popularity with the arrival of tools that produce browser-executable JavaScript.

[1] Available at https://www.ssw.uni-linz.ac.at/Research/Projects/Coco/

DOI: 10.1201/9781032614991-8

3. A *compiler* is a translator that converts code from high-level programming languages to low-level languages, such as assembly language or machine code.
4. An *interpreter* is a program that directly (instruction by instruction) executes code written in a certain high-level programming language.

This classification, to a large extent, is a matter of convention and context. For example, Emscripten[2], a tool for making C/C++ code executable by a web browser, is called "a compiler" in its documentation. By default, it outputs low-level WebAssembly code, but it can also "compile" to JavaScript, which is a higher-level language than C. In turn, the resulting JavaScript is executed by an interpreter that compiles certain code fragments on the fly (a process known as *just-in-time compilation*) to increase performance.

Some compilers combine various kinds of code translation to obtain executable code. Consider how the Unity Engine produces web apps. Unity scripts are converted by a C# compiler to low-level .NET Intermediate Language, which is then translated to high-level C++ by the IL2CPP scripting backend, to be finally compiled to low-level WebAssembly by Emscripten.

Compiler generators have been available for decades, including well-known tools like Bison and ANTLR. Coco/R is easy to use and thus perfectly suitable for our purposes. While making a compiler, it will be necessary to write some code in a general-purpose programming language, which has to be supported by the compiler generator. Coco/R is available for C#, Java, and C++, but fortunately, there is an unofficial Python-based version of Coco/R, which can be installed directly from GitHub using `pip`:

```
pip install git+https://github.com/hb9chm/CocoRPy3
```

8.2 THE COMPILER PIPELINE

A typical compiler pipeline includes at least three major functional blocks: a *lexical analyzer* (also known as a *scanner*), a parser, and a *code generator*.

8.2.1 SCANNER

The very first and arguably the least complex block is the *scanner*, which converts the source code into a sequence of meaningful symbols called *tokens*.[3]

While programming language keywords like `for` and `if` consist of individual characters, they are conceptually atomic. A compiler cannot extract any meaningful information from the fact that both of these keywords include the character `f`. Similarly,

[2] Available at https://emscripten.org

[3] Aho et al. [2, Sec. 3.1] distinguish "scanning" from "lexical analysis," but in Coco/R, the whole subsystem of lexical analysis is called "the scanner."

exponentiation in Python is an independent operation, and it is of no use to the compiler to know that the exponentiation operator looks like a double asterisk.

This way, the Python expression `5.4**3` contains six characters but only three meaningful tokens: a real number `5.4`, a mathematical operation `**`, and an integer `3`.

A scanner must be able to figure out that a certain sequence of characters comprises a token and to infer the token's type (a real number, an operation, an identifier), but it does not have to go any deeper. For instance, a scanner should be able to label `MyId_123` as a token representing a certain identifier. A scanner will not decide whether this identifier is the name of a variable, a class, or a function.

The functionality of a scanner sounds like the right job for regular expressions. This is indeed the case; it is often presumed that the set of valid tokens in a language forms a regular language that can be recognized with pattern matching [2, Sec. 3.3.3]. In Coco/R, tokens are defined with *Extended Backus-Naur Form* (EBNF) syntax. EBNF describes context-free languages in the same way as CFGs but with some syntactic sugar. Most notably, it has syntax for optional and repeating parts, which work like the `?` and `*` quantifiers in regular expressions.

Since Coco/R presumes that the language of valid tokens is regular, only regular EBNF productions are allowed in the scanner definition. As a technical note, the syntactic niceties of EBNF also simplify the development of the scanner. Imagine our goal is to detect tokens like `b`, `ab`, `aab`, and so on, consisting of an arbitrary number of characters `a` followed by a character `b`. One possible regular grammar for the language of such tokens is

$$
\begin{aligned}
S &\rightarrow B\mathtt{bd} \mid B\mathtt{bcd} \\
A &\rightarrow A\mathtt{a} \mid \varepsilon
\end{aligned}
$$

Unfortunately, it has a left-recursive rule that cannot be handled by a recursive descent parser. While it is possible to modify the input grammar, EBNF offers a better alternative:[4]

```
S = { "a" } "b" ["c"] "d".
```

Square brackets (`[]`) denote optional elements. Curly brackets (`{}`) represent the Kleene star, which corresponds to a simple loop in the parsing algorithm rather than infinite recursion [53].

This capability is helpful, for example, in the task of parsing arithmetic expressions. Recall the following LR(1) grammar from the previous chapter:

$$
\begin{aligned}
S &\rightarrow E \\
E &\rightarrow E\texttt{+}T \mid E\texttt{-}T \mid T \\
T &\rightarrow T\texttt{*}F \mid F \\
F &\rightarrow \texttt{(}E\texttt{)} \mid \mathtt{a} \mid \mathtt{b} \mid \mathtt{c}
\end{aligned}
$$

[4]Different tools use slightly different EBNF syntax. In Coco/R, terms are separated by spaces, strings are enclosed in quotation marks, and each production ends with a dot character.

We had difficulties transforming it into an LL(1) form while preserving associativity. However, this is easily achieved with EBNF:

```
S = E.
E = T { "+" T | "-" T }.
T = F { "*" F | "/" F }.
F = "(" E ")" | "a" | "b" | "c".
```

Coco/R produces a scanner that can be used on its own, independently from the parser and the code generator. Some compiler generators, like Bison, presume that a scanner is created by a separate tool (e.g., Flex).

8.2.2 PARSER

Compiler generators typically strive to produce fast and memory-efficient parsers, which is achieved by narrowing the class of supported formal languages. For instance, Coco/R produces a recursive descent parser, primarily designed to handle LL(1) languages. However, the user can provide a custom "resolver" procedure for cases where a one-symbol lookahead turns out to be insufficient. Such a resolver can examine subsequent input symbols (which extends the class of supported languages to LL(k)) or allow for more advanced semantic checks [50, Sec. 2.4.6].

In the previous chapter, we presumed that a parser processes strings consisting of symbols belonging to the alphabet of the given formal language. In a compiler pipeline, this presumption still holds: a parser processes scanner-prepared strings made up of tokens, which form the input alphabet.

8.2.3 CODE GENERATOR

The code generator is by far the most complex element of a compiler pipeline. It is also the place where the compiler developer has much freedom in choosing the goals to pursue. In Coco/R, a compiler is technically implemented by providing arbitrary *semantic actions* for each production rule recognized by the parser. These actions are coded using a conventional programming language, such as Python in the Python-based version of Coco/R (other options, as mentioned above, include C#, Java, and C++). The compiler generator imposes no restrictions on the action content: for instance, one can create a static code analyzer like Pylint rather than a compiler or an interpreter.

To put things into perspective, the discussion of code generation takes up around 80% of Cooper and Torczon's 760+ page volume on compiler development, while only the remaining 20% is devoted to scanning and parsing [14]. However, much of this complexity is connected with code optimization and runtime system organization,[5] which is not on our agenda.

---

[5] A runtime system determines, in particular, how data structures are represented in memory, how function calls are implemented, and how user code interacts with the operating system.

There are three primary kinds of systems a code generator may be designed to produce:

1. An interpreter, executing program statements as they are parsed.
2. A machine code compiler, producing platform-native binary executable files.
3. An intermediate code compiler, producing files that can be executed by a certain virtual machine.

Immediate interpretation was more common in the past. Parsing takes time, and there is a clear motivation to perform certain preprocessing before executing code. Imagine a certain arithmetic expression executed multiple times in a loop. An interpreter would have to parse it every time before each calculation.

Machine code is the standard target for the compilers of languages like C, C++, Rust, or Go. This option is perhaps the most daunting, but it is rare to see native machine code generation implemented directly in a parser. In the past, an easier option was to translate to a low-level language like C and then invoke a C compiler to generate machine code. A more contemporary choice is to translate to the LLVM Intermediate Representation (IR) language, which is further processed by the LLVM compiler infrastructure.[6]

One obvious advantage of having a certain kind of "intermediate representation" in the pipeline is the overall reduction of effort needed to support a variety of programming languages and target platforms. Imagine you need to compile programs written in four languages (C++, Rust, Go, JavaScript) for three target platforms (ARM, ×86, and WebAssembly). A straightforward approach would require three compilers per language, i.e., 12 tools in total. By organizing compilers as language-to-IR frontends and IR-to-platform backends, we reduce this number to 7 (4 frontends + 3 backends). Frontends and backends can be developed separately, so by creating a frontend for a certain language, you get immediate support for every platform for which a backend is available.

Intermediate representation is normally used in a compiler pipeline even in a single-language, single-platform scenario [14, Ch. 5]. In particular, certain significant code optimization techniques are applied at this level [2, Sec. 2.8.1].

An intermediate representation can also be directly executed by a "virtual machine," a kind of low-level interpreter. This approach is seen, for example, in the Java Virtual Machine or the .NET Common Language Runtime. Reasons to adopt virtual machines include, for example, more tools for security measures (sandboxing), easy portability (as in the old Java slogan "write once, run anywhere"), and extended capabilities of the runtime system, such as garbage collection [31]. Commonly used virtual machines employ just-in-time compilation and optimization to achieve near-native execution performance.

I think that the virtual machine-based approach is a good choice for educational projects, as it is easier than native code generation (even with LLVM) and splits the

[6]Check out the LLVM tutorials at https://llvm.org/docs/GettingStartedTutorials.html

resulting system nicely into "code generator" and "code runner" modules that can be developed and discussed independently.

8.3 DEVELOPING TINYCODE

Let's see how the scanner, parser, and code generator work together in a compiler pipeline. We will create a compiler for an extremely stripped-down (yet easily extensible) language called TinyCode. The following example should give an idea of TinyCode programming:

```
// countsum.tc

program CountSum.

// calculate 1 + 2 + 3 + 4 + 5

var sum: integer;
      c: integer;

begin
    let c := 1;

loop: let sum := sum + c;
      let c := c + 1;
      if c <= 5 goto loop;
      print sum;              // will print 15
end.
```

8.3.1 SYNTAX OF TINYCODE

Every TinyCode program starts with a header `program <Name>.` and ends with a concluding statement `end.`. The keywords `var` and `begin` introduce variable definitions and executable code, respectively.

TinyCode supports integer and Boolean variables and arrays that have to be declared right after the header, in the `var` section:

```
var a: integer;
    b: boolean;
    c: integer[5..10];
    d: boolean[-2..3];
```

Array bounds are arbitrary integer values. Handling out-of-range indices is a good example of a runtime system's responsibility. In Python, for instance, any attempt to access a non-existing list element produces an `IndexError` exception. In contrast, the C language runtime treats this situation as "undefined behavior" with unpredictable consequences.

The variable definition section is followed by the keyword `begin` and the main program body. The code consists of a sequence of statements. A statement may be prefixed with a label and must end with a semicolon. Four kinds of statements are supported:

```
let varName := expression;  // assignment
print expression;           // data output
if condition goto label;    // conditional jump
goto label;                 // unconditional jump
```

Expressions consist of numbers, variables, and Boolean constants, combined with arithmetic and logical operations. Comments start with the sequence `//` and span to the end of the line.

The dedicated assignment keyword `let` might seem redundant: at a glance, `c := 1;` is as good as `let c := 1;` but more concise. Unfortunately, an LL(1) parser will not be able to deduce whether `c` is a variable to be assigned or a statement label. The keyword `let` prevents ambiguity.

We will keep `let` in TinyCode as a practical example of the limitations of LL(1) parsing. However, there are at least two simple ways to remove it:

1. Introduce unique prefixes for labels. For example, if each label starts with `:`, the parser will be able to distinguish labels from variables.
2. Use a two-token lookahead (i.e., LL(2) parsing), which is possible with Coco/R resolvers. While `c` is ambiguous, the next token, either `:` or `:=`, uniquely identifies the context. Note that `:` and `:=` are distinct atomic elements for the parser; the scanner would recognize the two-character token `:=` before considering the single-character token `:`.

8.3.2 PARSING TINYCODE

Our next steps will be driven by the requirements of the Coco/R workflow. Coco/R reads EBNF productions of tokens and language structures from an input file and produces a package including a scanner, a parser, and an optional runner module. Therefore, our task is to prepare the input language definition file for Coco/R.

The first line of this file (let's name it `tinycode-parser.atg`) introduces the name of the formal grammar to be described:

```
COMPILER TinyCode
```

The next section defines character sets:

```
CHARACTERS
   letter = "A".."Z" + "a".."z".
   digit = "0".."9".
```

The purpose of character sets is convenience: it is now possible to use the set names `letter` and `digit` to denote arbitrary letters and digits. These names will prove useful in the following section:

```
TOKENS
   Identifier = letter {letter | digit}.
   Number = digit {digit}.
```

The `TOKENS` block is the foundation of the scanner. In TinyCode, we will only need to recognize variable identifiers and integer numbers. String literals (such as the keywords `let` or `goto`) can also be listed here, but this is not required. We will insert them directly into the production rules.

The next block declares that the sequence `//` and the newline character enclose comments:

```
COMMENTS FROM "//" TO "\n"
```

Coco/R-produced scanners ignore extra whitespace characters. We will also ignore tabs and newlines by specifying a custom `IGNORE` set:

```
IGNORE "\r\n\t"
```

Our next task is to express the grammar of TinyCode as a list of EBNF rules in the `PRODUCTIONS` block.

A TinyCode program consists of a header followed by the main body block:

```
PRODUCTIONS
   TinyCode = "program" Identifier "." ProgramBody.
```

In turn, the body starts with a variable declaration section and a list of instructions between the `begin` and `end.` statements:

```
ProgramBody = ["var" DeclareVar { DeclareVar }] "begin" { Statement } "end.".
```

A variable declaration consists of a variable name and a variable type:

```
DeclareVar = Identifier ":" DeclareVarBody ";".
```

TinyCode supports integer and Boolean variables and arrays:

```
DeclareVarBody = ("integer" | "boolean" ) [ "[" Number ".." Number "]" ].
```

The next nonterminal symbol to define is `Statement`:

```
Statement = [Identifier ":"] [StatementBody] ";".
```

The optional `Identifier` is for the label. The statement body is also optional (just like in the C language), making ; the only compulsory element of the statement.

TinyCode supports assignment, branching, print, and jump statements:

```
StatementBody = Assignment | Branching | Print | Goto.
```

Their high-level definitions are straightforward:

```
Assignment = "let" VarName ":=" Expr.
Branching = "if" Expr "goto" Identifier.
Print = "print" Expr.
Goto = "goto" Identifier.
```

These productions introduce two new nonterminals, a variable name `VarName` and an expression `Expr`. A variable name is not the same as `Identifier`, because we need to support both arrays and scalar variables. Thus, `VarName` should be able to match expressions like `arr[i]` and `x`:

```
VarName = Identifier ("[" Expr "]" | ).
```

Defining `Expr` is more complicated. Fortunately, we have already discussed how to declare arithmetic expressions using EBNF:

```
S = E.
E = T { "+" T | "-" T }.
T = F { "*" F | "/" F }.
F = "(" E ")" | "a" | "b" | "c".
```

This can be rewritten with dedicated nonterminals for arithmetic operations and supported values as follows:

```
S = E.
E = T { AddSub T }.
AddSub = "+" | "-".
T = F { MulDiv F }.
MulDiv = "*" | "/".
F = "(" E ")" | Value.

Value = VarName | Number | "true" | "false".
```

Let's add unary and Boolean operations to obtain TinyCode expressions:

```
Expr = E { BoolOp E }.
BoolOp = "and" | "or" | "<>" | "<" | "<=" | ">" | ">=" | "==".
E = T { AddSub T }.
AddSub = "+" | "-".
T = F { MulDiv F }.
MulDiv = "*" | "/".
F = UnOp F | Value | "(" Expr ")".
UnOp = "-" | "not".

Value = VarName | Number | "true" | "false".
```

Note that Boolean operations here have a lower priority than the four operations of arithmetic. Thus, expressions like `a < 5 and b > 6` will be processed correctly. Still, our expression grammar is quite simple. In particular, it is unable to detect type mismatches, such as in `5 + true or 3`. We will have to delegate this task to the runtime system.

The definition of the TinyCode grammar must be finished with the keyword `END`:

```
END TinyCode.
```

The complete grammar definition takes fewer than 40 lines:

```
COMPILER TinyCode

CHARACTERS
   letter = "A".."Z" + "a".."z".
   digit = "0".."9".

TOKENS
   Identifier = letter {letter | digit}.
   Number = digit {digit}.

COMMENTS FROM "//" TO "\n"
IGNORE "\r\n\t"

PRODUCTIONS
   TinyCode = "program" Identifier "." ProgramBody.
   ProgramBody = ["var" DeclareVar { DeclareVar }] "begin" { Statement } "end.".
   DeclareVar = Identifier ":" DeclareVarBody ";".
   DeclareVarBody = ("integer" | "boolean" ) [ "[" Number ".." Number "]" ].
   Statement = [Identifier ":"] [StatementBody] ";".
   StatementBody = Assignment | Branching | Print | Goto.
   Assignment = "let" VarName ":=" Expr.
   Branching = "if" Expr "goto" Identifier.
   Print = "print" Expr.
   Goto = "goto" Identifier.
   VarName = Identifier ("[" Expr "]" | ).

   Expr = E { BoolOp E }.
   BoolOp = "and" | "or" | "<>" | "<" | "<=" | ">" | ">=" | "==".
   E = T { AddSub T }.
   AddSub = "+" | "-".
   T = F { MulDiv F }.
   MulDiv = "*" | "/".
   F = UnOp F | Value | "(" Expr ")".
   UnOp = "-" | "not".

   Value = VarName | Number | "true" | "false".

END TinyCode.
```

8.3.3 TESTING THE PARSER

At this point, we can invoke Coco/R to generate a runnable parser pipeline as follows:

```
python -m CocoRPy3.Coco -c tinycode-parser.atg
```

The optional command-line argument `-c` instructs Coco/R to produce a simple runner module that binds the scanner and the parser together. This default runner takes a TinyCode program as input, parses it, and prints out any identified errors.

Let's test the parser by giving it some errors to detect:

```
// errors.tc

program Errors.

var s: integer[0..];      // missing upper limit
```

```
    d: integer[true..5]; // wrong limit type

begin
    let s := 0    // trailing semicolon missing
    let k := 1;   // ok
    let s[] = 2;  // array index missing
end.
```

The parser, invoked with

```
python TinyCode.py errors.tc
```

finds two errors:

```
file errors.tc : (5, 19) Number expected
file errors.tc : (6, 16) Number expected
2 errors detected
```

It correctly deduces that both variable declarations are missing a numerical value for one of the array boundaries. Let's fix the declarations:

```
var s: integer[0..10];
    d: integer[1..5];
```

The next run finds new errors:

```
file errors.tc : (10, 5) ";" expected
file errors.tc : (11, 11) invalid F
2 errors detected
```

The "missing semicolon" message was expected, but `invalid F` is somewhat less clear. It states that the square brackets in `s[]` must contain an arithmetic expression, which boils down to a nonterminal `F` that was not recognized by the parser at that position.

Note that the parser has no issues with the line

```
let k := 1;
```

It assigns a value to a non-existent variable, which is not considered an error, since the parser does not keep a list of declared variables. Similarly, the parser does not recognize the difference between scalar variables and arrays. Adding a semicolon at the end of line 5 fixes the error for that line:

```
let s := 0; // s is an array!
```

While such *semantic* errors can be delegated to the runtime system, there is still the code generation phase to be implemented, which may prove more suitable for dealing with semantics.

8.3.4 CHOOSING AN INTERMEDIATE REPRESENTATION

TinyCode programs will ultimately be run by a virtual machine we are going to develop. Thus, we have to choose an intermediate representation that can be easily executed. I think that *threaded code* [4] fits this description well. Each instruction in threaded code is a function call. Functions do not have arguments or return values; to pass data around, they use a global data stack instead.

The job of a code generator would be to produce the list of required functions and a sequence of calls corresponding to the input TinyCode program.

To understand how threaded code works, consider the following sample fragment:

```
// a and b are integers

let a := 1;
let b := 2 + a;
```

Let's presume that we only have scalar (non-array) variables, stored in a dictionary:

```
variables = { "a": 0, "b": 0 }
```

To execute the given fragment, we will need seven functions:

```
def op_read():
    name = pop() # pop from the data stack
    push(variables[name]) # push to the data stack

def op_let():
    v = pop()
    name = pop()
    variables[name] = v

def op_push_1():
    push(1)

def op_push_2():
    push(2)

def op_add():
    push(pop() + pop())

def op_push_a():
    push("a")

def op_push_b():
    push("b")
```

The corresponding threaded code consists entirely of function calls:

```
op_push_a()       # resulting stack: ["a"]
op_push_1()       # ["a", 1]
op_let()          # []; variables["a"] is now 1
op_push_b()       # ["b"]
op_push_2()       # ["b", 2]
```

```
op_push_a()       # ["b", 2, "a"]
op_read()         # ["b", 2, 1]
op_add()          # ["b", 3]
op_let()          # []; variables["b"] is now 3
```

Note that we will need to have a dedicated push function for each integer or Boolean value and each identifier found in the code. The list of these entities is finite and known to the parser, so generating the required functions is not challenging.

8.3.5 SETTING UP CODE GENERATION

A recursive descent parser produced by Coco/R performs certain actions for each production rule in the input grammar. These actions can be generated automatically because parsing is a well-defined process: the parser must check whether the input string conforms to the language grammar and identify meaningful pieces corresponding to nonterminal and terminal symbols.

Further actions depend on the intentions of the compiler designer. What exactly should happen when the compiler sees an instruction like `let k := 1;`? It is not for the parser generator to decide. For this reason, it is our responsibility to provide semantic actions to be performed in particular contexts.

In Coco/R, semantic actions (represented with Python code fragments) are inserted directly into the grammar definition between the markers `(.` and `.)`.[7] Inside such a block, we have access to the most recently recognized token value `self.token.val`. It is also possible to pass data from parent to child nonterminals and vice versa.

Semantic actions can be fairly complex and span multiple lines of code. Internally, Coco/R generates Python source code indented with 3 spaces,[8] so I would strongly recommend adhering to the same style. Required Python libraries can be imported before the `COMPILER` keyword. Coco/R-generated parsing functions are members of the `Parser` class, meaning that our semantic actions can use `self` to refer to the parser object itself.

As an example, let's process the header of a TinyCode program:

```
COMPILER TinyCode
   def initialize(self, name):
      self.name = name
...

PRODUCTIONS
   TinyCode = "program"
              Identifier          (. self.initialize(self.token.val) .)
              "."
              ProgramBody.
```

[7]Such an augmented grammar is known as an *attribute grammar*. [57].

[8]Three-space indentation is hardcoded in Coco/R:
https://github.com/hb9chm/CocoRPy3/blob/master/src/CocoRPy3/CodeGenberator.py

After recognizing `Identifier` after the keyword `program`, the parser calls the function `self.initialize()`, passing it the value of the recognized identifier. Next, this identifier is stored in the `Parser` object's member variable `name`.

Ultimately, the TinyCode compiler (i.e., the parser augmented with code generation) has to produce a list of function calls to be executed and the runtime system, consisting of function definitions and internal data structures, such as the global data stack.

Functions are first-class objects in Python. This means that a function, in particular, can be stored in a data structure just like any other object [3, Ch. 6]. Therefore, our threaded code can be represented simply as a list of functions to be called:

```
self.program = [op_push_a, op_push_1, op_let, ...]
```

To add new instructions, we will use a helper function `emit_op()`:

```
def emit_op(self, op):
   self.program.append(op)
```

We will also need stack `push()` and `pop()` operations:

```
def initialize(self, name):
   self.stack = []
   self.program = []
   self.name = name

def push(self, v):
   self.stack.append(v)

def pop(self):
   r, self.stack = self.stack[-1], self.stack[:-1]
   return r
```

As already noted, every identifier and value in the program needs its own dedicated `push()` function. Fortunately, this is easy to achieve in Python. The standard function `partial()` takes a function `f` and a list of argument values and returns an object that behaves like `f` called with the given arguments. Thus,

```
from functools import partial

push_5 = partial(self.push, 5)
```

will create a function `push_5()`, which calls `self.push(5)`. For further convenience, adding such customized push functions to the resulting code will be done via another helper function `emit_push()`:

```
# call, e.g., emit_push(5) to add push_5() instruction to the program
def emit_push(self, v):
   self.emit_op(partial(self.push, v))
```

Before proceeding to the actual code generation, let's dedicate a bit of effort to shortening the resulting compiler definition.

Our runtime system will have to rely on a few small functions similar to:

```
# push the sum of two topmost stack elements to the stack
def op_add():
    self.push(self.pop() + self.pop())
```

Merely ten functions like `op_add()` would contribute at least thirty lines to the program. To save space, we will use Python lambda expressions.[9]

Consider a function that returns its resulting value to the caller rather than placing it on the stack:

```
# return the sum of two topmost stack elements
def op_sum():
   return self.pop() + self.pop()
```

It can be added to our threaded code as follows:

```
self.emit_op(self.op_sum)
```

Alternatively, we can create an anonymous function using the `lambda` keyword and remove the definition of `op_sum()`:

```
self.emit_op(lambda: self.pop() + self.pop())
```

This way, it is possible to replace a call to `op_sum()` with a lambda expression. Our task, however, is to call a function like `op_sum()` and place the obtained result on the stack. Lambdas are not designed to manipulate data structures; they merely return the value of an expression for the supplied arguments.[10] To modify the data stack, we will need to combine a lambda expression with a push function using `partial()`:

```
def lop(self, op):
   return partial(self.push_result, op)

def push_result(self, op):
   self.push(op())
...

# we do not need op_add() anymore
self.emit_op(self.lop(lambda: self.pop() + self.pop()))
```

[9] We'll discuss the theory behind lambda expressions in Chapter 11.

[10] We are somewhat misusing lambdas by allowing them to modify the stack via `self.pop()`. In general, such *side effects* should be avoided [25].

8.3.6 GENERATING CODE

Let's now focus on the bulk of the code-generation functionality. We have already provided semantic actions for the program header and can now proceed to variable declarations:

```
COMPILER TinyCode
   def initialize(self, name):
      self.stack = []
      self.variables = {}
      self.constraints = {}
      self.labels = {}
      self.name = name
      self.program = []
      self.ip = 0 # instruction pointer

   def create_constraint(self, v, lbound, ubound):
      self.constraints[v] = range(lbound, ubound + 1)

   def create_var(self, v, value):
      self.variables[v] = value

PRODUCTIONS
...

   DeclareVar = Identifier         (. v = self.token.val .)
                ":"
                DeclareVarBody<v>
                ";".

   DeclareVarBody<v> =
                ("integer"         (. value = defaultdict(int) .)
                | "boolean"        (. value = defaultdict(bool) .)
                )                  (. lbound = ubound = 0 .)
                [
                "[" Number         (. lbound = int(self.token.val) .)
                ".." Number        (. ubound = int(self.token.val) .)
                "]"
                ]                  (. self.create_constraint(v, lbound, ubound)
                                      self.create_var(v, value) .)
                .
```

Variable declarations do not generate code; instead, they prepare the runtime system that will support code execution. In our case, each variable gets registered in the `self.variables` dictionary, receiving an initial value of 0 for integers and `False` for Booleans. For the sake of simplicity, we will represent each variable with a `defaultdict`. This gives us a convenient data structure for indexed arrays; scalar variables will be internally represented as single-element dictionaries. For array variables, we will also store admissible index ranges in `self.constraints`. These will be used by the runtime system to check for out-of-bounds errors.

As mentioned, Coco/R allows passing data between nonterminals. By listing nonterminal attributes in angle brackets (as in `DeclareVarBody<v> = ...`), we require the parent nonterminal to specify their values. In our case, `DeclareVar` stores the identified variable name in the local variable `v` and then passes its value to `DeclareVarBody`, where it is used to create a variable via the `self.create_var()` call.

Labels are processed in a similar way:

```
COMPILER TinyCode
   def initialize(self, name):
      ...
      self.labels = {}

   # label points to the current line of the program
   def create_label(self, label):
      self.labels[label] = len(self.program)

PRODUCTIONS
...

   Statement = [Identifier        (. self.create_label(self.token.val) .)
               ":"]
               [StatementBody]
               ";".
```

Now let's discuss how to handle assignment, which finally produces some code:

```
COMPILER TinyCode
...

   # assign value to name[idx]
   def op_let(self):
      value = self.pop()
      idx = self.pop()
      name = self.pop()
      self.check_bounds(name, idx)
      self.variables[name][idx] = value

   # place name[idx] on the stack
   def op_read(self):
      idx = self.pop()
      name = self.pop()
      self.check_bounds(name, idx)
      self.push(self.variables[name][idx])

   def check_bounds(self, name, idx):
      assert name in self.variables, f"var {name} not found"
      bounds = self.constraints[name]
      assert idx in bounds,  f"{name}[{idx}] is out of bounds"

PRODUCTIONS
...

   Assignment = "let"
                VarName
                ":=" Expr        (. self.emit_op(self.op_let) .)
                .
```

The key idea here is to place the `self.emit_op()` call after `VarName` and `Expr` to let their associated semantic actions be executed first. The task of `Expr` is to place the value of the calculated expression on the stack. Similarly, `VarName` will place the name and the index of the given variable on the stack. As a result, `op_let()` will be able to take everything it needs from the stack and perform the required assignment:

```
self.variables[name][idx] = value
```

Subsequent instructions are implemented using the same principle:

```
COMPILER TinyCode
...

   # if and goto modify the current instruction pointer
   def op_if(self):
      if_label = self.pop()
      if self.pop():
         self.ip = self.labels[if_label] - 1

   def op_goto(self):
      self.ip = self.labels[self.pop()] - 1

PRODUCTIONS
...

   PIdentifier = Identifier      (. self.emit_push(self.token.val) .)

   Branching = "if"
               Expr
               "goto"
               PIdentifier       (. self.emit_op(self.op_if) .)
               .

   Print = "print" Expr          (. self.emit_op(lambda: print(self.pop())) .)
           .

   Goto = "goto" PIdentifier     (. self.emit_op(self.op_goto) .)
          .
```

The function `op_if()` expects to find its jump destination label as well as its Boolean condition value on the stack. Not all identifiers need to be pushed (for instance, labels do not), so we need a separate "pushable" identifier type `PIdentifier` for `if` and `goto` instructions.

To wrap up assignment, we'll need to provide actions for `VarName`:

```
   VarName = PIdentifier
             ("[" Expr
             "]"
             |              (. self.emit_push(0) .)
             ).
```

A variable is described by its identifier and index. Scalar variables like `x` are considered equivalent to `x[0]`.

The final fragment of the code generator implements the expression calculator:

```
PRODUCTIONS
...

  Expr = E {
         BoolOp<out op> E        (. self.emit_op(op) .)
         }.

  BoolOp<out op> = "and" (. op = self.lop(lambda: self.pop() & self.pop()) .)
                 | "or"  (. op = self.lop(lambda: self.pop() | self.pop()) .)
                 | "<>"  (. op = self.lop(lambda: self.pop() != self.pop()) .)
                 | "<"   (. op = self.lop(lambda: self.pop() > self.pop()) .)
                 | "<="  (. op = self.lop(lambda: self.pop() >= self.pop()) .)
                 | ">"   (. op = self.lop(lambda: self.pop() < self.pop()) .)
                 | ">="  (. op = self.lop(lambda: self.pop() <= self.pop()) .)
                 | "=="  (. op = self.lop(lambda: self.pop() == self.pop()) .)
                 .

  E = T {
      AddSub<out op> T  (. self.emit_op(op) .)
      }.

  AddSub<out op> = "+"  (. op = self.lop(lambda: self.pop() + self.pop()) .)
                 | "-"  (. op = self.lop(lambda: -self.pop() + self.pop()) .)
                 .

  T = F {
      MulDiv<out op> F  (. self.emit_op(op) .)
      }.

  MulDiv<out op> = "*"  (. op = self.lop(lambda: self.pop() * self.pop()) .)
                 | "/"  (. op = self.lop(lambda: 1 / self.pop() *
                 self.pop()) .)
                 .

  F = UnOp<out op> F    (. self.emit_op(op) .)
    |   Value
    | "(" Expr ")"
    .

  UnOp<out op> = "-"      (. op = self.lop(lambda: -self.pop()) .)
               | "not"    (. op = self.lop(lambda: not self.pop()) .)
               .

  Value = VarName                (. self.emit_op(self.op_read) .)
        | Number                 (. self.emit_push(int(self.token.val)) .)
        | "true"                 (. self.emit_push(True) .)
        | "false"                (. self.emit_push(False) .)
        .
```

Every operation of the calculator works in a straightforward way by taking its operands from the stack and pushing back the resulting value. Output attributes (marked with the keyword `out`) are used to pass data back to the parent nonterminal. Note that `and` and `or` use bitwise rather than conventional logical operators:

```
  BoolOp<out op> = "and" (. op = self.lop(lambda: self.pop() & self.pop()) .)
```

```
                | "or"  (. op = self.lop(lambda: self.pop() | self.pop()) .)
```

In Python, the logical `and` and `or` operators perform short-circuit evaluation. For example, if `a` in `a or b` is `True`, then the whole expression is `True`, and there is no reason to evaluate `b`. In our case, this is not desirable, as the value for `b` would be left on the stack. Therefore, it is necessary to use the bitwise operators `|` and `&`, which always evaluate both of their arguments.

8.3.7 EXECUTING CODE

Threaded code is easy to run. The interpreter simply calls code functions in sequence as long as the instruction pointer is valid:

```
COMPILER TinyCode
...

   def run(self):
      print(f"Running {self.name}")
      while self.ip < len(self.program):
         self.program[self.ip]()
         self.ip += 1
```

Note that `op_goto()` sets the instruction pointer to the statement preceding the jump label:

```
def op_goto(self):
   self.ip = self.labels[self.pop()] - 1
```

This is correct because `run()` increases `self.ip` after each function call. The same technique is used in `op_if()`.

In principle, it would be natural to run the obtained code right after parsing in `TinyCode.py`. Alternatively, we can specify `self.run()` as a semantic action for the last statement of the program:

```
PRODUCTIONS
...

   ProgramBody = ["var"
                 DeclareVar
                 { DeclareVar }]
                 "begin"
                 { Statement }
                 "end."          (. self.run() .)
                 .
```

The complete TinyCode compiler takes fewer than 200 lines of code:

```
from functools import partial
from collections import defaultdict

COMPILER TinyCode
```

```
def initialize(self, name):
    self.stack = []
    self.variables = {}
    self.constraints = {}
    self.labels = {}
    self.name = name
    self.program = []
    self.ip = 0

def run(self):
    print(f"Running {self.name}")
    while self.ip < len(self.program):
        self.program[self.ip]()
        self.ip += 1

def create_constraint(self, v, lbound, ubound):
    self.constraints[v] = range(lbound, ubound + 1)

def create_var(self, v, value):
    self.variables[v] = value

def create_label(self, label):
    self.labels[label] = len(self.program)

def emit_op(self, op):
    self.program.append(op)

def emit_push(self, v):
    self.emit_op(partial(self.push, v))

def lop(self, op):
    return partial(self.push_result, op)

def push_result(self, op):
    self.push(op())

def push(self, v):
    self.stack.append(v)

def pop(self):
    r, self.stack = self.stack[-1], self.stack[:-1]
    return r

def op_goto(self):
    self.ip = self.labels[self.pop()] - 1

def check_bounds(self, name, idx):
    assert name in self.variables, f"var {name} not found"
    bounds = self.constraints[name]
    assert idx in bounds,  f"{name}[{idx}] is out of bounds"

def op_let(self):
    value = self.pop()
    idx = self.pop()
    name = self.pop()
    self.check_bounds(name, idx)
    self.variables[name][idx] = value
```

```
    def op_read(self):
        idx = self.pop()
        name = self.pop()
        self.check_bounds(name, idx)
        self.push(self.variables[name][idx])

    def op_if(self):
        if_label = self.pop()
        if self.pop():
            self.ip = self.labels[if_label] - 1

CHARACTERS
    letter = "A".."Z" + "a".."z".
    digit = "0".."9".

TOKENS
    Identifier = letter {letter | digit}.
    Number = digit {digit}.

COMMENTS FROM "//" TO "\n"
IGNORE "\r\n\t"

PRODUCTIONS
   TinyCode = "program"
              Identifier         (. self.initialize(self.token.val) .)
              "."
              ProgramBody.

   ProgramBody = ["var"
                DeclareVar
                { DeclareVar }]
                "begin"
                { Statement }
                "end."           (. self.run() .)
                .

   DeclareVar = Identifier       (. v = self.token.val .)
               ":"
               DeclareVarBody<v>
               ";".

   DeclareVarBody<v> =
               ("integer"        (. value = defaultdict(int) .)
               | "boolean"       (. value = defaultdict(bool) .)
               )                 (. lbound = ubound = 0 .)
               [
               "[" Number        (. lbound = int(self.token.val) .)
               ".." Number       (. ubound = int(self.token.val) .)
               "]"
               ]                 (. self.create_constraint(v, lbound, ubound)
                                    self.create_var(v, value) .)
               .

   Statement = [Identifier       (. self.create_label(self.token.val) .)
              ":"]
              [StatementBody]
```

```
            ";".

StatementBody = Assignment
              | Branching
              | Print
              | Goto
              .

Assignment = "let"
             VarName
             ":=" Expr        (. self.emit_op(self.op_let) .)
             .

PIdentifier = Identifier      (. self.emit_push(self.token.val) .)
              .

Branching = "if"
            Expr
            "goto"
            PIdentifier       (. self.emit_op(self.op_if) .)
            .

Print = "print" Expr          (. self.emit_op(lambda: print(self.pop())) .)
        .

Goto = "goto" PIdentifier     (. self.emit_op(self.op_goto) .)
       .

VarName = PIdentifier
          ("[" Expr
          "]"
          |             (. self.emit_push(0) .)
          ).

Expr = E {
       BoolOp<out op> E       (. self.emit_op(op) .)
       }.

BoolOp<out op> = "and" (. op = self.lop(lambda: self.pop() & self.pop()) .)
               | "or"  (. op = self.lop(lambda: self.pop() | self.pop()) .)
               | "<>"  (. op = self.lop(lambda: self.pop() != self.pop()) .)
               | "<"   (. op = self.lop(lambda: self.pop() > self.pop()) .)
               | "<="  (. op = self.lop(lambda: self.pop() >= self.pop()) .)
               | ">"   (. op = self.lop(lambda: self.pop() < self.pop()) .)
               | ">="  (. op = self.lop(lambda: self.pop() <= self.pop()) .)
               | "=="  (. op = self.lop(lambda: self.pop() == self.pop()) .)
               .

E = T {
    AddSub<out op> T  (. self.emit_op(op) .)
    }.

AddSub<out op> = "+"  (. op = self.lop(lambda: self.pop() + self.pop()) .)
               | "-"  (. op = self.lop(lambda: -self.pop() + self.pop()) .)
               .

T = F {
```

```
        MulDiv<out op> F  (. self.emit_op(op) .)
        }.

    MulDiv<out op> = "*"  (. op = self.lop(lambda: self.pop() * self.pop()) .)
                   | "/"  (. op = self.lop(lambda: 1 / self.pop() * self.
                   pop()) .)
                   .

    F = UnOp<out op> F    (. self.emit_op(op) .)
      |   Value
      | "(" Expr ")"
      .

    UnOp<out op> = "-"      (. op = self.lop(lambda: -self.pop()) .)
                 | "not"    (. op = self.lop(lambda: not self.pop()) .)
                 .

    Value = VarName             (. self.emit_op(self.op_read) .)
          | Number              (. self.emit_push(int(self.token.val)) .)
          | "true"              (. self.emit_push(True) .)
          | "false"             (. self.emit_push(False) .)
          .

END TinyCode.
```

A test run of `countsum.tc` produces the expected output:

```
python TinyCode.py countsum.tc
Running CountSum
15
0 errors detected
```

As a more advanced example, let's find all prime numbers no larger than 100 using the sieve of Eratosthenes algorithm [69]:

```
// sieve.tc

program Sieve.

var A: boolean[2..100];
    i: integer;
    j: integer;
    N: integer;

begin
    let N := 100;

    // set each A[i] to true ("is prime")
    let i := 2;
aloop:
    let A[i] := true;
    let i := i + 1;
    if i <= N goto aloop;

    // loop for i = 2 to sqrt(N)
    let i := 2;
```

```
sloop:
    if not A[i] goto skip;

    // mark multiples of i as non-prime
    let j := i * i;
jloop:
    let A[j] := false;
    let j := j + i;
    if j <= N goto jloop;

skip:
    let i := i + 1;
    if i * i <= N goto sloop;

    // print out identified primes
    let i := 2;
ploop:
    if not A[i] goto pskip;
    print i;
pskip:
    let i := i + 1;
    if i <= N goto ploop;
end.
```

It correctly identifies 25 prime numbers:

```
python TinyCode.py sieve.tc
Running Sieve
2
3
5
7
11
13
17
19
23
29
31
37
41
43
47
53
59
61
67
71
73
79
83
89
97
0 errors detected
```

8.4 TAKEAWAYS

1. Classic methods of compiler development rely on tools already familiar to us, such as regular expressions, finite automata, formal grammars, pushdown automata, and recursive parsers.
2. Some essential parts of a compiler, such as a scanner and a parser, can be generated automatically from a certain formal description.
3. A formal description for a scanner typically relies on regular expressions or regular EBNF productions, defining the set of programming language tokens. The resulting scanner usually implements a variation of a finite state machine.
4. A formal description for a parser requires a more advanced instrument, typically equivalent to a certain type of context-free grammar. The generated parser is often based on the pushdown automaton model or implements a simpler approach, such as recursive descent.
5. Semantic actions that turn a parser into an actual compiler are typically written in a general-purpose programming language, such as C, C#, or Python.

9 The Lindenmayer systems

Formal grammars are most commonly used to describe the structure of a formal language and to facilitate parsing. The LR(1) parsing algorithm we discussed in Chapter 7 relies on context-free production rules to identify meaningful constituents of the input.

It is also possible to use the definition of a certain formal language to generate strings belonging to that language. Such use cases are well beyond the scope of this book, but before moving on to the next topic, let's take a quick excursion into the world of *Lindenmayer systems* (or *L-systems*) and see how formal grammars can produce complex and beautiful objects.

9.1 EVOLVING PLANTS

The inventor of L-systems, Aristid Lindenmayer, was interested in studying the developmental process of plants and similar organisms [60]. Among the most apparent properties of a plant's shape are *symmetry* and *self-similarity*. Axial symmetry is commonly seen in leaves, which consist of two mirror-image parts on either side of the midrib. Flowers typically exhibit "floral" symmetry, being made up of similar parts connected to the center. Self-similarity is a more elusive concept that describes a structure consisting of elements that look similar to the whole. For example, a tree is "self-similar" because its branches are organized in the same way as the tree itself. Likewise, a compound leaf (such as a fern leaf) consists of leaflets that look similar to the whole leaf. The complexity of a plant's structure appears to be an emergent property, arising naturally in the course of normal plant growth.

L-systems are based on three foundational ideas. The first is to represent a plant's structure with a string of characters. For example, suppose that a certain type of plant is made of three kinds of elements: a trunk element I, a left leaf L, and a right leaf R. A small specimen of this plant, consisting of a single trunk element and two leaves, can be described with the string LRI (see Figure 9.1).

This figure, however, is just an illustration of one of many possible appearances of the LRI plant. The textual description does not really dictate any particular appearance; it only defines the internal structure of the entity we are describing.

With enough patience, one can create fairly complicated plants using this approach, but in practice, the description strings quickly become long and difficult to

FIGURE 9.1: An LRI plant.

DOI: 10.1201/9781032614991-9

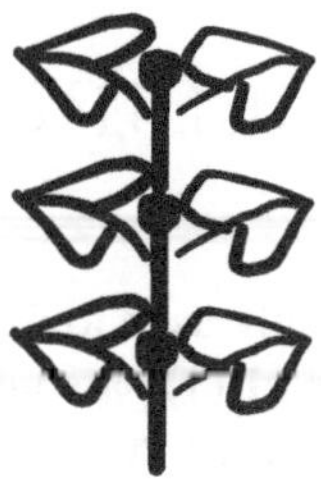

FIGURE 9.2: An ALRILRILRI plant (the root element A is invisible).

work with. Thus, the second foundational idea is to specify the developmental rules of the plant in the form:

$$predecessor \rightarrow successor$$

We can make our LRI plant growable by introducing a new element A (a "root") and specifying its developmental rule:

$$A \rightarrow ALRI$$

Now let's "seed" an initial plant consisting only of the root element A. After three applications of the developmental rule, we will obtain a "triple-LRI" plant (see Figure 9.2):

$$A \rightarrow ALRI \rightarrow ALRILRI \rightarrow ALRILRILRI$$

The third foundational idea is to treat the textual description of a plant's structure as a script executable by a certain visualization module. We will discuss this a bit later.

Summing up, an L-system is a description of a plant structure consisting of an initial string (called an *axiom*) and a set of *production rules* that determine how individual symbols "grow" into strings. Within the context of *deterministic, context-free (D0L) systems,*[1] it is also presumed that no rules are in conflict, so if we have a rule $A \rightarrow B$, there should be no alternative rule $A \rightarrow C$.

9.2 GENERATING STRINGS

Clearly, the production rules of a D0L system are the rules of a context-free grammar with an additional ban on alternative right-hand sides. For further discussion, let's presume that Latin characters represent nonterminal symbols of a D0L, while the rest of the ASCII chart represents terminals. Instead of a start symbol, a D0L has its

[1] "D0L" stands for a **D**eterministic **L**-system with **0** interactions (i.e., context-free), but the spelling "DOL" is also very common.

axiom, but we can always introduce a production rule like $S \rightarrow$ axiom to create a "proper" start symbol.

We have already discussed in Chapter 5 that the production rules of a formal grammar define the set of allowed nonterminal-to-string transformations. For instance, the rules

$$S \rightarrow A\_N$$
$$A \rightarrow \texttt{brave} \mid \texttt{lazy} \mid \texttt{hungry}$$
$$N \rightarrow \texttt{cat} \mid \texttt{dog} \mid \texttt{bear}$$

state that S can be replaced with the sequence A_N, where A can be `brave`, `lazy`, or `hungry`, and N can be `cat`, `dog`, or `bear`. Therefore, the string `brave_dog` belongs to the given language.

Having a grammar is necessary but not sufficient for generating language strings; a generator needs certain guiding principles to choose the sequence of replacements to make. This point is hardly new to us: parsers address a similar issue by relying on principles like "process data from left to right" and "aim for the leftmost derivation." Likewise, a generator can impose additional rules directing the process of string construction. For example, it can choose `dog` twice as often as `cat` when expanding the nonterminal N. By fine-tuning string generation, it is possible to obtain diverse sets of strings belonging to the given formal language.

The L-system string generator constructs the output string by replacing *all* nonterminal symbols in the input string according to the production rules. By invoking the generator with the axiom string as input, we obtain the "generation 1" string, which, in turn, can be passed to the generator to obtain the "generation 2" string, and so on.

Consider, for example, the evolution of the axiom `g` according to the production rule `g` → `g[+g][-g]`:

```
gen 0: g
gen 1: g[+g][-g]
gen 2: g[+g][-g][+g[+g][-g]][-g[+g][-g]]
```

Every occurrence of `g` in the input string becomes `g[+g][-g]` in the output. This process can go on forever, but in practice, it is usually interesting to watch the evolution of a certain axiom over N generations or to simply visualize the N-th generation string without intermediate steps.

9.3 VISUALIZING STRINGS

A string of characters can be treated as a sequence of drawing control commands. This idea is used, for instance, in Microsoft QBasic and some earlier BASIC dialects:

```
DRAW "U50R100D50L100"
```

Here, the `DRAW` statement[2] moves the drawing pen `U`p by 50 pixels, then `R`ight by 100 pixels, then `D`own by 50 pixels, and finally `L`eft by 100 pixels, thus drawing a rectangle. A more recent example of the same approach is G-code, used to control 3D printers [52].

L-systems do not define any single "right" method to interpret plant description strings. However, a commonly suggested way to get started is to treat individual characters as turtle commands. As a reminder, *turtle graphics* (available in Python via the `turtle` module) is a method of drawing lines by issuing commands to a virtual, pen-carrying, turtle-like robot. The list of supported turtle commands varies across implementations, and some L-system visualizers may provide control characters not found in alternative tools.

The L-systems toolbox in JFLAP is fairly basic but sufficient for our needs (see Table 9.1).

TABLE 9.1: Commonly used turtle commands in JFLAP.

Command	Description
`g`	Go `distance` points forward while drawing (default value: 15 pixels).
`+`	Turn by `angle` degrees clockwise (default value: 20 degrees).
`-`	Turn by `angle` degrees counterclockwise.
`%`	Turn by 180 degrees.
`[`	Start a new branch (pass control to a new clone of the current turtle).
`]`	End a branch (pass control to the previously active turtle).
`{`	Start a filled-in polygon.
`}`	End a filled-in polygon.
`!`	Increase line width.
`~`	Decrease line width.

The visualizer starts with a single turtle located at the bottom center of the screen and pointing upward. We will only discuss 2D visualization, but in principle, JFLAP turtles can turn around any axis of the 3D space. All unrecognized characters are ignored.

Now let's discuss how to use JFLAP to visualize an arbitrary L-system. Let's start JFLAP and choose **L-System** from the main menu. The next screen is an editor where the axiom and production rules must be entered. For now, let's proceed with the axiom

[2]See https://www.qbasic.net/en/reference/qb11/Statement/DRAW.htm

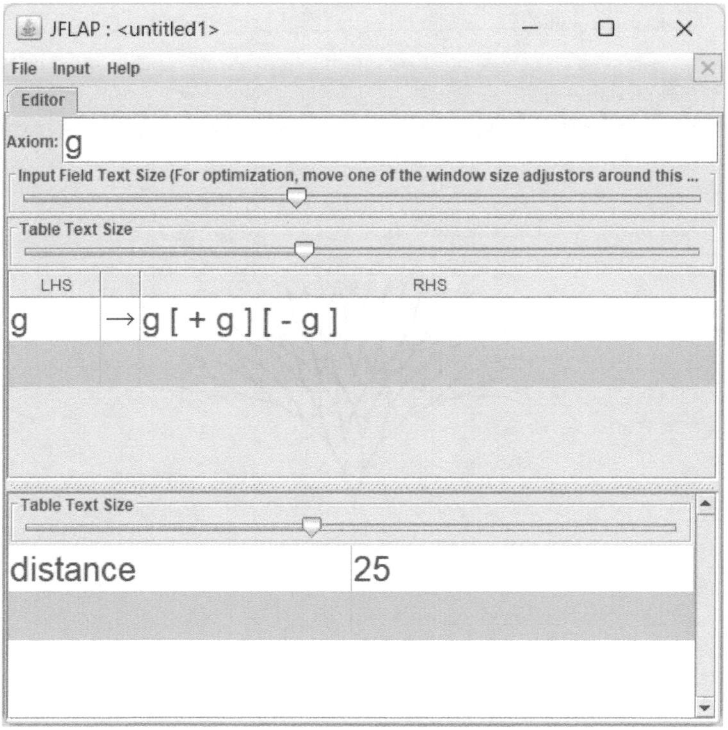

FIGURE 9.3: The JFLAP L-system editor.

g and the single production rule `g` → `g[+g] [-g]` (note that JFLAP requires the individual symbols to be separated by spaces). Finally, let's use the bottom part of the editor to override the default value of `distance`, setting it to 25 pixels (see Figure 9.3).

The resulting L-system can be rendered via the **Input, Render System** menu option. The spin edit control on the right-hand side of the new **L-S Render** tab can be used to set the generation to be rendered. For example, Figure 9.4 shows generation 7 of our plant. To return to the editor, simply close the **L-S Renderer** tab.

It is also interesting to examine the evolution of our L-system (see Table 9.2).

The axiom `g` is easy to render: by executing the command `g`, the turtle draws a single vertical line. The next string, `g[+g] [-g]`, is more interesting. The first `g` corresponds to a vertical line, just like before. The next symbol `[` starts a branch: a new turtle appears at the current position, turns `angle` degrees clockwise (the `+` command), and draws a line (the `g` command). The branch ends here, and control is passed to the previous turtle. Then the left branch is drawn in the same manner.

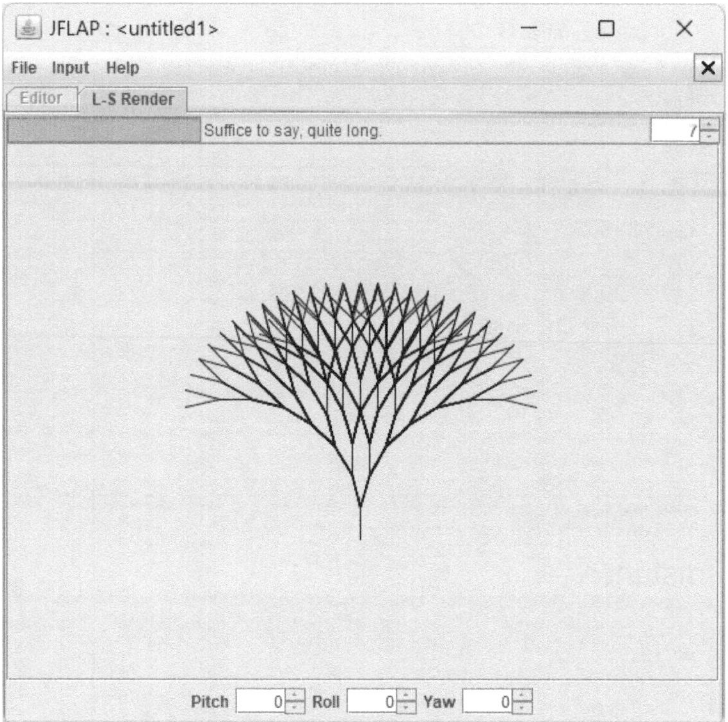

FIGURE 9.4: Visualizing a simple L-system with JFLAP.

TABLE 9.2: The visualized evolution of a simple L-system.

Generation	String	Visualization
0	g	
1	g[+g][-g]	
2	g[+g][-g][+g[+g][-g]][-g[+g][-g]]	

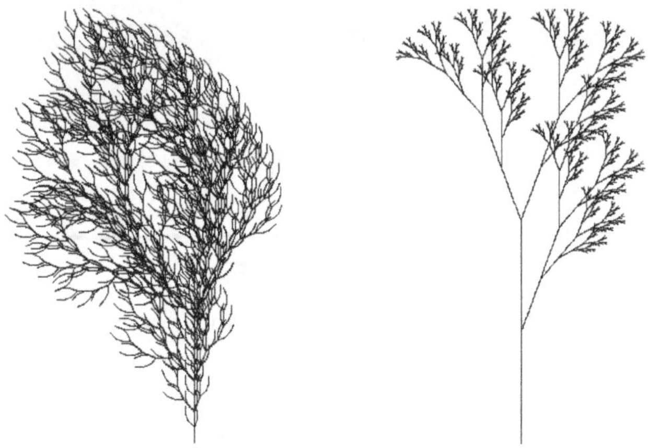

axiom: g
rules: g → gg-[-g+g+g]+[+g-g-g]
angle: 22.5, distance: 8, gen: 4

axiom: X
rules: X → g[+X]g[-X]+X
g → gg
angle: 20, distance: 2, gen: 7

FIGURE 9.5: Two plants produced by L-systems.

The process of visualization can be inefficient in certain cases. For example, the generation 2 plant starts with the already-familiar fragment `g[+g][-g]`. After finishing it, the turtle proceeds to a more complex structure `[+g[+g][-g]][-g[+g][-g]]`, which is drawn right on top of the previous fragment, meaning that the same lines are painted many times. The generation 1 plant consists of three lines, and its description has three `g` symbols. Generation 2 needs nine `g` symbols to draw seven lines. The L-system can be optimized by introducing a "plant bud" symbol `A` as follows:

Axiom: `A`
Production rule: `A` → `g[+A][-A]`

The development of this modified system takes place only in buds (which are not recognized as control characters by the turtle and are thus ignored):

```
step 0: A
step 1: g[+A][-A]
step 2: g[+g[+A][-A]][-g[+A][-A]]
step 3: g[+g[+g[+A][-A]][-g[+A][-A]]][-g[+g[+A][-A]][-g[+A][-A]]]
...
```

Figure 9.5 demonstrates that even slightly more complex L-systems can already produce realistic, plant-like objects.

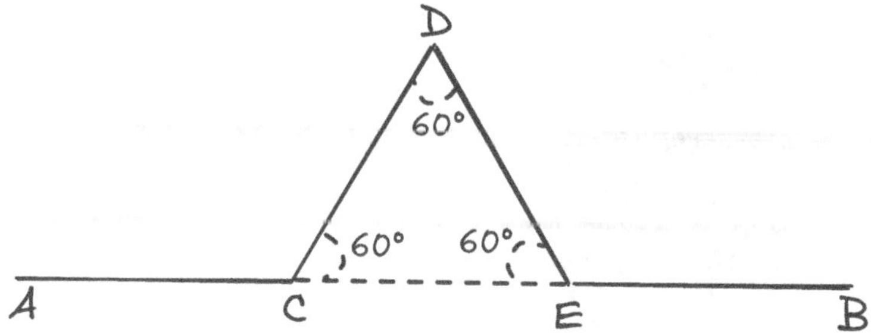

FIGURE 9.6: Constructing the Koch curve.

9.4 FRACTAL PATTERNS

Prusinkiewicz and Lindenmayer suggested that real plants can be modeled by mathematical structures known as *fractals*, which possess the property of self-similarity [60, Ch. 8]. It was shown that L-systems are able to represent many classic fractals, not necessarily plant-like [59]. Let's briefly explore this capability by constructing two simple fractal objects: the Koch curve and the Sierpiński triangle.

The Koch curve can be constructed as follows: 1. Start with a single line segment AB. 2. Replace AB with four segments of the same size, AC, CD, DE, and EB, as shown in Figure 9.6. 3. Repeat step 2 for each of the four new segments to obtain a more accurate approximation.

It takes an infinite number of steps to construct the perfect Koch curve. Our task is to draw a version of the curve obtained after a user-specified number of steps.

Consider a k-th step approximation of the Koch curve. Each of its segments is drawn with the turtle command `g`. For step $k + 1$, `g` has to be replaced with a four-segment turtle path:

```
go straight
turn 60° counterclockwise
go straight
turn 120° clockwise
go straight
turn 60° counterclockwise
go straight
```

This principle can be encoded within a single production rule:

```
g → g-g++g-g
```

To render this L-system correctly in JFLAP, it is also necessary to set the value of `angle` to 60 (see Figure 9.7).

Note that while the shape of the obtained curve is correct, its size does not reflect the iterative derivation process: the value of `distance` should be divided by 3 at each successive step. We will return to this task a bit later.

Constructing the Sierpiński triangle is a bit more challenging:

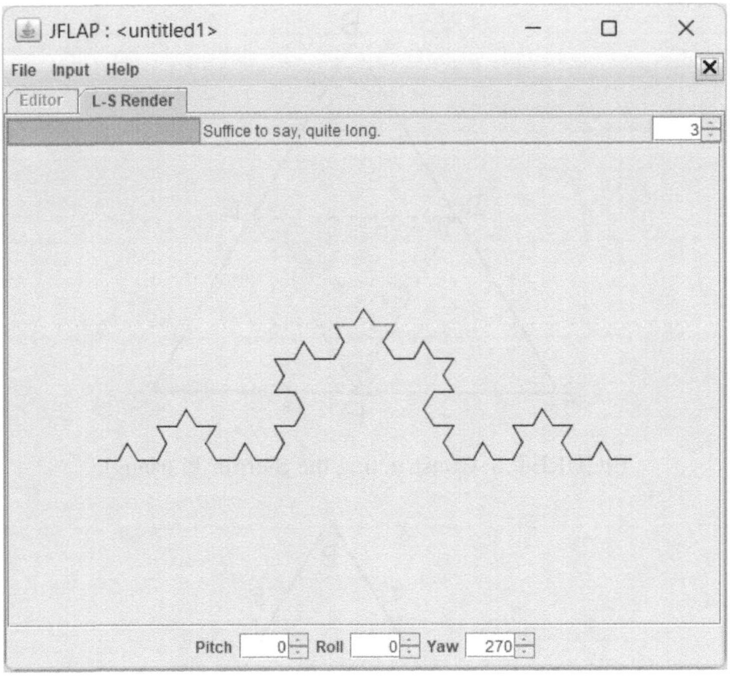

FIGURE 9.7: The Koch curve of the third order rendered by JFLAP.

1. Start with an equilateral triangle ABC.
2. "Cut out" the central triangle DEF, as shown in Figure 9.8.
3. Repeat step 2 for each of the three remaining triangles, ADF, DBE, and FEC, to obtain a more accurate approximation.

The axiom of the corresponding L-system should represent a triangle ABC that can be further sliced into four pieces. Since the turtle can only move `distance` points forward at a time, the length of each side of ABC has to be twice the `distance`.

Consider the axiom `gXg-gg-gg` (Figure 9.9). If `angle` is 120, the turtle will draw an equilateral triangle with a point X marking the start of the future cutout DEF.

Now, imagine the turtle stops at X on its way from A to C. To draw a new triangle in the center, it would need to turn 120° counterclockwise and move to the midpoint between A and B, then proceed to the midpoint between B and C, and finally return to X. This maneuver, however, would not create X-points for subsequent cutouts. What we really need is the shape shown in Figure 9.10.

Just as in the case of the axiom, each X-marked line has to be at least twice the `distance` long. Hence, we will need a rule to double the length of every line of the drawing:

```
g → gg
```

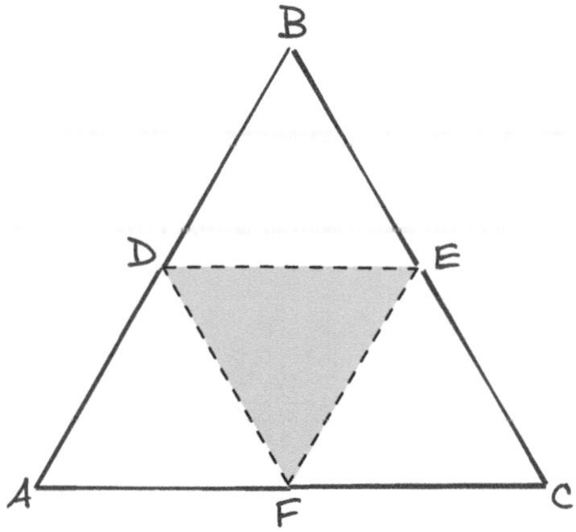

FIGURE 9.8: Constructing the Sierpiński triangle.

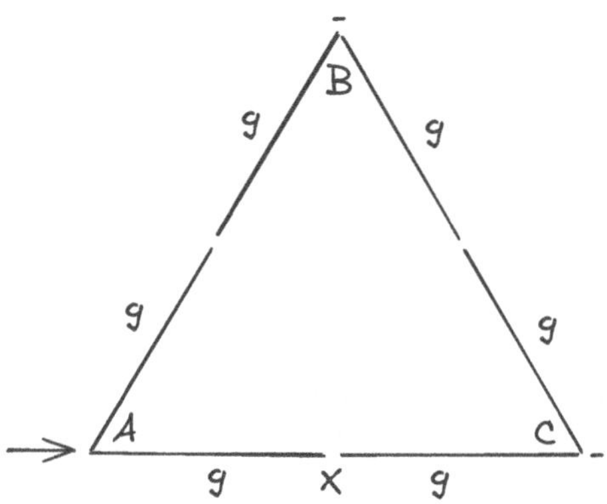

FIGURE 9.9: The axiom for the Sierpiński triangle L-system.

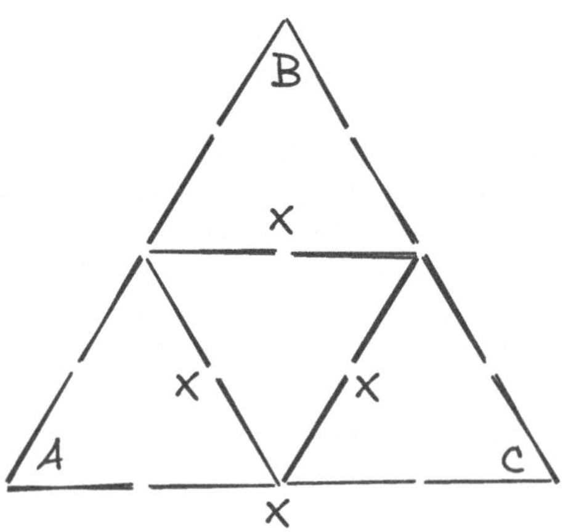

FIGURE 9.10: Sierpiński triangle: creating the cutout.

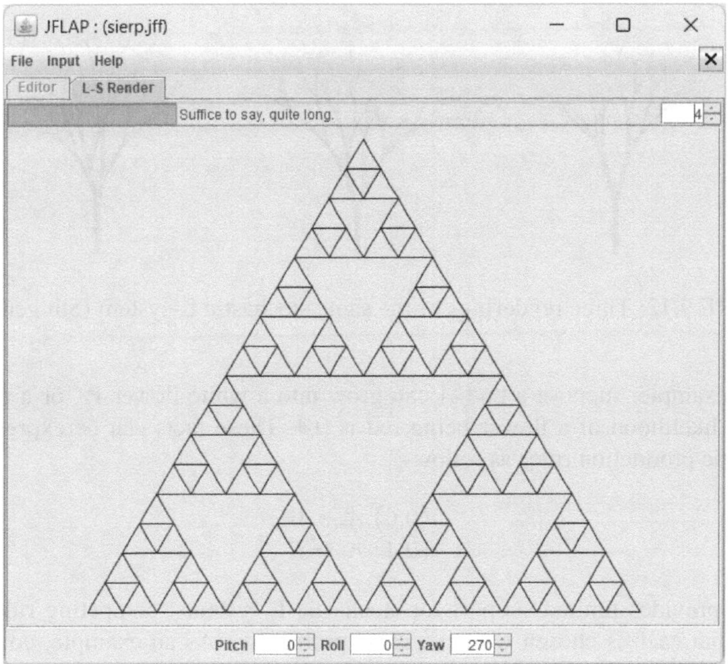

FIGURE 9.11: A Sierpiński triangle of the fourth order rendered by JFLAP.

Finally, let's create a rule for the central triangular cutout:

```
X → -gXg+gXg+gXg-
```

The JFLAP visualization of the obtained results is shown in Figure 9.11.

9.5 BEYOND D0LS

The Koch curve-generating L-system has already demonstrated certain limitations of D0L systems. In particular, simple context-free rules cannot express gradual changes in `distance`. Another limitation is determinism, which works well for mathematical fractals but is hardly suitable for generating groups of plant-like objects that exhibit certain individual differences. D0L systems represent the simplest type of L-systems. More advanced types also deserve a brief discussion.

9.5.1 STOCHASTIC L-SYSTEMS

Stochastic L-systems add variation to the process of string generation by allowing competing production rules. Competing productions can be marked with probabilities, determining the likelihood of choosing a particular rule.

FIGURE 9.12: Three renderings of the same stochastic L-system (8th generation).

For example, suppose a bud A can grow into a white flower W or a red flower R. The likelihood of a flower being red is 0.4. These facts can be expressed with stochastic production rules as follows:

$$(0.6)\ A \rightarrow W$$
$$(0.4)\ A \rightarrow R$$

JFLAP provides limited support for stochastic L-systems: competing rules are allowed, but each is chosen with the same probability. As an example, consider the following L-system:

Axiom: `R~B`
Productions:
```
B → [~TLL-B++B]
L → [{-g++g%-g}]
R → !R
T → Tg
T → T
```

Different runs of the renderer produce slightly different variations of the resulting plant (see Figure 9.12).

9.5.2 CONTEXT-SENSITIVE RULES

Consider a new kind of plant. A bud A produces a flower W if there are already two sibling flowers. However, the same bud produces a leaf L if there are already two sibling leaves. These rules can be formalized as follows:

$$1\ WAW \rightarrow W$$
$$1\ LAL \rightarrow L$$

The left-hand side still denotes a symbol to be transformed, but this time it must be surrounded by a specific "context." The number i preceding the rule states that the transformation is applied to the i-th symbol of the left-hand side. In our case,

1 WAW means that the 1st symbol (A) will be transformed into W, while the 0th and 2nd symbols form the required context.

According to Prusinkiewicz and Lindenmayer [60], *context-sensitive* rules are useful for modeling signal propagation. Imagine, for example, a plant stem consisting of individual chunks: $CCCCCC$. A certain "signal" is initiated at the root: $SCCCCC$. To deliver this signal to the tip of the plant, we can use the following rules:

$$1\ SC \to S$$
$$S \to C$$

By applying these rules, we propagate the signal S across the stem with every new generation:

$$SCCCCC \to CSCCCC \to CCSCCC \to CCCSCC \ldots$$

JFLAP supports context-sensitive rules in the form described above. However, practical examples require more advanced capabilities, found, for example, in the vlab / L-studio suite[3] or SideFX Houdini.[4] In particular, these tools allow for excluding certain symbols or sibling nodes from the context.

Imagine that the plant stem in the "signal propagation" example is slightly curvy:

$$C\text{-}C\text{+}C\text{-}C\text{+}C\text{-}C$$

The turtle commands `-` and `+` might be important for the outward appearance of the plant but not for the context-sensitive rules. Likewise, it is possible to imagine rules taking into account the existence of an adjacent branch `[...]` while ignoring the actual structure of that branch.[5]

9.5.3 PARAMETRIC L-SYSTEMS

Another useful improvement over basic D0Ls is represented by *parametric L-systems*, which associate numeric data with symbols. For example, a flower F can be smaller, such as $F(0.8)$, or larger, such as $F(1.5)$. The production rules of parametric L-systems can manipulate this data. Suppose a bud A produces a certain plant fragment F with a new bud at the tip:

$$A \to FA$$

We can specify the initial fragment size and make subsequent fragments smaller by parameterizing the axiom and the production rule:

Axiom: $A(50)$
Productions: $A(x) \to F(0.8x)A(0.8x)$

---

[3] https://algorithmicbotany.org/virtual_laboratory/

[4] https://www.sidefx.com/products/houdini/

[5] See, e.g., the **Context Includes Siblings** option in Houdini:

Production rules of parametric L-systems can be made conditional. The following rule is applicable only if $x > 5$:

$$A(x), x > 5 \rightarrow F(0.8x)A(0.8x)$$

JFLAP does not support parametric L-systems as such, but it is possible to achieve similar results by manipulating global variables with turtle commands.[6] The JFLAP turtle can assign the value of a given expression to a global variable. For example, the current value of `distance` can be decreased by issuing the turtle command `distance=distance-1`.

Consider how this capability allows us to produce successive generations of the Koch curve while preserving its original bounding rectangle:

Axiom: `Mg`
Productions:
`g` → `g-g++g-g`
`M` → `M distance=distance/3`

The n-th generation of the Koch curve produced with this system starts with n assignments `distance=distance/3`, ultimately setting the correct length of the baseline segment.

9.6 TAKEAWAYS

1. L-systems demonstrate how formal grammars can be used in *procedural content generation*—a domain quite distinct from parsing or compiler development.
2. Parsing algorithms discover the sequence of grammar productions leading to a given string. L-systems, operating in the opposite direction, produce valid strings of the specified formal language.
3. The obtained strings can be treated as a sequence of commands for a turtle-based visualization subsystem. This way, a seemingly meaningless character string can be turned into a beautiful plant or a fractal.
4. The basic D0L variation of L-systems can be enhanced with advanced capabilities, such as stochastic rule selection, numeric parameters, or context-sensitive productions.

---

https://www.sidefx.com/docs/houdini/nodes/sop/lsystem.html

[6]See
https://research.cs.vt.edu/AVresearch/openalgoviz/JFLAP/trunk/DOCS/gui.lsystem.DisplayPane.html

10 Turing machines

One of the major themes of this book is "problem-solving devices." We have examined the capabilities and limitations of finite state machines and pushdown automata, and we are about to consider a more powerful device: the Turing machine.

This abstract computational machine plays an important role in theoretical computer science but is hardly useful in practice. Our further goal will be to explore the limits of computing machines, but in this chapter, we will approach the Turing machine merely as an extension of the concept of a finite state machine.

10.1 BEYOND CONTEXT-FREE LANGUAGES

In earlier chapters, we examined various devices capable of recognizing formal languages. We started with finite automata, employing them for the task of detecting even binary numbers. This example demonstrated that finite automata are able to recognize *some* languages. Later, we saw that some other languages, like $L = \{\varepsilon, \texttt{ab}, \texttt{aabb}, \texttt{aaabbb}, \dots\}$, are not "pumpable" and thus cannot be recognized by finite automata. However, it turned out that certain non-pumpable languages can be recognized by more sophisticated pushdown automata, which are equipped with stack memory. In a few moments, we will consider languages that are beyond the grasp of nondeterministic pushdown automata, the most capable devices on our list so far.

This discussion takes on new dimensions once we realize that any *decision problem* (a "yes/no" question) can be reframed as a language-recognition problem. At a glance, it might seem that the ability to decide whether a given string belongs to a given language is mostly of interest in compiler development or data validation tasks. Yet, imagine a language of strings that encode the locations of individual chess pieces on a board. Does the White player have a winning strategy in the given string-encoded position? This question can be reformulated as a language-recognition problem: "Does the given string belong to the language of positions where the White player has a winning strategy?" As mentioned in Chapter 5, decision problems are found in all complexity classes and thus can be used to study complexity without loss of generality. Consequently, language-recognition devices are "problem solvers" possessing particular traits that allow them to tackle problems of a certain complexity class.

So far, our most powerful instrument for describing formal languages has been the context-free grammar. In Chapter 5, we used a context-free grammar to describe the language $L = \{\texttt{a}^n\texttt{b}^n\}$, made up of strings consisting of characters a followed by the same number of characters b. By extending these strings with the same number of characters c, we obtain a slightly more complex language $L' = \{\texttt{a}^n\texttt{b}^n\texttt{c}^n\}$. Perhaps counter-intuitively, the language L' is not context-free and cannot be

DOI: 10.1201/9781032614991-10

described with a context-free grammar. Instead, it belongs to a wider class of *context-sensitive* languages, which can be described with *context-sensitive grammars* (CSGs).

We have already seen how context-sensitive rules work in L-systems. In context-sensitive grammars, production rules take the form of

$$\alpha A\beta \rightarrow \alpha c\beta$$

As before, A is a nonterminal symbol that is replaced by the string c, which consists of both terminal and nonterminal symbols. The rule is only applicable when A is surrounded by strings α and β over the alphabet $\Sigma \cup V$. Both α and β can be empty; in this case, we have a context-free production rule (and thus context-free grammars are just special cases of context-sensitive grammars). The string c cannot be empty, but the rule $S \rightarrow \varepsilon$ is allowed if S does not appear on the right-hand side of any rule.

The following context-sensitive grammar describes the language L':

$$\begin{aligned}
&S \rightarrow P \mid \varepsilon \\
&P \rightarrow \mathtt{a}P B\mathtt{c} \mid \mathtt{abc} \\
&\mathtt{c}B \rightarrow B\mathtt{c} \\
&\mathtt{b}B \rightarrow \mathtt{bb}
\end{aligned}$$

The rule $P \rightarrow \mathtt{a}PB\mathtt{c}$ generates an equal number of as and cs, and a placeholder nonterminal B. The rule $\mathtt{c}B \rightarrow B\mathtt{c}$ then allows the Bs to migrate to the left across any cs. Finally, $\mathtt{b}B \rightarrow \mathtt{bb}$ converts the placeholders into the required bs between the as and cs.

Figure 10.1 shows an example derivation obtained with the production rules of this grammar.

10.2 THE PUMPING LEMMA FOR CONTEXT-FREE LANGUAGES

Like regular languages, context-free languages possess their own variation of the "pumping property", established by the *pumping lemma for context-free languages*:

There exists an integer p such that any string s in a context-free language L with a length of at least p can be represented as a concatenation of five strings $vwxyz$ in such a way that:

1. at least one of the substrings w and y is not empty;
2. the length of the substring wxy does not exceed p;
3. the strings vw^ixy^iz for any $i \geq 0$ also belong to L.

In other words, any sufficiently long string of a context-free language contains two substrings w and y that can be removed or repeated ("pumped") any number of times to produce strings that also belong to L.

Let's recall why regular languages are pumpable. Regular languages can be recognized by finite automata. Any sufficiently long string of a regular language will inevitably cause the state machine to revisit a certain state. A portion of the string corresponding to this loop can be removed or pumped.

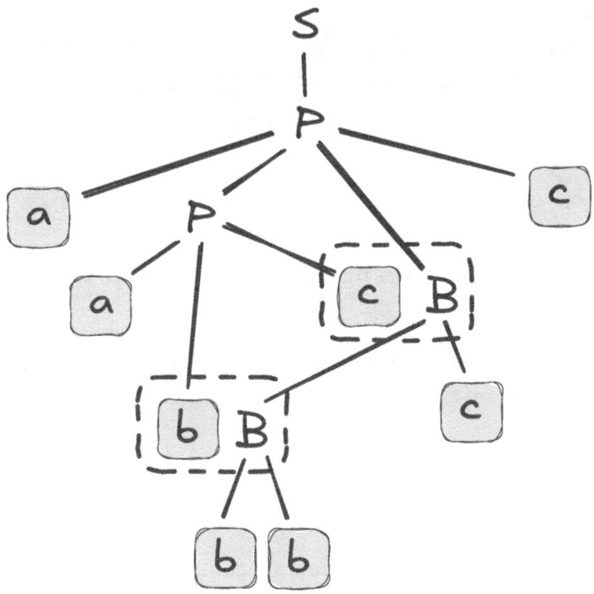

FIGURE 10.1: Derivation of the string aabbcc.

Similar reasoning can be applied to context-free languages. A context-free language is described with a grammar having a finite number of nonterminals. A parse tree of any sufficiently long string of a context-free language will inevitably contain a derivation path from S to a certain terminal symbol that contains a certain nonterminal X at least twice. For example, look again at Figure 7.7. The grammar used to produce this parse tree has only four nonterminals: S, E, T, and F. Thus, a large parse tree will include at least one path from S to a certain terminal with two Es, Ts, or Fs.

If a nonterminal X appears twice in the path, it means that X can eventually produce a string of symbols having X inside: $X \rightarrow \ldots \rightarrow wXy$. Applying this observation, we can replace X with wXy and still obtain strings belonging to L: $wwXyy$, $wwwXyyy$, …, thus "pumping" strings w and y. Since we cannot expand X forever, there should be an alternative way to terminate X via a certain path $X \rightarrow \ldots \rightarrow x$. This way, it is also possible to remove w and y altogether, leaving only x.

To show that $L' = \{a^n b^n c^n\}$ is not pumpable and thus is not context-free, we can again use a proof by contradiction. Assume L' is context-free and has a pumping length p. Consider a string $s = a^p b^p c^p$, which belongs to L'. According to the pumping lemma, we should be able to split it into five substrings $vwxyz$ so that the length of wxy does not exceed p, while w and y are nonempty and pumpable. In this case, wxy cannot contain both as and cs, because they are separated by p symbols b.

Suppose that wxy does not contain as. Then by pumping w and y we will only increase the number of bs and/or cs. Similarly, if we presume that wxy does not contain

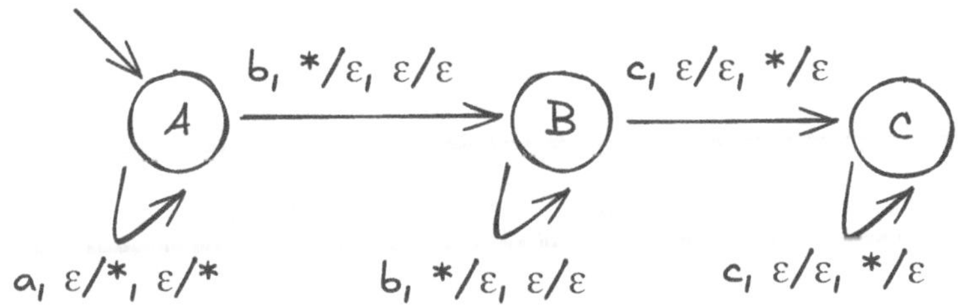

FIGURE 10.2: A 2-PDA recognizing the language $L' = \{a^n b^n c^n\}$

cs, by pumping w and y we will only increase the number of as and/or bs. In either case it means that $vw^i xy^i z$ cannot be in L', contradicting the assumption that L' is context-free.

10.3 TWO-STACK PDAS

The most straightforward way to obtain a machine capable of recognizing context-sensitive languages is to equip a deterministic pushdown automaton with a second stack. As a reminder, the transition rules of a PDA have the form of $(A, c, s) \rightarrow (A', s')$, where A is the current state, c is the next input symbol, s is the symbol on top of the stack, A' is the target state, and s' is the string replacing s on the stack. A two-stack PDA ("2-PDA") introduces a new symbol p, denoting the top element of the second stack, and the string p' that replaces it: $(A, c, s, p) \rightarrow (A', s', p')$. In the case of acceptance by empty stack, both stacks must be cleared to accept the input string.

Figure 10.2 shows a device recognizing the language $L' = \{a^n b^n c^n\}$. It is very similar to the pushdown automaton shown in Figure 6.3, but it uses two stacks to count the expected characters b and c. The 2-PDA starts by placing as many asterisks on each stack as there are a characters in the input string. Next, it reads bs, each time removing one asterisk from the first stack. Finally, it reads cs, each time removing one asterisk from the second stack. Only strings belonging to L' leave both stacks empty.

Most books on the theory of computation, however, barely examine two-stack pushdown devices. Historically, the mainstream discussion has focused mostly on their computationally equivalent alternatives, Turing machines.

10.4 DETERMINISTIC TURING MACHINES

A *Turing machine* (TM) is another simple computational device that operates quite differently from the kinds of finite automata we have considered so far (see Figure 10.3).

Like an FA, a TM is always in a certain state. The number of possible states is finite. However, the TM has explicit accepting and rejecting states (labeled Y and N in the sketch). Once either of these states is reached, the machine ceases to operate

(1, ◇)	(N, ◇, ▷)
(3, ◇)	(1, ◇, ▷)
(4, ◇)	(3, ◇, ▷)
(3, A)	(1, C, ▷)
(3, □)	(Y, C, ▷)

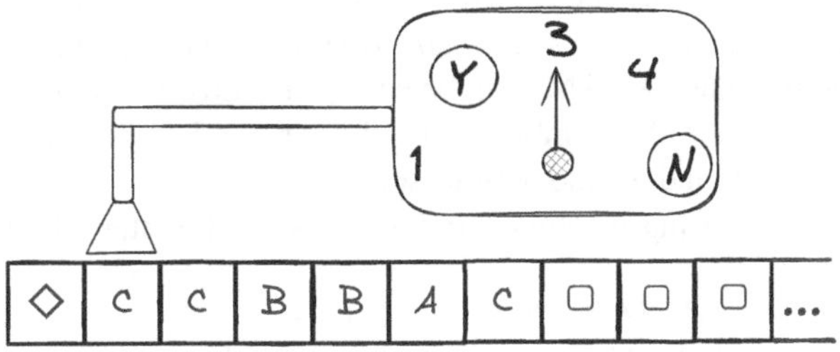

FIGURE 10.3: A sketch of a Turing machine.

("halts"). Abnormal situations caused by missing transition rules can be treated as halting in a rejecting state.

Most notably, the TM is equipped with a read/write head that can move along the input tape in either direction. All of our previous finite automata were only able to read input symbols sequentially from the beginning to the end of the tape. The Turing machine has no such limitation: it can both read and write data located anywhere on an infinite tape. The tape has a beginning (marked with a sentinel symbol ◇) but no right-hand border. Empty cells are presumed to be filled with blank characters, □.

The transition rules of a TM associate pairs of (*state*, *symbol*) with triplets of (*state'*, *symbol'*, *action*). Just as before, a pair (*state*, *symbol*) describes the current situation, here composed of the device's state and the symbol under the head. As a result of a transition, the machine switches into the state *state'*, and the symbol *symbol'* is written to the tape cell currently under the head. The third component, *action*, determines the position of the head after the transition as follows:

- ◁: the head moves to the adjacent left cell;
- ▷: the head moves to the adjacent right cell.

Unlike finite automata, a TM does not consume its input: its read/write head can move in both directions and modify the tape's content. Thus, the TM halts by entering its accepting or rejecting states rather than by exhausting the input data.

The definition of the language recognized by a TM still holds: it is the set of strings the TM accepts. However, in the case of TMs, "non-acceptance" can be due to explicit

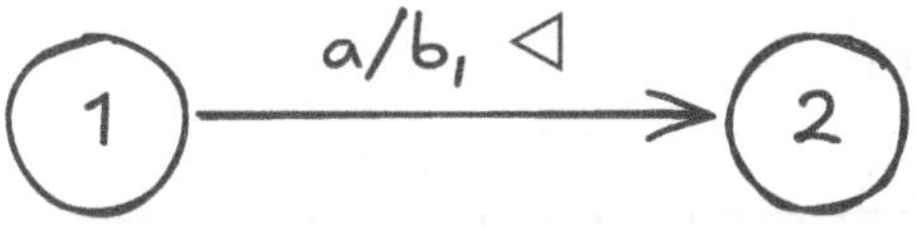

FIGURE 10.4: A sketch of the transition rule (1, a) → (2, b, ◁).

rejection or *looping*. Imagine a machine that processes the input string ab by endlessly moving its head right and left without ever entering an accepting or rejecting state. In this case, the string ab does not belong to the language recognized by the given TM. TMs that always halt on any input form a useful class of machines called *deciders*.

For now, we will focus on *deterministic Turing machines*, which contain no conflicting transitions. Like FAs, TMs can be easily visualized as a directed graph. Each edge label must include the symbol currently expected to be under the read/write head, its replacement, and a head action (see Figure 10.4).

More formally, a Turing machine can be represented by the following elements:

1. A finite set of states $Q = \{q_1, q_2, \dots, q_n\}$.
2. A finite set of tape symbols $\Sigma = \{a_1, a_2, \dots, a_m\}$.
3. The start state q_s, belonging to Q.
4. An accepting state q_y and a rejecting state q_n, both belonging to Q.
5. A transition function $\delta(q_i, a) = (q_j, b, \text{action})$, mapping a pair (*state*, *symbol*) to a triplet (*state'*, *symbol'*, *action*).

Note that both the sentinel ◇ and blank □ characters are presumed to be reliable markers of the beginning and the end of the input data. They should not appear inside the input.

10.5 REPRESENTING TMS WITH 2-PDAS

Some authors note that Turing machines don't fit well into the series of progressively more capable finite state machines [43]. We started with a finite automaton having states but no memory, then moved to a pushdown automaton equipped with a stack, and, finally, discussed a more advanced PDA version having two stacks. Each expansion provided new computing capabilities without changing the basic architecture of the original machine. We could observe that while subsequent devices were able to recognize new kinds of formal languages, the general operating principle remained intact: a 2-PDA is merely a DFA with two stacks. The Turing machine, with its moving head and random-access memory, feels like a different type of machine. To bridge the gap between TMs and finite automata, let's discuss how a 2-PDA can be used to simulate a TM's behavior.

The first stack of the 2-PDA represents the portion of the Turing machine's tape to the left of the head, with the top-stack element being closest to the head. The second stack of the 2-PDA represents the remainder of the tape, with the top-stack element being the one directly under the head (see Figure 10.5).

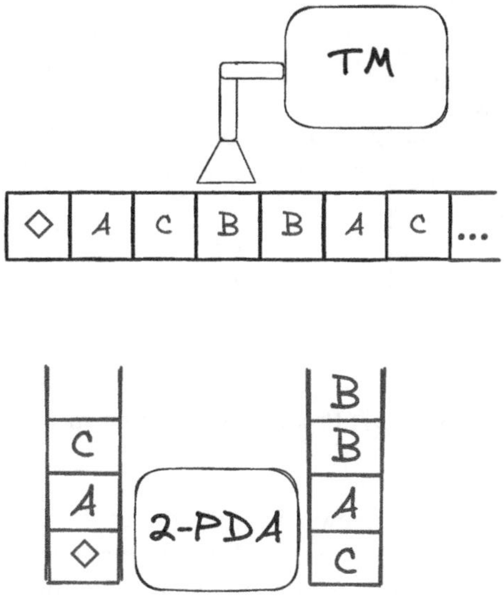

FIGURE 10.5: Representing a TM tape with two stacks.

Since a TM tape begins with a ◇ symbol and has no right-hand border, we can presume that the first stack of the 2-PDA contains the ◇ symbol and that the second stack has an infinite supply of □ symbols, meaning that a pop operation from an empty second stack returns □.

We can presume that the stacks of the 2-PDA already contain the necessary input data. Alternatively, it is possible to populate them from an input string that ends with a special symbol $, which does not belong to the input alphabet Σ. We will need a three-state 2-PDA, as shown in Figure 10.6. Transitions of the kind $(1, x, \varepsilon, \varepsilon) \rightarrow (1, x, \varepsilon)$ and $(2, \varepsilon, x, \varepsilon) \rightarrow (2, \varepsilon, x)$ must be created for each $x \in \Sigma$.

Consider the input string abc$ that has to be transformed into a TM tape. The transition from state 1 to state 2 consumes the three input symbols a, b, and c and

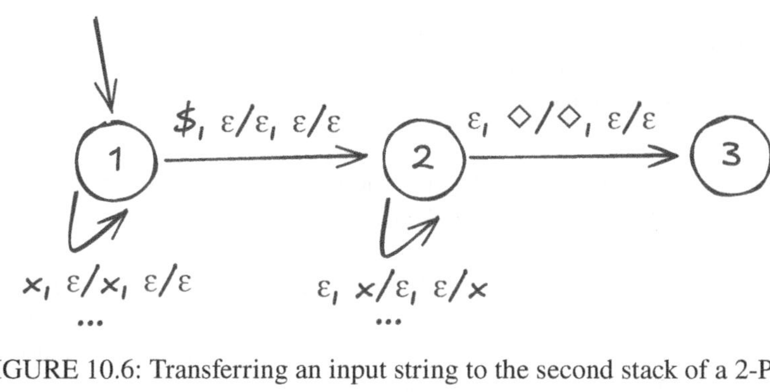

FIGURE 10.6: Transferring an input string to the second stack of a 2-PDA.

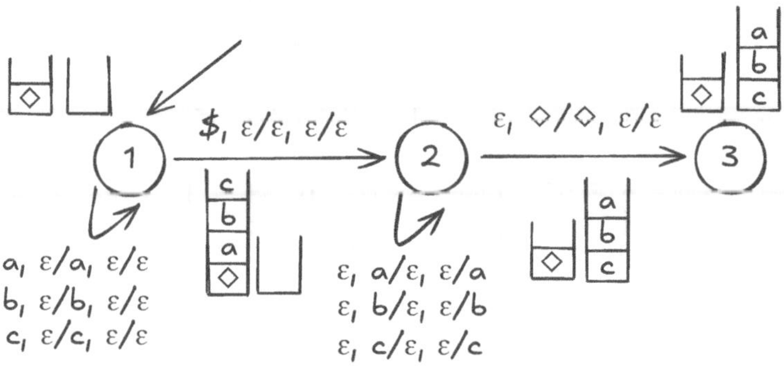

FIGURE 10.7: Processing the input string abc$.

places them on the first stack. Now c is at the top of the first stack. The next input symbol, $, switches the 2-PDA into state 2, where it removes the elements from the first stack and places them on the second stack in reverse order. As soon as the stack sentinel symbol ◇ is reached, the machine switches into state 3 (see Figure 10.7).

At this point, the device will stop operating because the whole input string has been consumed. The easiest way to prevent this and to get some actual work done is to add yet another special symbol $ to the end of the input. The machine will halt after reading it.

The Turing machine supports only two directions of head movements.

Each rule $(S, a) \to (S', b, \triangleright)$ creates a 2-PDA transition $(S, \varepsilon, \varepsilon, a) \to (S', b, \varepsilon)$, where

- a is popped from the second stack;
- b is pushed onto the first stack.

Each rule $(S, a) \to (S', b, \triangleleft)$ creates a set of 2-PDA transitions $(S, \varepsilon, x, a) \to (S', \varepsilon, xb)$, one for each symbol $x \in \Sigma$, where

- a is popped from the second stack;
- x is popped from the first stack;
- xb is pushed onto the second stack.

If a certain state Q of the Turing machine is designated as accepting, the 2-PDA can consume the last remaining input symbol $ and switch to its own designated favorable state F using the rule $(Q, \$, \varepsilon, \varepsilon) \to (F, \varepsilon, \varepsilon)$.

Summing up, we can conclude that 2-PDAs and Turing machines are more similar than they might seem at a glance. It is also interesting (and practically important) that the computational power of a Turing machine can be achieved without random-access memory; it is enough to have two stacks.

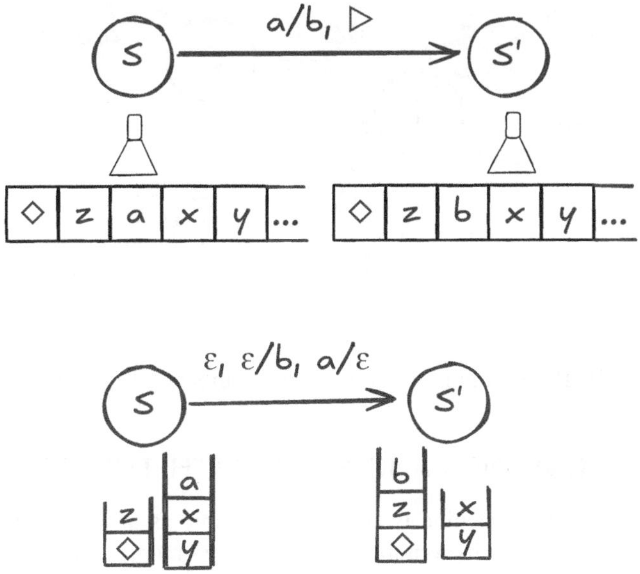

FIGURE 10.8: Implementing the transition rule $(S, \texttt{a}) \rightarrow (S', \texttt{b}, \triangleright)$ in a 2-PDA.

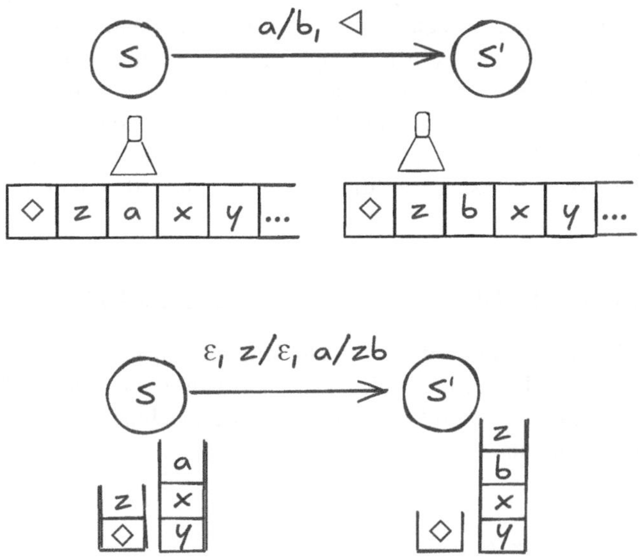

FIGURE 10.9: Implementing the transition rule $(S, \texttt{a}) \rightarrow (S', \texttt{b}, \triangleleft)$ in a 2-PDA.

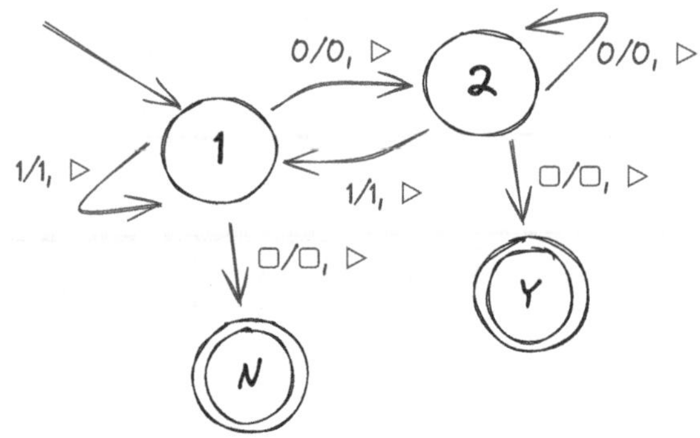

FIGURE 10.10: Recognizing even binary numbers with a Turing machine.

10.6 RECOGNIZING LANGUAGES WITH TURING MACHINES

Intuitively, the Turing machine is at least as capable as any other device we have discussed so far, thanks to its writable, random-access memory. However, let's revisit several familiar formal languages and see how a Turing machine recognizes them.

10.6.1 RECOGNIZING A REGULAR LANGUAGE

We will start with the basic example of a regular language of even binary numbers. Being a regular language, it requires only FA-like functionality (see Figure 10.10).

The Turing machine moves its head rightward until it hits a blank cell. The value of the last non-blank cell determines whether the machine halts in state Y or state N. To simplify the machine a bit, we can remove the N state and its associated transition $(1, \square) \rightarrow (N, \square, \triangleright)$. In this case, a blank cell under the head in state 1 will cause an abnormal situation (a missing transition), which is treated as halting in a rejecting state.

10.6.2 RECOGNIZING A CONTEXT-FREE LANGUAGE

Let's proceed to an example of a more challenging context-free language, $\{\mathtt{a}^n\mathtt{b}^n\}$, which was shown to be recognizable by a pushdown automaton in Chapter 5. The PDA approach has to be modified, since a Turing machine uses tape-based rather than stack-based memory:

```
LOOP
    IF the tape is empty
        accept the input
    IF the first non-space character is a AND the last non-space character is b
        replace both characters with spaces
    ELSE
        reject the input
END LOOP
```

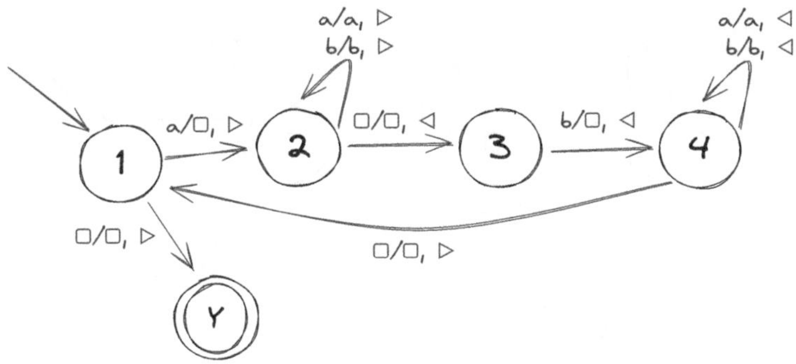

FIGURE 10.11: Recognizing the language $\{a^n b^n\}$ with a Turing machine.

Checking whether a and b constitute the ends of the input string can be done as follows:

```
// check whether the input starts with "a"
move left until a space is under the head
move right
check that "a" is under the head

// check whether the input ends with "b"
move right until a space symbol is under the head
move left
check that "b" is under the head
```

In the start state, the character under the head is expected to be a, so we can begin by replacing it with a space, then proceed to the right-hand end of the input. The resulting Turing machine is shown in Figure 10.11.

10.6.3 RECOGNIZING A CONTEXT-SENSITIVE LANGUAGE

Clearly, the Turing machine is able to recognize some context-free languages. Our next step is to recognize an even more challenging context-sensitive language, $\{a^n b^n c^n\}$. We will use the following straightforward procedure:

```
LOOP
    WHILE the current tape symbol is "*"
        move the head right
    IF the current tape symbol is space
        accept the input
    replace "a" under the head with "*", move the head right

    WHILE the current tape symbol is "a" or "*"
        move the head right
    replace "b" under the head with "*", move the head right

    WHILE the current tape symbol is "b" or "*"
        move the head right
    replace "c" under the head with "*", move the head right
```

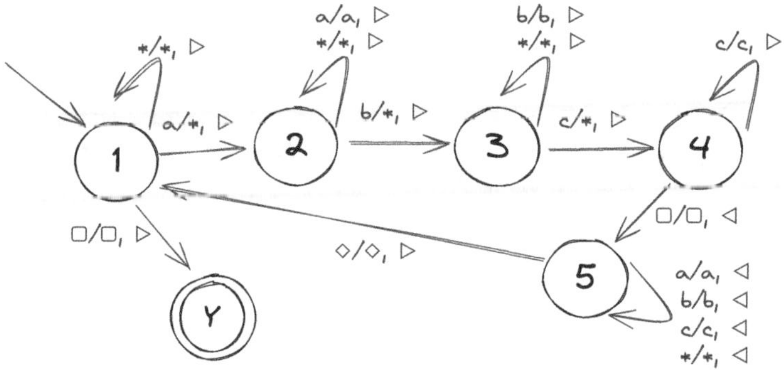

FIGURE 10.12: Recognizing the language $\{a^n b^n c^n\}$ with a Turing machine.

```
    WHILE the current tape symbol is "c"
        move the head right
    check that the current tape symbol is space, move the head left

    move the head to the beginning of the tape
END LOOP
```

Every iteration of the outer loop replaces three symbols a, b, c with asterisks. If the tape contains nothing but spaces and asterisks, the input is accepted. Any unexpected situation leads to string rejection. Consider how tape contents change during processing of the input string aaabbbccc:

```
◇aaabbbccc□
◇*aabbbccc□
◇*aa*bbccc□
◇*aa*bb*cc□
◇**a*bb*cc□
◇**a**b*cc□
◇**a**b**c□
◇*****b**c□
◇********c□
◇*********□
```

Figure 10.12 shows the Turing machine implementing this algorithm. Note that, just like finite automata, any particular Turing machine is designed to perform a specific task. Different tasks require different machines.

10.7 TMS IN PYTHON

Before exploring further capabilities of the Turing machine, let's consider a Python-based simulator, which will help us test various TM configurations. The emulator can be obtained by modifying the DFA implementation from Chapter 2.

```
from dataclasses import dataclass
```

```
from collections import defaultdict


@dataclass
class TM:
    rules: defaultdict
    state_y: int
    state_n: int
    start: int
    tape: str = ""

    def accepts(self, tape):
        self.tape = "#" + tape

        state = self.start
        pos = 1

        try:
            while True:
                if state == self.state_y:
                    return True
                if state == self.state_n:
                    return False
                if pos >= len(self.tape):
                    self.tape += " "

                state, c, a = self.rules[(state, self.tape[pos])]
                self.tape = self.tape[:pos] + c + self.tape[pos + 1 :]
                pos = pos - 1 if a == "L" else pos + 1
        except KeyError:
            return False
```

This code uses # as a tape sentinel symbol, a space character as a “tape space” □, and the characters L and R as actions. The tape is expanded to the right every time the machine needs to read from an out-of-bounds location.

As an example, let’s process several input strings using the machine from Figure 10.12:

```
...

tm = TM(
    {
        (1, " "): (6, " ", "R"),
        (1, "*"): (1, "*", "R"),
        (1, "a"): (2, "*", "R"),
        (2, "b"): (3, "*", "R"),
        (2, "*"): (2, "*", "R"),
        (2, "a"): (2, "a", "R"),
        (3, "c"): (4, "*", "R"),
        (3, "*"): (3, "*", "R"),
        (3, "b"): (3, "b", "R"),
        (4, "c"): (4, "c", "R"),
        (4, " "): (5, " ", "L"),
        (5, "a"): (5, "a", "L"),
        (5, "b"): (5, "b", "L"),
        (5, "c"): (5, "c", "L"),
```

```
        (5, "*"): (5, "*", "L"),
        (5, "#"): (1, "#", "R"),
    },
    6,
    None,
    1,
)

print(tm.accepts(""))  # True
print(tm.accepts("aaabbbccc"))  # True
print(tm.accepts("aaabbbcc"))  # False
print(tm.accepts("abcabc"))  # False
```

10.8 COMPUTING WITH TMS

The ability to rewrite tape content makes Turing machines suitable for solving computational problems of a more general kind than language recognition. In addition to a yes/no output, we can use the tape to prepare output data. For example, it is possible to design a Turing machine that produces the result of an arithmetic expression provided as input before proceeding to the accepting state.

Let's examine several simple Turing machines capable of performing general computing tasks.

10.8.1 SUBTRACTING NUMBERS

We will start with a machine that calculates the difference between two given numbers. Its tape would originally contain an expression `a-b=`, where `a` and `b` are integers. The machine would replace it with the difference and halt in its accepting state.

For the sake of simplicity, we will represent numbers using a unary numeral system: a number N will be encoded with N dots on the tape. We will also presume that the resulting difference will be non-negative. Thus, the expression `5-2=` will be encoded as

```
●●●●●-●●=
```

Our machine (see Figure 10.13) will implement the following subtraction procedure:

```
LOOP
    IF the symbol to the left of "=" is "-"
        replace "-" and "=" with □, then transit to the accepting state
    replace "=" with □, move the head left, write "="
    replace the last dot before "-" with □
END LOOP
```

While calculating the difference between 5 and 2, the machine will modify its tape as follows:

```
◇●●●●●-●●=
◇●●●●□-●=
◇●●●□□-=
◇●●●
```

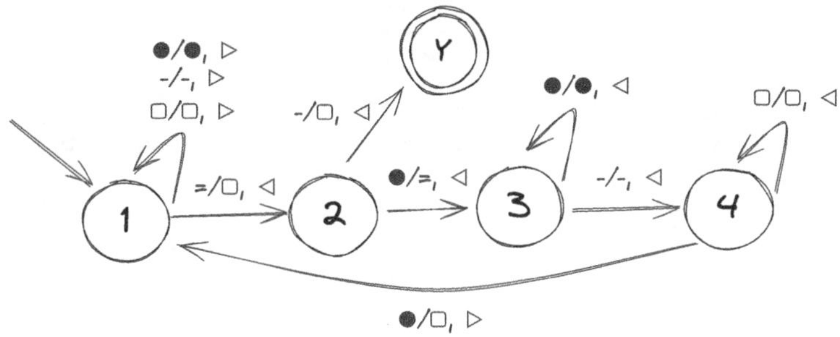

FIGURE 10.13: Subtracting numbers with a Turing machine.

10.8.2 DUPLICATING AN INPUT STRING

The next machine we are going to develop will duplicate the contents of an input string. For example, if it is `aabba`, the output will be `aabbaaabba`. Presuming that the input alphabet consists of the symbols `a` and `b` only, we can implement the following approach:

```
WHILE the input string contains at least one lowercase symbol
    IF the leftmost lowercase symbol is "a"
        replace it with "A" and add "A" to the end of the string
    IF the leftmost lowercase symbol is "b"
        replace it with "B" and add "B" to the end of the string
END LOOP
replace all uppercase symbols with their lowercase versions
transition to the accepting state
```

The resulting machine is shown in Figure 10.14.

10.8.3 SORTING TAPE CONTENT

The last example will illustrate the capability of the Turing machine to sort data. Let's again presume that the tape contains a string consisting of the characters `a` and `b`. Our task is to move all `a`s closer to the beginning of the tape and all `b`s closer to the end. One possible way to achieve this is to perform a simple kind of exchange sort:

```
WHILE the tape contains at least one sequence "ba"
    replace "ba" with "ab"
transition to the accepting state
```

The machine shown in Figure 10.15 implements this routine. States 1 and 2 are used to skip `a`s and `b`s. State 3 is activated by the character `a` immediately after a `b`. Here, `ba` is replaced with `ab`, and the head is moved to the left edge of the tape before restarting the process from state 1.

These examples are intended to show that the Turing machine is quite versatile, able to tackle a large variety of diverse computational problems. Before discussing the kinds of languages it is able to recognize and the tasks beyond its grasp, let's consider certain common variations of the basic TM formula.

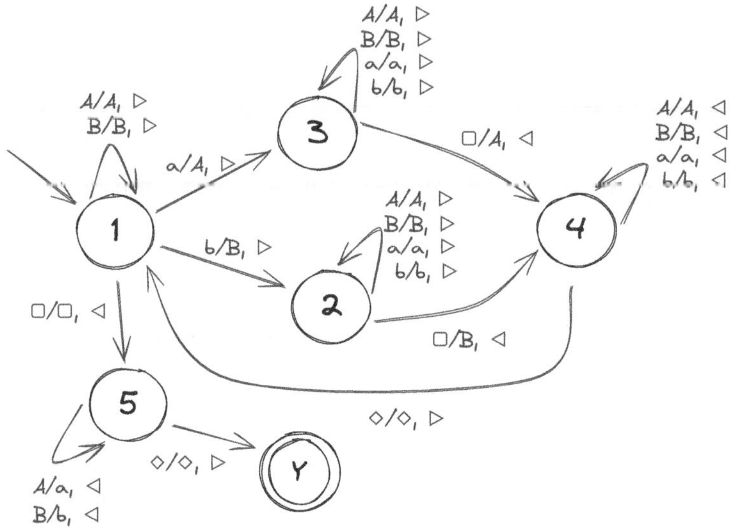

FIGURE 10.14: Duplicating the input with a Turing machine.

10.9 SUBTRACTING NUMBERS WITH A 2-PDA

As an additional example, let's convert the number-subtracting Turing machine (Figure 10.13) into a 2-PDA device and check how it works. The TM-to-2-PDA conversion is straightforward (see Figure 10.16). States 1 and 2 are responsible for placing the input string on the second stack of the 2-PDA, while the actual subtraction takes place in states 3 to 7. State 7 corresponds to the accepting state of the original Turing machine. Here its task is to consume the last remaining $ symbol of the input and halt the device.

Simulating a 2-PDA in Python takes more effort compared to a Turing machine (see Listing 10.1).

Listing 10.1: 2-PDA Simulator.

```
from dataclasses import dataclass
from collections import defaultdict


@dataclass
class TwoPDA:
    rules: defaultdict
    favstates: set
    start: int
    state: int = 0
    input: str = ""
    stacks: list = None

    # pqr: p must be on top
    def push(self, i, v):
        self.stacks[i] += v[::-1]
```

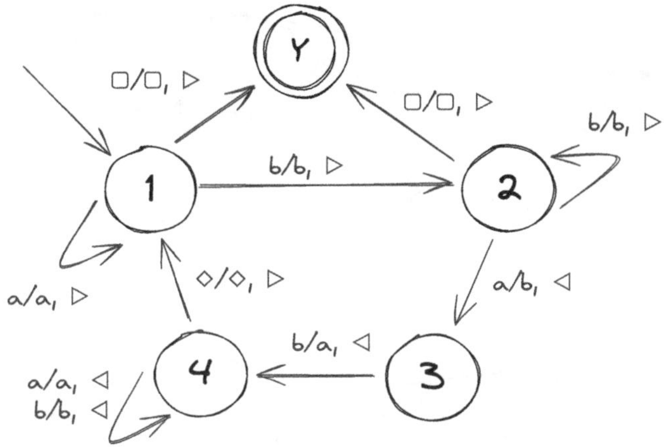

FIGURE 10.15: Sorting data with a Turing machine.

```
def pop(self, i, s):
    r = self.stacks[i][len(self.stacks[i]) - len(s) :]
    self.stacks[i] = self.stacks[i][: len(self.stacks[i]) - len(s)]
    return r

def apply_rule(self, c, s, p):
    self.state, ns, np = self.rules[(self.state, c, s, p)]
    self.input = self.input[len(c) :]

    self.pop(0, s)
    self.push(0, ns)

    self.pop(1, p)
    self.push(1, np)

def choose_rule(self):
    for c in ("", self.input[0]):
        for s in ("", self.stacks[0][-1]):
            for p in ("", self.stacks[1][-1]):
                if (self.state, c, s, p) in self.rules:
                    self.apply_rule(c, s, p)
                    return
    raise KeyError()

def accepts(self, input):
    self.input = input
    self.state = self.start
    self.stacks = ["#", ""]

    try:
        while self.input:
            self.stacks[1] = self.stacks[1] if self.stacks[1] else " "
            self.choose_rule()
        return self.state in self.favstates

    except KeyError:
        return False
```

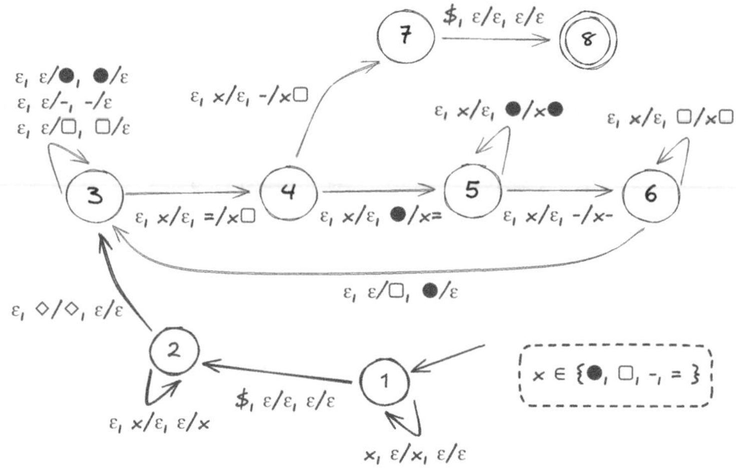

FIGURE 10.16: Subtracting numbers with a 2-PDA.

A `TwoPDA` object has to be initialized with a set of transition rules, a set of favorable states, and a start state. String processing is invoked by calling the `accepts()` method. It starts by initializing both stacks, represented here as strings. The first stack contains the beginning-of-tape marker `#`. The second stack is empty.

The main `while` loop ensures there is always a space symbol on top of the second stack and chooses the next transition rule to apply. This process requires three loops because of ε-elements. Suppose the current state is A, the next input character is c, and the top-stack elements are s and p. It is not enough to try to find a rule with a left-hand side of (A, c, s, p). Any instance of c, s, or p can be replaced with an ε-string, so we have to check all relevant combinations. Fortunately, since the 2-PDA is presumed to be deterministic, it is enough to find only the first match.

The methods `apply_rule()`, `push()`, and `pop()` are designed to support empty strings. Note that `push()` reverses its argument `v` before placing it on the stack to maintain the correct order when pushing multi-character strings (see Figure 6.2).

Before testing the machine shown in Figure 10.16, we will need an additional utility function `expand_rule()`:

```
def expand_rule(lhs, rhs):
    return {
        (
            lhs[0],
            lhs[1].replace("x", c),
            lhs[2].replace("x", c),
            lhs[3].replace("x", c),
        ): (rhs[0], rhs[1].replace("x", c), rhs[2].replace("x", c))
        for c in ". -="
    }
```

Each rule that includes the symbol x has to be replaced with four rules, where x becomes •, □, −, or =. The task of `expand_rule()` is to generate these four versions instead of the original rule description, making the resulting definition of the 2-PDA more concise:

```
pda = TwoPDA(
    expand_rule((1, "x", "", ""), (1, "x", ""))
    | {(1, "$", "", ""): (2, "", "")}
    | expand_rule((2, "", "x", ""), (2, "", "x"))
    | {
        (2, "", "#", ""): (3, "#", ""),
        (3, "", "", "."): (3, ".", ""),
        (3, "", "", "-"): (3, "-", ""),
        (3, "", "", " "): (3, " ", ""),
    }
    | expand_rule((3, "", "x", "="), (4, "", "x "))
    | expand_rule((4, "", "x", "-"), (7, "", "x "))
    | expand_rule((4, "", "x", "."), (5, "", "x="))
    | expand_rule((5, "", "x", "."), (5, "", "x."))
    | expand_rule((5, "", "x", "-"), (6, "", "x-"))
    | expand_rule((6, "", "x", " "), (6, "", "x "))
    | {(6, "", "", "."): (3, " ", ""), (7, "$", "", ""): (8, "", "")},
    {8},
    1,
)

# calculate 5-2
print(pda.accepts(".....-..=$$")) # True
print(pda.stacks) # ['#... ', '      ']
```

10.10 NONDETERMINISTIC TURING MACHINE

Like other devices we have discussed, the Turing machine can be nondeterministic. In this case, the TM definition may contain different rules with the same left-hand sides:

$$(1, b) \to (2, b, \lhd)$$
$$(1, b) \to (3, c, \rhd)$$

A nondeterministic Turing machine behaves in the same way as other nondeterministic devices we discussed earlier. Every possible choice between transitions produces a different computation path. The input string is considered accepted if it is accepted on at least one path.

Just as with finite automata, nondeterminism does not increase the computational power of the Turing machine. This property is handy, for example, for proving that a certain language can be recognized by a Turing machine. Nondeterministic rules often make the construction of the recognition device simpler.

For example, suppose we need to prove that a TM can decide whether a given input represents a composite number, i.e., it has divisors other than 1 and itself. One option would be to implement a division algorithm, then use it to try dividing the input number by successive integers starting from 2. However, nondeterministic behavior offers a simpler alternative.

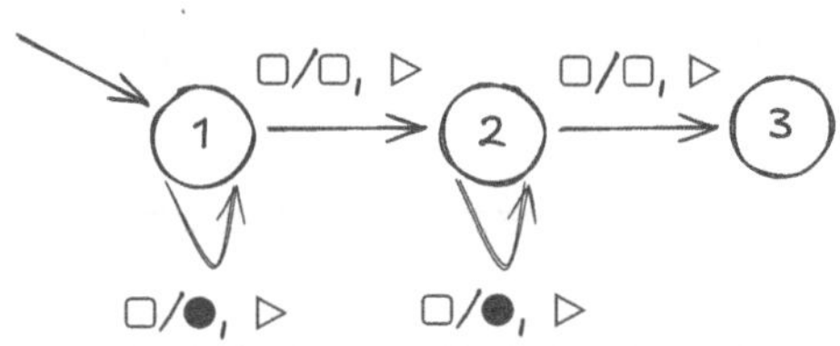

FIGURE 10.17: Generating integers with a nondeterministic Turing machine.

Suppose the input number is provided in the unary numeral system (as in our subtraction example). Next, suppose we have already implemented the multiplication of two numbers, which is much easier to do than division. Then, we'll need a machine that nondeterministically generates two space-separated integer numbers (see Figure 10.17).

Every action taken in state 1 generates two computation paths: one path generates the next digit, •, and another path proceeds to state 2, where the second number is generated. In state 3, the Turing machine has three space-separated numbers on its tape: a, b, and c. Now it can calculate $b \times c$ and accept the input if the result is equal to a. To ensure halting when a is a prime number, we also have to modify the machine so that it never generates numbers longer than a.

Clearly, such a brute-force approach to divisibility checking is not practical, but it is perfectly suitable as a theoretical proof. If a nondeterministic Turing machine can determine whether a number is composite, a deterministic Turing machine can do it as well.

10.11 MULTIPLE HEADS AND TAPES

Various authors often introduce modifications to the basic TM formula. These variations are aimed at simplifying the construction of machines that need to perform certain tasks, but none of these modifications extend the computing capabilities of the basic Turing machine. As Sipser puts it, *"Turing machines have an astonishing degree of robustness"* [68, Sec. 3.2]: it is nearly impossible to suggest a modification that would affect the class of languages recognizable by the TM.

The most popular modification makes the tape infinite in both directions (see Figure 10.18). In this scheme, it is not possible to cause an error by moving the head to the left of the leftmost cell. It is also not possible to refer to cells as the "first" or "second"; it is the user's responsibility to introduce any markup symbols.

Another common extension is a multi-track tape (see Figure 10.19). Here, each cell of the tape is presumed to contain k symbols, or "tracks," and transition rules read or modify all of them at once:

$$(\text{state}, \langle s_1, \ldots, s_k \rangle) \to (\text{state}', \langle s_1', \ldots, s_k' \rangle, \text{action})$$

The next extension introduces additional heads to the Turing machine (see Figure 10.20). At the start state, all the heads are located over the same tape cell. Only

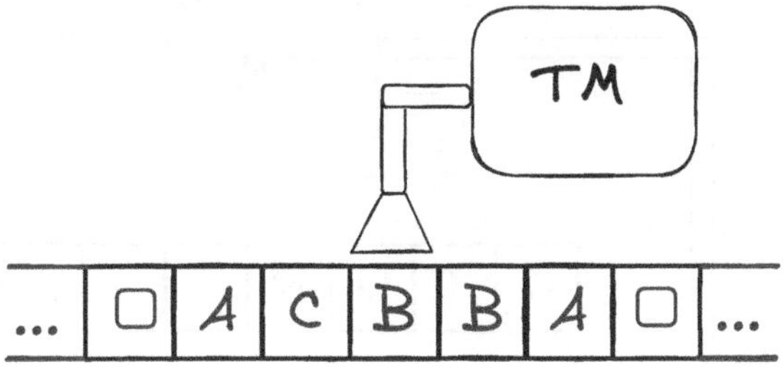

FIGURE 10.18: A Turing machine with a doubly infinite tape.

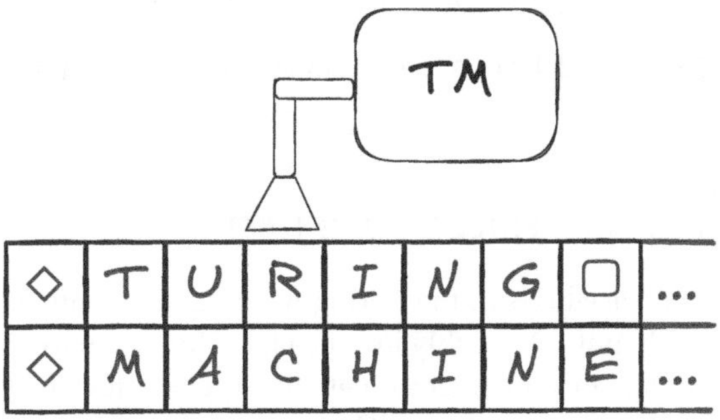

FIGURE 10.19: A Turing machine with a two-track tape.

one head operates at a time, so each transition rule now has to specify the head performing the action:

$$(\text{state}, \text{symbol}) \to (\text{state}', \text{head}, \text{symbol}', \text{action})$$

Yet another common idea is to provide a dedicated tape for each head of a multiple-head Turing machine (see Figure 10.21). In this "multi-tape" variation, all heads can perform their actions simultaneously:

$$(\text{state}, \langle s_1, \ldots, s_k \rangle) \to (\text{state}', \langle s_1', \ldots, s_k' \rangle, \langle \text{action}_1, \ldots, \text{action}_k \rangle)$$

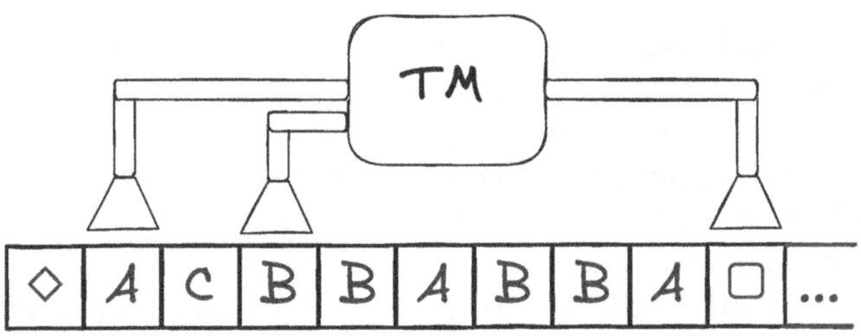

FIGURE 10.20: A Turing machine with three heads.

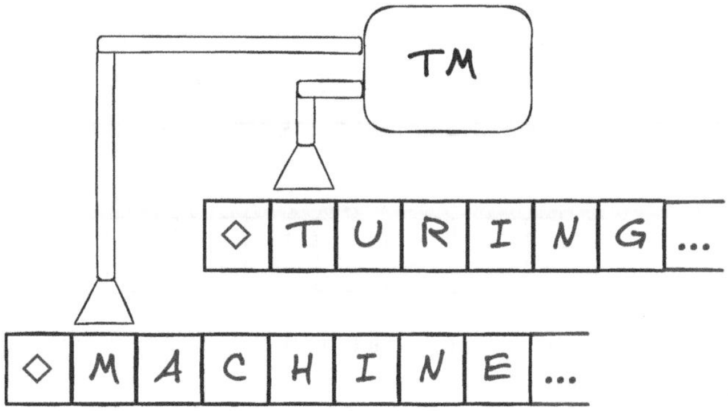

FIGURE 10.21: A Turing machine with two tapes.

10.12 TURING MACHINES IN JFLAP

JFLAP supports two variations of the Turing machine: one with a single doubly infinite tape and one with multiple doubly infinite tapes. Since we were primarily focused on the basic single-tape machine, let's create this type of device by selecting **Turing Machine** from the JFLAP main menu. The states and transitions of the machine are created just as in the case of a finite state machine. Transition labels include three elements: the symbol to be read, the symbol to be written, and the head action. In JFLAP, three actions are available: move **L**eft, move **R**ight, or **S**tay. Blank tape cells are rendered as white square symbols. Turing machines in JFLAP do not have explicit accepting or rejecting states; the machine should leave any obtained computational results on the tape before halting.

As an example, consider the familiar number-subtracting machine (Figure 10.22).

To test this machine, choose **Input, Fast Run**, type `00000-00=`, and press **OK**. JFLAP will display the tape content for the identified accepting configuration (see Figure 10.23).

10.13 UNIVERSAL TURING MACHINE

Throughout this book, computational machines have always been treated separately from the data they process. There have been devices made up of states and transitions, and there have been strings to be accepted or rejected by these devices. However, computational devices themselves can be encoded as strings. This is hardly new: Section 10.7 includes a fragment of Python code that represents a Turing machine able to recognize the formal language $\{a^n b^n c^n\}$.

Fragments of Python code are strings, so it is possible to imagine a Turing machine analyzing a string that represents another (or even the same) Turing machine. In the next chapter, we will discuss whether any interesting properties of the encoded

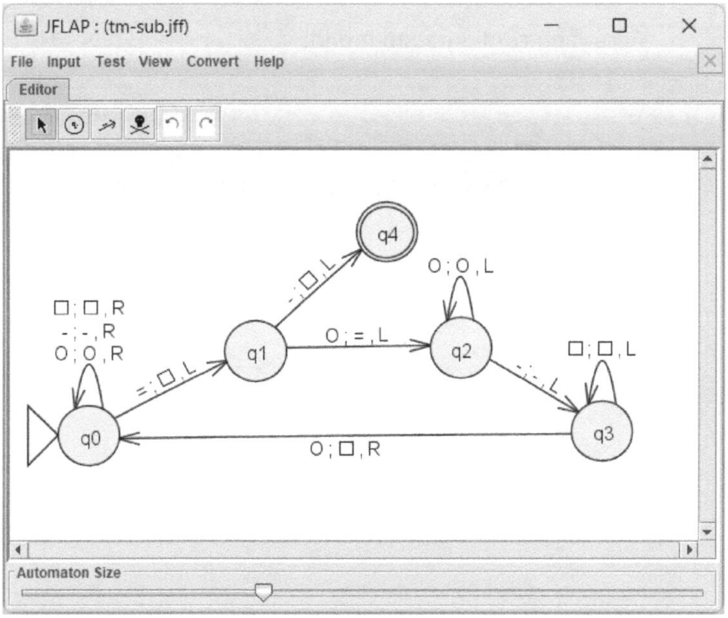

FIGURE 10.22: Subtracting numbers with a Turing machine (JFLAP).

machine can be revealed with such an analysis. For now, let's propose a fairly straightforward idea: a Turing machine can be used to simulate the behavior of an encoded machine on a given input.

The possibility of creating such a simulator can be demonstrated by actually constructing it. This is not as difficult to do as it might seem, especially with a multi-tape version of the Turing machine (see, e.g., [36, Sec. 9.2.3]). The resulting simulator is known as a *universal Turing machine* (UTM). Since a UTM is itself a Turing machine, it is perfectly possible to use a UTM to simulate its own behavior by feeding it a string-encoded UTM as input.

10.14 TAKEAWAYS

1. The Turing machine is a device with computing capabilities equal to those of a pushdown automaton with two stacks. These are the most capable machines in our lineup.
2. The Turing machine is able to recognize at least some languages that are not context-free (such as the context-sensitive language $\{a^n b^n c^n\}$).
3. The Turing machine can be nondeterministic, just like finite automata. Nondeterministic behavior does not extend the class of languages recognized by the Turing machine.

FIGURE 10.23: Accepting configuration with ooo on the TM tape.

4. The Turing machine is robust: its numerous variations recognize the same class of languages as the basic version.
5. The Turing machine is powerful enough to simulate another Turing machine encoded as a string. Such a simulator is known as a universal Turing machine.

11 Decidability and complexity

In the previous chapter, we discussed the inner workings of the Turing machine without examining the class of languages it is able to recognize. Clearly, the TM is able to recognize certain context-sensitive languages, but what are its limits?

In this chapter, we will examine the limits of the TM and the extent of its computing capability. We will also discuss the importance of the TM, venturing into the *computational theory of complexity* and its basic concepts.

11.1 DECIDABILITY OF LANGUAGES

Languages that can be recognized by a Turing machine that always halts in its accepting or rejecting state are called *recursive* or *decidable*. Languages that can be recognized by a Turing machine that halts for the input strings it accepts are called *recursively enumerable* or *partially decidable*. \index{language!partially decidable|see {recursively enumerable}

Recursively enumerable languages form a wider class than recursive languages. A language L is recursive if it is possible to construct a Turing machine that explicitly accepts all strings belonging to L and explicitly rejects all other strings. In the case of a recursively enumerable language R, it is enough to accept all the strings belonging to R. Any other string can be "non-accepted" by either rejecting it or by looping.

Table 11.1 provides a revised list of formal languages and their respective recognition devices.

TABLE 11.1: Formal languages and recognition devices.

Language	Recognition device
Regular	Finite automaton
Deterministic	Deterministic pushdown automaton
Context-free	Nondeterministic pushdown automaton
Context-sensitive	Linear bounded automaton (LBA)
Recursive	Turing machine with an infinite tape
Recursively enumerable	Turing machine with an infinite tape
Undecidable	Unknown

At this point, we can finally make a distinction between context-sensitive and recursive languages. Recursive languages require a Turing machine with an infinite tape, as described in the previous chapter. Context-sensitive languages can be recognized by a *linear bounded automaton*, which is a Turing machine with a tape of a length sufficient to store the given input string.

A less strict definition allows the LBA to use at most $k \times N$ tape cells for processing an input of size N [35, Chapter 9]. These extra cells, however, do not provide

DOI: 10.1201/9781032614991-11

computational advantages, since a shortage of tape cells can be compensated for with extra states and a larger alphabet.

Similarly, the *Chomsky hierarchy*, shown in Table 11.2, shows the correspondence between formal languages and grammars. Recursively enumerable languages can be described with an *unrestricted grammar*, where any nonempty string p can be transformed into the string q with a production rule $p \rightarrow q$.

TABLE 11.2: The Chomsky hierarchy.

Language	Formal grammar
Regular	Type 3: regular
Context-free	Type 2: context-free
Context-sensitive	Type 1: context-sensitive
Recursively enumerable	Type 0: unrestricted

Table 11.1 introduces one new class of formal languages: *undecidable languages*. Given that the most powerful recognition device we have discussed so far is the Turing machine, the term "undecidable" should be understood as "undecidable by a Turing machine."

11.2 THE HALTING PROBLEM

Our next goal is to show the limitations of the Turing machine by providing an example of an undecidable language. One classic method is to employ the *halting problem*, stated by Martin Davis in 1958 [45]:

Determine whether a given TM, placed in a given initial state, will eventually halt. [20, Ch. 5]

Let's unpack this definition. We know that any Turing machine can be converted into a string. Such strings are read, for example, by the universal Turing machine. The challenge of the halting problem is to construct a Turing machine $H(m, s)$ that would process any given string-encoded machine m along with its input s and decide whether m halts.

Such a machine H would be able to recognize the following formal language: *the set of string-encoded Turing machines (with their inputs) that eventually halt.*

Proving the decidability of a given language is often a straightforward process: it is enough to construct a Turing machine that is able to decide it. Undecidability is harder to prove, but this is fortunately not the case with the halting problem.

Let's presume that the Turing machine $H(m, s)$, able to solve the halting problem, exists. This machine switches into the accepting state q_y if m halts or into the rejecting state q_n otherwise. Note that H always halts. Let's construct another Turing machine $T(r)$, performing the following actions:

```
run H(r, r) until it halts

IF H is in qn
```

```
    switch into q_y
ELSE
    perform an endless loop
```

$T(r)$ follows the IF branch and halts in q_y if its input machine r loops (as identified by $H(r,r)$, which halts in q_n). Otherwise, $T(r)$ loops by following the ELSE branch.

Now let's try to figure out whether machine T halts on the input string t_{str}, representing a string-encoded T. Let's consider both possibilities. Not halting ("looping") means that $H(t_{str}, t_{str})$ must halt in q_n (by the definition of H). However, in this case, T follows the IF branch and halts. The same contradiction occurs if we consider the alternative. Suppose that T halts on t_{str}. In this case, $H(t_{str}, t_{str})$ must halt in q_y. This means, in turn, that T follows the ELSE branch and loops.

In short, T is designed to do the opposite of what the perfect halt-checker H predicts: it halts if H says it will loop, and it loops if H says it will halt. An attempt to use H to predict the behavior of T processing its own string-encoded definition creates an inescapable logical contradiction.

The root cause of this contradiction is our presumption that a machine H able to solve the halting problem exists. Thus, we must conclude that H does not exist.

This result can be used to prove a more general *Rice's theorem*, which states that *all* "nontrivial" properties of recursively enumerable languages are undecidable [35, Ch. 8].

This statement should be understood as follows. A "property" is simply a definition of a certain subset of recursively enumerable languages. It is "nontrivial" if the subset we define includes *some* but not *all* recursively enumerable languages. Suppose that the given Turing machine M recognizes the language $L(M)$. Rice's theorem states that it is not possible to decide whether $L(M)$ possesses a property of interest by analyzing the string representation of machine M.

For example, consider the following property: "consists of single-character strings." Some languages like {`a`, `b`, `d`} or {`c`, `e`} possess this property; others like {`aa`, `ced`} do not. Generally, it is not possible to decide whether a given string represents a Turing machine that recognizes a language consisting of single-character strings.

11.3 THE TURING MACHINE AND DECIDABILITY

The Turing machine is not the first device unable to recognize a certain class of languages, but this time, the lack of computational power is a fundamentally different kind of problem, not the same as it was in the case of finite or pushdown automata. With Turing machines, we have reached the end of the line: there are no known devices of higher computational power, so any language undecidable by the Turing machine is effectively undecidable.

11.3.1 THE ORIGINS OF THE TURING MACHINE

Alan Turing's original goal was to attack David Hilbert's "decision problem" (*Das Entscheidungsproblem*), which is *"solved once we know a procedure that allows us to decide, by means of finitely many operations, whether a given logical expression is universally valid or, alternatively, satisfiable.*" [16] Logic is well beyond the scope of our discussion, but fortunately, the *Entscheidungsproblem* has an easier-to-understand related predecessor, Hilbert's "tenth problem":

"Given a Diophantine equation with any number of unknown quantities and with rational integral numerical coefficients: to devise a process according to which it can be determined by a finite number of operations whether the equation is solvable in rational integers." [19]

In turn, this problem can be rephrased as follows. Consider a *polynomial*, which is a sum of terms $t_1, \ldots, t_n$, multiplied by integer coefficients $C_1, \ldots, C_n$:

$$P(\text{variables}) = C_1 t_1 + \cdots + C_n t_n$$

Each term is a product of variables; for example, t_1 could be $x \cdot x \cdot y \cdot z$, t_2 could be $y \cdot z \cdot z \cdot z$, and so on. The task is, for any given polynomial P, to find a combination of integer values for its variables that makes the resulting value of P zero. For example, if $P(x, y, z) = 5 \cdot x \cdot x \cdot z - 2 \cdot y \cdot z$, one possible desired combination is $x = 2, y = 10, z = 1$.

Note that both of Hilbert's problems require one to "know a procedure" or "devise a process." To a certain degree, the idea of a "procedure" or an *algorithm* can be explained informally. Introductory books on programming typically explain that algorithms are similar to cooking instructions, for example. While this approach helps to build intuition, it also leads to a slippery slope, as it is unclear what kind of "instructions" can be treated as "algorithms" or "procedures." The "procedure" might involve "thinking hard" to win a game of chess or "aiming accurately" to score in basketball.

Appealing to intuition becomes even more slippery if the goal is to show that a certain procedure *cannot* be devised at all. Apparently, Hilbert expected the *Entscheidungsproblem* to be eventually solved. In contrast, Turing's project was to prove it unsolvable. At this point, it is essential to define what exactly is understood by the term "process" or "procedure." In Turing's words, *"All arguments which can be given are bound to be, fundamentally, appeals to intuition, and for this reason rather unsatisfactory mathematically. The real question at issue is 'What are the possible processes which can be carried out in computing a number?' "* [73]

Turing's solution was to formalize the concept of a "process" (or an *algorithm*) as a configuration of his "L.C.M." (*logical computing machine*, known to us as the Turing machine). Then he could proceed to proving that no L.C.M. is able to solve the *Entscheidungsproblem*.

As a side note, the tenth problem was eventually solved (proven undecidable). The solution required a whole series of efforts, with the final piece of the puzzle being obtained in 1970 [47].

11.3.2 THE CHURCH-TURING THESIS

Clearly, Turing's proof hinges on the proposal that the notion of a computational procedure can be formalized as the Turing machine. In other words, these two statements are equivalent:

1) There exists an algorithm that can sort the given array.
2) There exists a Turing machine that can sort the given array.

Turing provided some arguments in favor of his proposal (known today as the *Church-Turing thesis*), but no formal proof was given:

Any "effective computation" can be performed by a Turing machine.

There are certain variations of the thesis, but the general message remains the same: if something can be computed in principle, it can be computed by a Turing machine. The term *effective computation* refers to a procedure that can, in principle, be performed in a finite number of steps by a human being equipped with paper, a pencil, and precise instructions, without resorting to intuition or insight [15].

As Turing put it, *"It is possible to produce the effect of a computing machine by writing down a set of rules of procedure and asking a man to carry them out. Such a combination of a man with written instructions will be called a 'Paper Machine'. A man provided with paper, pencil, and rubber, and subject to strict discipline, is in effect a universal machine."* [74, Chapter 10]

11.3.3 TURING MACHINES AND COMPUTERS

Turing machines are, in some sense, quite terrible computing devices. They lack even random-access memory, to say nothing of real-time keyboard input or 4K video playback. However, in terms of language-recognition capabilities (and problem-solving capabilities), our conventional computers offer no advantages. Being equipped with finite rather than infinite memory, they are technically closer to linear bounded automata. However, for most practical purposes where infinite memory cannot be expected, computers can be considered the computational equivalents of Turing machines.

Since the Turing machine is a formalization of the concept of an algorithm, it would be more precise to imagine different Turing machines as different pieces of (e.g., Python) code. A computer, capable of running any given piece of code, is closer to the idea of the universal Turing machine.

In the world of conventional computers, the inconvenience of undecidability quickly becomes apparent. Let's rephrase Rice's theorem in terms of programs rather than Turing machines:

Suppose that a piece of code M prints `Y` for any input string taken from the set of strings $L(M)$ and `N` for any other string. Any nontrivial property of $L(M)$ is undecidable.

As an example, consider again the property "consists of single-character strings." The task of M is to print `Y` if it is supplied with a single-character input string, and `N` in any other case. *Will M actually do this?* In other words, *is M correct or buggy?* Rice's theorem states that it is not possible to reveal the properties of the actual language $L(M)$ recognized by M. Therefore, it is not possible to find bugs in M by analyzing its source code.

This statement might sound counter-intuitive: after all, *we* seem to be able to understand what a given piece of code is supposed to do and to debug it when necessary. However, there is no contradiction: Rice's theorem asserts that *some* pieces of code are impossible to debug, not *all* of them. Clearly, the code

```
def M(s):
    print("Y")
```

is buggy: it prints `Y` for any given input. Imagine, however, Python code that uses a complex neural network to determine whether its input is a single-character string. Debugging such a network would be a daunting task even for an expert programmer.

The undecidability of the halting problem can also be easily shown using computer programs rather than Turing machines. Let's presume that there exists a Python function `Halts(m, s)` that returns `True` if the given string-encoded Python function `m` halts on its input string `s`, and `False` otherwise. Now consider the function `Test(r)`, defined as follows:

```
def Test(r):
    if not Halts(r, r):
        return True
    else:
        while True:
            pass
```

By examining the possible outcomes of the call `Test(t_str)`, where `t_str` is a string-encoded definition of `Test`, we will face the same contradiction as with Turing machines before: `Test(t_str)` must halt, and `Test(t_str)` must loop. The only way to resolve the contradiction is to reject the initial presumption that `Halts(m, s)` can actually be implemented.

Now let's revisit the example of the program M that is expected to print `Y` when it receives a single-character input string. The following Python solution is correct:

```
def M(s):
    return "Y" if len(s) == 1 else "N"
```

However, a minor modification changes everything:

```
def Test():
    ...


def M(s):
    Test()
    return "Y" if len(s) == 1 else "N"
```

Now the outcome depends on whether `Test()` halts or not. Since the halting problem is generally undecidable, there is no way to decide whether `M()` is correct anymore.

11.3.4 CHECKING CODE PROPERTIES

Statements like "the halting problem is undecidable" or "nontrivial properties of languages are undecidable" are correct in general: it is indeed impossible to design an algorithm that would decide whether *any given piece of code* halts or prints `Y`. However, partial solutions can be offered, and code can often be deliberately designed to simplify the analysis of its properties.

Consider, for example, the case of a program that only needs a fixed-size memory block for its variables and arrays. For the sake of simplicity, let's presume there are no function calls, so we don't have to deal with passing arguments and call/return operations. Suppose the program starts executing from the first instruction ($i = 1$), and its variables have initial values of $v_1, \ldots, v_k$.

The complete state of such a program will be defined by the values $(v_1, \ldots, v_k, i)$. Since the process of code execution is deterministic, it is possible to predict the state of the program after completing the current instruction i. Let's look at the following Python code:

```
a, b = 1, 1  # i = 1
a = 5        # i = 2
b = 7        # i = 3
a = a + b    # i = 4
```

When line 2 becomes current, the state of this program is $(a = 1, b = 1, i = 2)$. By executing line 2, we arrive at the state $(a = 5, b = 1, i = 3)$. To determine any subsequent state, we only need to know the current state and the instruction to be executed.

Since the code operates with a fixed amount of memory, the number of such states is finite. Eventually, we'll either arrive at a point where the program halts or at a previously encountered state, which means that the program loops. Thus, we have just solved the halting problem for the case of fixed memory. These situations are illustrated in Listing 11.1 and Figure 11.1.

Listing 11.1: Example Python programs operating with fixed memory.

```
# halting example
a = 0           # i = 1
while a < 2:    # i = 2
    a += 1      # i = 3

# looping example
a = 0            # i = 1
while a < 2:     # i = 2
    a += 1       # i = 3
    if a == 2:   # i = 4
        a = 0    # i = 5
```

By exploring the state space of the given code, it is also possible to examine its semantic properties, for example, to discover whether it executes the line that prints `Y`.

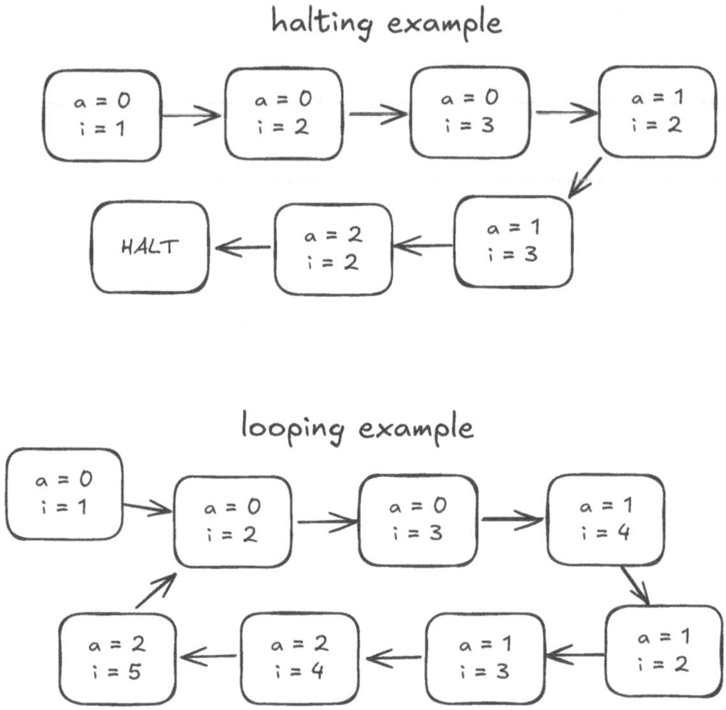

FIGURE 11.1: Exploring the state space of the example programs.

While this approach might sound like a purely theoretical possibility, it is at the heart of *model checking* systems such as SPIN[^spin] or TLA+.[^tla] These tools are used to formally prove that a certain *model* of a software system satisfies a given specification.

In most everyday cases, we are content with finding bugs by testing and are used to regular patches delivered over the net. However, in certain scenarios, testing can be especially unreliable, or patching can be hardly possible. For example, the behavior of multi-threaded programs often depends on timing. If process A writes `1` into a certain memory cell while process B simultaneously writes `2` into the same cell, the resulting value will depend on whether A or B wrote its value first (this situation is known as a *race condition*). A test run might reveal some unexpected execution sequences, but there is no guarantee of catching them all. Patching may prove difficult if the code is part of a hardware chip or a piece of equipment not really designed to receive updates.

Model checking systems typically analyze simplified versions (*models*) of real software systems, representing processes that need to be verified. The user can express certain properties of the system to be checked. For example, consider a printer driver. It has to handle all kinds of situations triggered by pushing buttons, changing the toner cartridge, and so on. However, in no case should the printer be in the state of printing if either the toner cartridge or paper is missing. A system like SPIN can be instructed to find code paths leading to a state that violates such a property.

Note again that the state space diagrams of sequential (non-concurrent) programs are simple paths, just like the ones shown in Figure 11.1. Each state is unambiguously determined by its preceding state. Concurrent programs quickly branch into alternative execution paths. The value of a certain variable might depend on which process accessed it first, and the model checker has to consider every possibility.

11.3.5 THE STRONG CHURCH-TURING THESIS

The Church-Turing thesis states that the computational power of the Turing machine is sufficient to perform any "effective computation." While it is still technically a "thesis" (or a "conjecture"), no practical computational model proposed since 1936 has managed to surpass the Turing machine. It seems that the instruction set of the Turing machine is indeed "complete": no additions can extend its computational power in a meaningful way. Therefore, any computational model is either *Turing-complete* (i.e., computationally equivalent to the Turing machine) or not. Two-stack pushdown automata are Turing-complete; finite automata are not.

Since the term "effective computation" is somewhat informal, the Church-Turing thesis can be reversed to define it precisely:

Effective computation is any computation that can be performed by a Turing machine.

This definition naturally opens up a deeper question: is any imaginable computation "effective"? The Turing machine cannot rely on intuition or insight, but *we* seemingly can, which makes the relation between the computational power of the Turing machine and the human mind far from obvious.

The limits of insight can be demonstrated with the following example. Presuming that variables can hold arbitrarily large values, does the code from Listing 11.2 halt or not?

Listing 11.2: Searching for an odd perfect number.

```python
# return True if the sum of divisors of k is equal to k
def is_perfect(k):
    s = 0
    for i in range(1, k // 2 + 1):
        if k % i == 0:
            s += i
    return s == k

num = 1
while True:
    if is_perfect(num):
        break
    num += 2
```

Any number that is equal to the sum of its divisors (excluding itself) is known as a *perfect number*. For example, $6 = 1 + 2 + 3$; $28 = 1 + 2 + 4 + 7 + 14$. As of today, it is not known if there are any odd perfect numbers. At least, none have been found among numbers up to 10^{1500} [55]. Therefore, we don't really know whether the given code halts or not.

Clearly, the powers of insight or intuition cannot help in this case, but it is an open question whether they might make a difference in other scenarios. The idea that our whole universe (and our minds as a part of it) is computationally equivalent to the Turing machine is known as the *strong Church-Turing thesis*. Even if there are natural processes that are computationally more capable than the Turing machine, it is still possible that our minds do not rely on these capabilities. The hypothesis of a "non-Turing mind," surpassing the computational power of the Turing machine, is advocated, for instance, by Sir Roger Penrose [58], but it has received a mostly lukewarm reception among experts [62, Sec. 7.2].

11.4 CHURCH'S FORMALISM AND FUNCTIONAL PROGRAMMING

The general operating principles of the Turing machine vaguely resemble the organization of a conventional computer. There is a writable memory, a set of instructions the machine can execute, and a configuration forming the "program" being run. Surrounded by computers, we are accustomed to the idea of a "computation" as something that is performed by a code-executing computing device and might need to make an effort to imagine possible alternatives.

One such alternative is *untyped lambda calculus*, invented by Alonzo Church. His original motivation was *"the study of the general properties of functions"* [12]. In particular, he attempted to develop a precise formal language for defining and transforming functions.

Conventional mathematical notation relies on context and implicit assumptions. For example, we usually presume that $f(x)$ is a function of a single argument, while $f(x_0)$ is the value of a function f calculated at the given point x_0. Likewise, we are supposed to deduce from the context whether $x(t-1)$ is the value of the function x at the point $t-1$ or an arithmetic expression "x times $t-1$."

Lambda calculus removes such ambiguities and provides a unified syntax for mathematical operations by introducing the concepts of *lambda expressions* and *reduction operations*. It was proposed that any computation can be represented with reductions applied to lambda expressions.

11.4.1 LAMBDA EXPRESSIONS

Lambda expressions can be described by the following context-free grammar:

$$E \to V \mid (\lambda V.E) \mid (EE)$$

Here, E is a lambda expression, and V is a certain identifier (i.e., a variable name). For practical purposes, it is usually allowed to replace variables with numerals and arithmetic expressions, even though they were not used in the original lambda calculus.

The expression $(\lambda V.E)$ is Church's syntax for defining an anonymous ("lambda") function. Each lambda function has one argument, V, and a body, E. For example, the function $f(x) = 5 \cdot x$ can be described as a lambda expression as follows:

$$f = (\lambda x.5 \cdot x)$$

To define a function having more than one argument, two options are available.

One option is to treat several arguments as a single "list of arguments" object, which can be "unpacked" inside a function when necessary. With this method, $f(x, y) = 5 \cdot x + y$ becomes

$$f = (\lambda p.5 \cdot p_1 + p_2)$$

Another option (known as *currying*) is to chain lambda expressions as follows:

$$f = (\lambda x.(\lambda y.5 \cdot x + y))$$

11.4.2 THE β-REDUCTION RULE

Lambda calculus introduces several kinds of conversions. Our purposes are covered by the β-reduction rule. It says that a lambda expression of the type $((\lambda V.E)E')$ can be transformed into an expression obtained by replacing every instance of V in E with E'.

For example, consider the lambda expression

$$((\lambda x.5 \cdot x)3)$$

Here, V is x, E is $5 \cdot x$, and E' is 3. By replacing every instance of x in $5 \cdot x$ with 3, we obtain $5 \cdot 3$. Now let's examine a more complex example:

$$((\lambda x.((\lambda y.5 \cdot x + y)1))2)$$

Here, V is x, E is $((\lambda y.5 \cdot x + y)1)$, and E' is 2. By replacing x with 2 everywhere in $((\lambda y.5 \cdot x + y)1)$, we obtain

$$((\lambda y.5 \cdot 2 + y)1)$$

Finally, we can replace y with 1 in $5 \cdot 2 + y$ to obtain the final expression $5 \cdot 2 + 1$.

11.4.3 DECLARATIVE COMPUTING

Summing up, lambda calculus provides a syntax for declaring lambda expressions (anonymous functions) and a rule for transforming a given expression $((\lambda V.E)E')$ into a modified version of E'. Note that lambda calculus does not explicitly define "actions" or "instructions," which are central to the Turing machine. A declaration of a lambda expression like

$$f = (\lambda x.(\lambda y.5 \cdot x + y))$$

merely states that f is now a shortcut for $(\lambda x.(\lambda y.5 \cdot x + y))$. It is not an assignment where the content of a certain memory cell is copied into another memory cell. Likewise, the β-reduction rule states that

$$((\lambda x.((\lambda y.5 \cdot x + y)1))2) = 5 \cdot 2 + 1$$

In other words, $((\lambda x.((\lambda y.5 \cdot x + y)1))2)$ is the same as $5 \cdot 2 + 1$, and both expressions can be used interchangeably.

This is a notable feature of the mathematical concept of a function: by saying that $\sin(\pi/2) = 1$, we state that $\sin(\pi/2)$ is the same as 1, and therefore we can replace $\sin(\pi/2)$ with 1 or vice versa everywhere. In programming, only *pure functions* possess such a property. Some functions, like Python's `math.sin()`, are pure; other functions are not. For example, the line-reading function `readline()` has *side effects* and thus is not pure:

```
f = open("words.txt", "r")
print(f.readline())
print(f.readline())
```

Suppose the first `print()` statement displays the word `cat` on the screen. It does not mean, however, that the expression `f.readline()` is equivalent to `cat`: the next `print()` statement might yield a completely different output.

Using lambda expressions, it is possible to state that something we are looking for can be obtained from something else, which, in turn, can be obtained from something else, and so on, until we reach a known variable or a constant. This approach to laying out a solution to a computational problem is the basis of *functional programming*, which can be considered one of the methods of *declarative programming*.

Functional programming possesses a number of attractive features [37]. One obvious advantage is functional purity, mentioned above. If a certain function has provided the correct output for a certain input, we can be sure that it will always provide the same output for the same input. Another clear advantage is the ease of creating, modifying, and combining anonymous functions.

Note that the term "declarative programming" refers to the way a program is written. Such a program provides a plan for subsequent evaluation: once we know how something we need can be obtained from something else, it is time to do the actual computation. Since our computers are essentially Turing machines, this stage still means executing instructions. In addition, certain operations (such as file input-output) are inherently impure, requiring specialized instruments to handle them [56, Ch. 7].

Practical functional programming maintains a strong connection with its theoretical foundation. As Hudak puts it, *"rather than changing or compromising those ideas, modern functional languages are best classified as embellishments of a certain set of ideals (...) they have so effectively held on to pure mathematical principles in a way shared by very few other languages"* [38].

11.5 FUNCTIONAL PROGRAMMING IN PYTHON

While classic functional programming languages like Haskell remain niche, elements of the functional style are found in most mainstream languages, including Python. Let's consider several simple examples demonstrating the functional approach to writing code.

11.5.1 CALCULATING THE FACTORIAL

We will start with the very simple task of computing the factorial of a given number:

$$n! = 1 \cdot 2 \cdot \dots \cdot n$$

By convention, $0! = 1$.

The most straightforward way to calculate a factorial in Python is to use a loop:

```
def factorial(n):
    r = 1
    for i in range(1, n + 1):
        r *= i
    return r
```

Since there is no concept of a loop in functional programming, we'll have to define the factorial using a recurrence relation:

$$\text{factorial}(n) = \begin{cases} 1, & n = 0 \\ n \cdot \text{factorial}(n-1), & n > 0 \end{cases}$$

This expression can be translated into Haskell nearly verbatim:

```
factorial 0 = 1
factorial n = n * factorial (n - 1)
```

A Haskell interpreter matches alternative definitions of the same function sequentially in a top-down order. Therefore, it chooses the definition `factorial 0 = 1` when the task is to calculate `factorial 0` and proceeds to the next definition in any other case. In Python, the closest equivalent of this fragment would be:

```
factorial = lambda n: 1 if n == 0 else (
                    n * factorial(n - 1))

print(factorial(8)) # prints 40320
```

11.5.2 CONDITIONAL EXPRESSIONS

While functional programming languages do not support imperative loops (like `for` or `while` loops in Python), conditional expressions fit well into the functional approach. Here we have to distinguish between *conditional statements* and *conditional expressions*.

Conditional statements control the flow of the program, typically taking a form similar to "if *condition*, do *this*; else, do *that*":

```
if x > 5:
    do_this()
else:
    do_that()
```

In contrast, conditional expressions are functions of three arguments, returning their second or third argument depending on the value of their first argument. In Python, such conditionals are written as:

```
r = x if condition else y
```

Here, `r` is assigned the value of `x` or `y` depending on whether `condition` is `True`.

Note that conditional expressions are not much different from commonly used functions like `max(a, b)`, which returns either `a` or `b` depending on whether `a` is larger than `b`.

We can implement our own version of `max()` using a conditional expression:

```
my_max = lambda x, y: x if x > y else y
```

New lambda expressions can be derived from existing lambda expressions. For example, suppose we need to "clip" a given value, making sure it is never negative. The function `clip0` can be defined in terms of `my_max` as follows:

```
clip0 = lambda y: my_max(0, y)
```

11.5.3 PROCESSING LISTS

The most common data structure for representing a collection of items in functional languages is the list. A non-empty list is typically treated as a combination of a "head" item and a "tail," which represents the list of the remaining items. Let's adhere to this convention and introduce two helper functions:

```
h = lambda lst: lst[0]    # head
t = lambda lst: lst[1:]   # tail
```

Now let's develop a function `member()` that tests whether a given value `e` belongs to a given list `lst`. It will rely on the following logic:

1. `e` is not a member of an empty list.
2. `e` is a member of `lst` if `h(lst)` is `e`.
3. `e` is a member of `lst` if `member(e, t(lst))` is `True`.

This can be translated into Python in a straightforward manner:

```
member = lambda e, lst: False if not lst else (
                        True if e == h(lst) else
                        member(e, t(lst))
                        )

print(member(4, [1, 6, 4, 2])) # prints True
```

For people used to command-based *imperative* programming, the most natural way to interpret this fragment is as a recursive function: if the first two options fail, `member()` calls itself with a shorter list `t(lst)`. Naturally, this is exactly what is happening here, but the right way to approach this code from the functional programming perspective is to treat it as a declarative statement that membership in a given list can be derived from membership in the list's tail, in the same way that factorial(n) is defined in terms of factorial$(n-1)$.

Our next task will be more challenging: to sort a list in ascending order.

First, we will need to define the concept of the smallest list item:

```
listmin = lambda lst: h(lst) if not t(lst) else (
                        h(lst) if h(lst) < listmin(t(lst)) else
                        listmin(t(lst))
                        )
```

Let's unpack this definition. If the list consists of only one item (so its tail is empty), the head is the smallest item. If the tail is not empty, the smallest item is the head if it is smaller than anything in the tail, or it is the smallest item in the tail.

Next, let's create the function `without(e, lst)` that returns the list `lst` without the first occurrence of `e`:

```
without = lambda e, lst: [] if not lst else (
                        t(lst) if e == h(lst) else
                        [h(lst)] + without(e, t(lst))
                        )
```

If `e` is head element of `lst`, we can simply return the tail of `lst`. Otherwise, we need the head attached to the tail without `e`.

Finally, the concept of a sorted list can be expressed as follows: a non-empty sorted list consists of the smallest item in the original list, followed by the sorted version of the rest of the list. Let's translate this into Python:

```
sorted = lambda lst: [] if not lst else (
                    [listmin(lst)] + sorted(without(listmin(lst), lst))
                    )

print(sorted([3, 2, 6, 4, 2])) # prints [2, 2, 3, 4, 6]
```

This function works as expected, but it is not very efficient. To obtain every successive item of the resulting sorted list, we have to search for the smallest item in the remaining tail. This approach is a variation of *selection sort*, which has *quadratic complexity*: its total running time is proportional to the square of the input list's length. In contrast, fast algorithms, such as *quicksort*, have *quasilinear* (almost linear) complexity.

It is safe to say that declarative programs focus on end results rather than the means to achieve them. However, some authors phrase this statement as if we can focus solely on the goals and leave the job of achieving them to the computer. Unfortunately, our example shows this is not quite so: a declarative program still has a *procedural meaning*, defining the actual sequence of processor instructions to be executed. Therefore, we still have to keep in mind that some declarations produce less efficient code, non-halting code, or code that requires excessive memory.

This conclusion is somewhat frustrating. One might ask, what is the point of declarative programming if it cannot take away the need to think about down-to-earth technical details? Bratko [7, Sec. 2.6.3] offers the following response: "the philosophy adopted by many is that it is better to have at least *some* declarative meaning rather than *none*."

11.5.4 MAPPING

Our final example of functional programming shows the use of *higher-order functions*, which are functions that take other functions as arguments or return functions as their results. The ability to pass functions as arguments or results is yet another tool that makes combining functions together easier and is also commonly employed in conventional imperative code.

Consider a very simple function `fmap()` that applies a given function f to each element of a given list $[e_1, \ldots, e_n]$, producing the resulting list $[f(e_1), \ldots, f(e_n)]$:

```
fmap = lambda f, lst: [] if not lst else (
                      [f(h(lst))] + fmap(f, t(lst))
                      )
```

Now any function that transforms individual elements of a list can be passed as an argument to `fmap()`:

```
print(fmap(lambda x: x * x, [1, 2, 3, 4, 5])) # prints [1, 4, 9, 16, 25]

print(fmap(sorted, [[5, 2, 3], [7, 1, 6]])) # prints [[2, 3, 5], [1, 6, 7]]
```

11.6 COMPLEXITY

In this chapter, we have finally reached the limits of what is computable. The Turing machine serves as an instrument used to categorize decision problems as decidable or undecidable (such as the halting problem). From a practical standpoint, however, not all decidable problems are equal. Some of them are *intractable*, requiring an inordinate number of computational operations to complete.

The classification of problems according to the use of resources, such as time and memory, is the task of the *computational theory of complexity*. The distinction between "tractable" and "intractable" problems is probably the most important one and is well worthy of our attention.

11.6.1 TIME COMPLEXITY

We have already used terms like "linear complexity" or "exponential complexity" when discussing finite state machines. For example, a DFA consumes exactly one symbol from the input tape on every computational step and halts after processing the whole input string. A DFA needs to perform twice as many operations to process a string twice as long, and so on.

Complexity estimates rarely, if ever, mention the specific number of required operations. Consider the following Python code:

```
def listmin(lst):
    r = lst[0]
    for v in lst:
        if v < r:
            r = v
    return r
```

How many operations does this function need to perform for a given list having N elements? The answer is not really straightforward. We may treat `r = lst[0]` as an atomic assignment operation or as two separate operations: 1) reading the first element of `lst` and 2) assigning its value to `r`. How would the total number of operations change if we additionally decided to check whether `lst` is empty and return a special error value in that case? What kind of low-level operations does a Python interpreter actually perform when executing instructions such as `if` and `for`?

The precise answer depends on the computer architecture used, the programming language, and the implementation details. A more practically useful task would be to estimate the *asymptotic complexity*, which shows the "order of growth" of the algorithm. Ideally, we should be able to point to a simple function that grows as fast as the time required to perform the algorithm as the input length increases.

For example, the running time of the Python function `listmin()`, provided above, grows as fast as a linear function $f(n) = kn$: every new element in the input list `lst` brings a fixed cost to the overall running time.

A standard way to declare the asymptotic complexity of a given algorithm is to use *big O notation*, which focuses on the basic growth principle and ignores constants and non-dominating terms, as they become insignificant for large inputs. For example, if a certain algorithm requires $15n + 3$ operations to process an input of n elements, its running time still grows linearly, so we can estimate it as $O(n)$ ("growing at most as fast as n") using big O notation. Similarly, an algorithm requiring $n^2 + 3n - 2$ operations can be estimated as $O(n^2)$, because $3n - 2$ grows more slowly than n^2 and thus does not change the basic growth rate.

The most important growth rates for our purposes are *polynomial*, $O(n^k)$, and *exponential*, $O(k^n)$. Polynomial growth rates include linear, quadratic, cubic, and so on. An algorithm is considered "polynomial-time" if its running time grows *no faster* than a polynomial function. For this reason, faster algorithms, for example, those having a growth rate of $O(\log n)$, are also "polynomial-time."

In practice, the gap between, say, $O(\log n)$, $O(n)$, and $O(n^2)$ is substantial. It can literally mark the difference between acceptable and unacceptable performance. For us, however, all polynomial-time algorithms will be treated as "tractable": even if slow, obtaining a solution with a polynomial-time algorithm is usually within our grasp for realistic input sizes.

In contrast, exponential-time algorithms can be considered mostly intractable: their running time grows too fast to be acceptable even for relatively small input sizes. Intractability is not necessarily a negative property. The only known way to "recover" a password for data encrypted with any modern cryptographic algorithm is to use an intractable brute-force search. This can be done for a four-digit password (where we only have to test 10,000 combinations in total), but it would literally take ages for long combinations of letters, digits, and special characters.

11.6.2 COMPLEXITY CLASSES P AND NP

Two of the most important classes of decision problems studied in the computational theory of complexity are named P and NP. Their definitions are simple: P is the set of decision problems decidable in **p**olynomial time by a deterministic Turing machine; NP is the set of decision problems decidable in **p**olynomial time by a **n**ondeterministic Turing machine.

An alternative definition states that P-class problems can be solved in polynomial time, and NP-class problems can be verified in polynomial time on a deterministic Turing machine. "Verification" here is the process of checking whether a given candidate solution is correct.

As stated in the previous chapter, all definitions of the Turing machine are computationally equivalent. Additional tapes or heads do not affect the set of decidable problems. For our current discussion, it is important that all "reasonable" deterministic computational models are also polynomially equivalent. This means that an extra head or tape might help in designing a faster algorithm, but it may only bring a polynomial-time improvement. For example, any algorithm that runs in $O(t(n))$ time on a multi-tape Turing machine can be executed in $O(t^2(n))$ time on a single-tape Turing machine [68, Sec. 7.1]. This means that a polynomial-time algorithm cannot become exponential-time when ported to a less efficient computational device.

The previous chapter provided some examples of P-class algorithms. Consider the Turing machine for recognizing a context-sensitive language $\{\mathtt{a}^n\mathtt{b}^n\mathtt{c}^n\}$ (Section 10.6.3). It moves its head over the tape, sequentially replacing the symbols a, b, and c with asterisks. If the input string belongs to the language $\{\mathtt{a}^n\mathtt{b}^n\mathtt{c}^n\}$, each iteration produces exactly three asterisks, until no letter symbols remain. For an input string of length N, a single "trip" across the tape takes N operations. Replacing all letters with asterisks requires $N/3$ trips, yielding $N^2/3$ operations in total ($O(n^2)$).

Quite obviously, any P-class problem also belongs to the NP class: if something can be done in polynomial time with a deterministic Turing machine, it can also be done in polynomial time with a nondeterministic Turing machine. It is much harder to figure out whether NP-class problems also belong to the P class.

Essentially, this is the famous "P versus NP problem," one of the unsolved Millennium Prize Problems. The Clay Mathematics Institute offers a $1 million US dollar prize for its solution.[1] It is safe to say that P ≠ NP is the prevailing opinion among

[1] See https://www.claymath.org/millennium-problems/

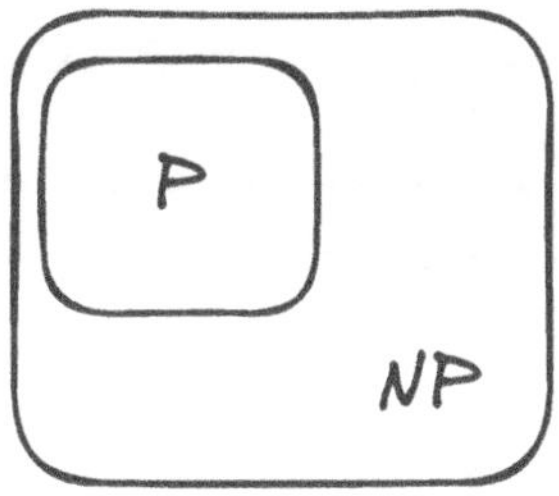

FIGURE 11.2: The complexity classes P and NP.

specialists [28]. While there is no strict mathematical proof as of today, a large number of well-researched NP problems do not have known polynomial-time solutions. Therefore, we will rely on the working hypothesis that P is not equal to NP (see Figure 11.2).

Let's consider some classic examples of NP-class problems that have no known polynomial-time solutions.

Boolean satisfiability problem (SAT). Given an expression consisting of Boolean variables and operations, determine whether it is "satisfiable," i.e., true for a certain combination of variables. For example, the expression $(x \text{ OR } y) \text{ AND } z$ is satisfied by the combination $(x = \text{True}, y = \text{True}, z = \text{True})$. In contrast, the expression $x \text{ AND } (\text{NOT } x)$ is not satisfiable.

Traveling salesman problem (TSP). A salesman must travel through N cities, visiting each of them only once, and then return to the first city of departure. Determine whether there exists a route cheaper than K, given the cost of a trip between any two cities.

Knapsack problem (KS). Given the weight and the price of each object from a given list of N objects, determine whether there exists a combination of objects having a total weight of at most K and a total price of at least V.

Each of these problems can be easily solved in polynomial time with a nondeterministic Turing machine. Consider, for example, the knapsack problem. The algorithm would go through the list of the given objects and produce separate timelines for the cases where the i-th object is taken or not (see Figure 11.3). After N steps, the Turing machine will be able to confirm whether any of the timelines produces an affirmative answer.

These timelines can be examined using a deterministic Turing machine. As discussed before, this is an exponential-time algorithm. Imagine, for example, that each step of the nondeterministic Turing machine produces two timelines. Then the total number of outcomes to be examined after N steps would be 2^N.

Let's take a moment to appreciate what exponential-time complexity, or "intractability," means in practice. Suppose we are using an exponential-time algorithm to solve a certain task, and we are satisfied with the time it spends to process inputs of size 1 to 18. However, for $N = 19$, the performance is no longer adequate. If the complexity of the algorithm is $O(2^N)$, we'll have to speed up the code by a factor

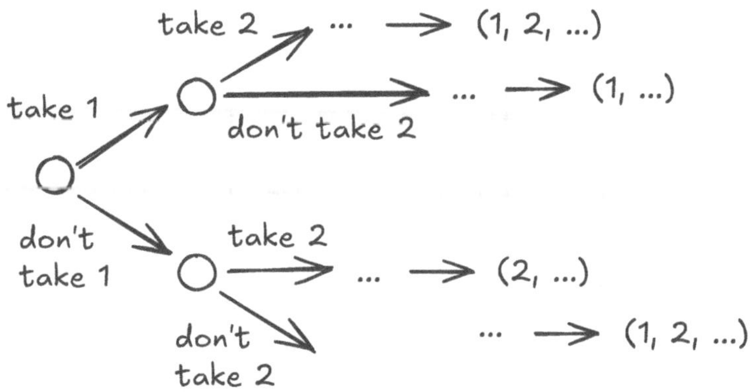

FIGURE 11.3: A nondeterministic solution to the knapsack problem.

of two to keep it under the required time constraints. To process an input of size 20, we'll have to make the code work four times faster, and for $N = 21$, the code has to be eight times faster!

There are methods (such as *branch-and-bound* [13]) that are able to reduce brute-force search by identifying dead ends early. They cannot change the asymptotic complexity of an exponential-time algorithm, but they can sometimes expand the range of tractable inputs enough to make a practical difference.

Many intractable problems have "optimization" versions, where the goal is to find the best possible solution. For example, the optimization version of the traveling salesman problem requires finding the cheapest route through N cities. Similarly, the optimization version of the knapsack problem asks for the most expensive combination of objects having a total weight of at most K.

Such optimization versions can often be solved approximately with polynomial-time algorithms. For instance, the Christofides algorithm [11] can find an approximate solution for the traveling salesman problem in $O(N^3)$ time. It is guaranteed that the obtained route will be at worst 1.5 times more expensive than the optimal solution.

11.6.3 POLYNOMIAL-TIME REDUCTIONS

Exponential-time algorithms that solve such NP-class problems as SAT, TSP, and KS are very similar brute-force search routines. Essentially, in every case, we have to generate every possible solution to the given problem and check whether a certain criterion is met. This similarity hints at a deep connection between the problems comprising the NP class.

In an old joke, a mathematician solves the task of boiling some water by filling an empty kettle with water and placing it on a stove. When given a kettle with water, the mathematician empties it and proclaims the task done because it has now been reduced to a previously solved problem.

Jokes aside, such reductions indeed help to identify related problems and to reuse existing solutions. For the purposes of computational complexity analysis, it is important to know the complexity of the method used to reduce one task to another, to take into account the computational effort required to perform the reduction. We will only discuss *polynomial-time reductions*, which require a polynomial-time algorithm to transform an input for decision problem A into an input for decision problem B, such that the answer ("yes/no") to problem B on this input also applies to the original problem A.

Such reductions can be tricky to construct. As a standard textbook example, let's discuss how to reduce the 3-SAT problem to the KS problem. The 3-SAT problem is a variation of the Boolean satisfiability problem with the following restrictions:

- The Boolean formula is represented with AND-combined clauses:

$$C_1 \text{ AND } C_2 \text{ AND } \dots \text{ AND } C_m$$

- Each clause consists of OR-combined literals represented by variables (like x) or their negations (like NOT x).
- Each clause consists of exactly three elements, for example,

$$C_1 = x_1 \text{ OR NOT } x_2 \text{ OR } x_3$$

  In terms of complexity, 3-SAT is equivalent to SAT, and it can be shown that any Boolean formula can be transformed to the 3-literal *conjunctive normal form* described above.

Our task is to demonstrate that it's possible to reuse a "black-box" Knapsack problem solver to solve any given instance of 3-SAT. To do this, we will first convert a 3-SAT formula with n variables and m clauses into a set of $2(n + m)$ numbers, consisting of $n + m$ digits each.

For each variable x_i we create two "literal items":

- A number labeled "x_i" with digit i set to 1, and with digit $n + j$ set to 1 for each clause C_j containing x_i.
- A number labeled "NOT x_i" with digit i set to 1, and with digit $n + j$ set to 1 for each clause C_j containing NOT x_i.

For each clause C_j we create two "slack items":

- A number labeled "$S_{j,1}$" with digit $n + j$ set to 1.
- A number labeled "$S_{j,2}$" with digit $n + j$ set to 2.

All other digits in these numbers should be set to 0.

Finally, we will need a "target number" T that has the first n digits set to 1, and the remaining m digits set to 3.

For example, a 3-SAT formula

$$(x_1 \text{ OR } x_2 \text{ OR NOT } x_3) \text{ AND } (\text{NOT } x_1 \text{ OR NOT } x_2 \text{ OR } x_3)$$

with $n = 3$ and $m = 2$ yields:

Item	Digit 1	Digit 2	Digit 3	Digit 4	Digit 5
x_1	1	0	0	1	0
NOT x_1	1	0	0	0	1
x_2	0	1	0	1	0
NOT x_2	0	1	0	0	1
x_3	0	0	1	0	1
NOT x_3	0	0	1	1	0
$S_{1,1}$	0	0	0	1	0
$S_{1,2}$	0	0	0	2	0
$S_{2,1}$	0	0	0	0	1
$S_{2,2}$	0	0	0	0	2
T	1	1	1	3	3

Now consider the following problem: *for the obtained set of numbers, find a subset that sums exactly to T*. This task is known as a *subset sum problem*, which is a close relative of a Knapsack problem. Let's treat each element in the constructed set as a knapsack item. The number corresponding to each item will serve as both weight and price of the item. Is it possible to find a combination of items having a total weight of at most T and a total price of at least T?

The resulting combination of knapsack items will also serve as a solution for the original 3-SAT instance. In our example, the elements to be taken into the knapsack are x_1, NOT x_2, x_3, $S_{1,2}$, and $S_{2,1}$. Indeed, their sum is equal to T: $10010 + 01001 + 00101 + 00020 + 00001 = 11133$. The original 3-SAT instance is satisfied by the combination $x_1 = True, x_2 = False, x_3 = True$.

The structure of T ensures that a valid truth assignment for the 3-SAT formula corresponds to a solution for the subset sum, and vice versa. The first n digits of T that correspond to variables $x_1, \ldots, x_n$ are set to 1. The only way to achieve this sum is to select exactly one option from x_i and NOT x_i for each variable x_i.

The next m elements of T are set to 3. Any valid 3-SAT solution has every C_j satisfied. By including a literal item into a solution, we obtain 1 in digits corresponding to every clause where this item is found. The trouble is that certain clauses might be satisfied by two or three literals, which will bring the total sum for such a clause to 2 or 3. The purpose of slack items is to provide extra "padding" values of 1 and 2 which can be used to obtain the resulting sum of exactly 3.

Therefore, a subset of items add up to T if and only if it corresponds to selecting exactly one literal for each variable, and for every clause, the sum of chosen literals is at least one. This is precisely the condition for a satisfying assignment in 3-SAT.

To prepare knapsack items, we have to fill out a table of $2(n + m) \times (n + m)$ elements, which is clearly a polynomial-time process.

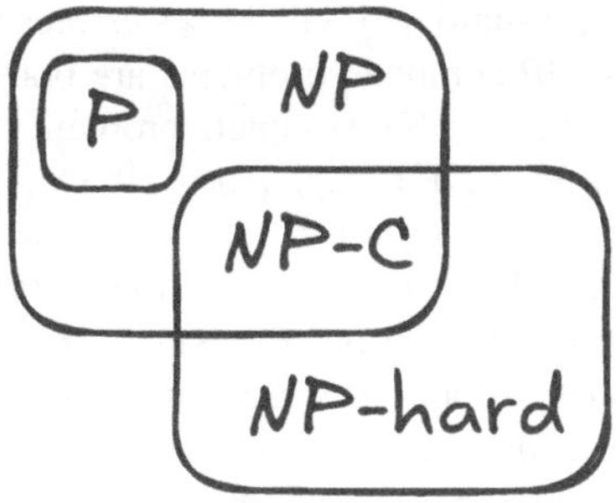

FIGURE 11.4: The complexity classes P, NP, NP-complete, and NP-hard.

11.6.4 NP-HARD AND NP-COMPLETE PROBLEMS

Polynomial-time reductions may help to identify the complexity class of a given problem. If its solution can be obtained via a polynomial-time reduction to a known P-class problem, the given problem also belongs to the class P, because it can be solved with two polynomial-time steps. Similarly, by reducing a given problem to a known NP-class problem, we can show that it belongs to the class NP. An exponential-time algorithm with a polynomial-time preparation step still takes exponential time to run.

Now, let's recall that the classes P and NP do not correspond to "tractable" and "intractable" problems. If P is not equal to NP (as shown in Figure 11.2), then NP includes both tractable and intractable problems. To isolate intractable problems, we will need to define a new complexity class, called *NP-hard.* A given problem belongs to the class NP-hard if any NP-class problem can be reduced to it in polynomial time. In other words, NP-hard problems are at least as hard as anything found in the NP class. Importantly, representatives of the NP-hard class are not limited to decision problems.

Suppose we need to identify the complexity class of the following simple problem: *find out whether the sum of all the items in a given list is at least V.* It can be easily reduced to the knapsack problem: presuming that every item of the list has a weight of 0, find out whether it is possible to find a combination of items with a total value of at least V. This reduction puts the original problem into the class NP, which is technically correct but practically not very helpful.

The concept of NP-hardness resolves this issue. Presumably, P does not belong to NP-hard, i.e., it is not possible to reduce a typical "intractable" problem such as SAT or KS to a P-class problem solvable by means of a polynomial-time algorithm. There are also decision problems that belong to NP-hard but not to NP (see Figure 11.4). A simple example is the halting problem: it is undecidable and thus does not belong to NP. However, it is NP-hard: it is easy to reduce a problem like SAT to the halting problem. Imagine code that halts if a given Boolean formula is satisfiable. Then solving the halting problem for this code is equivalent to solving SAT.

The intersection of the NP-hard and NP classes creates an important class of *NP-complete* problems. Since NP-complete problems are both in NP and NP-hard, any NP problem can be reduced to any NP-complete problem. This observation provides an actual instrument for proving NP-completeness: if a known NP-complete problem can be reduced to the given task in polynomial time (and the task itself is in NP), then it is also NP-complete. The *Cook-Levin theorem* states that the SAT problem is NP-complete, so it is possible to prove the NP-completeness of a given problem by reducing SAT to it. Such reductions were constructed for KS and TSP, so these problems are NP-complete. Since all NP-complete problems can be reduced to each other, it would be enough to solve any of them with a polynomial-time algorithm to show that P = NP. Conversely, if someone were to ever prove that a certain NP-complete problem can only be solved with an exponential-time algorithm, it would mean that P ≠ NP.

Ladner's theorem [44] states that if P ≠ NP, there are problems in NP that are neither in P nor NP-complete. Such problems are known as *NP-intermediate*. Strictly speaking, since we do not know whether P = NP, there are no known NP-intermediate problems either. However, there are some strong candidates, such as the *prime factorization decision problem*: given integers n and k, decide whether n has a prime factor no larger than k [51]. For example, for $n = 35$ and $k = 6$, the answer is yes, because 35 is divisible by the prime number 5.

11.6.5 COMPLEXITY CLASSES PSPACE AND EXP

The halting problem is a correct yet somewhat unsatisfying example of a problem that is NP-hard but not NP-complete. It would be far more interesting to identify decidable problems that are harder than NP.

The complexity classes P and NP were defined on the basis of the time required to obtain a solution. Time was "tractable" (polynomial) or "intractable" (exponential). Alternatively, we can focus on *space* or memory requirements. Note that even presumably intractable problems like KS or SAT require an amount of memory comparable to the size of the input. A brute-force approach requires us to prepare a candidate solution having at most as many elements as the input, test it, and proceed to the next candidate solution if necessary. Therefore, both P and NP problems seem to exist in the same "space-tractable" territory.

This is not a coincidence: it seems that "time-tractability" is harder to satisfy *"because space can be reused whereas time cannot"* [68, Ch. 8]. Brute-force search methods require us to work with one solution at a time. Once a candidate solution is rejected, we can reuse the same memory to process the next candidate solution. Time, on the other hand, cannot be reclaimed.

The notion of space complexity gives us an instrument for introducing the complexity class *PSPACE*, defined as decision problems solvable using $O(n^k)$ space for an input of size n. This definition applies to both deterministic and nondeterministic Turing machines. According to *Savitch's theorem* [67], any problem that can be solved using $f(n)$ space on a nondeterministic Turing machine can be solved using $f(n)^2$

space on a deterministic Turing machine. Therefore, nondeterministic polynomial-space solutions remain polynomial-space for deterministic computing machines.

As in the case of P vs. NP, it is not known (but widely believed) whether PSPACE ≠ NP. A standard example of a problem that is in PSPACE but probably not in NP is the DFA intersection problem: given k DFAs, decide whether there is a string accepted by all of them. It is decidable but likely not in polynomial time, even using a nondeterministic Turing machine.

Even more complex yet solvable problems can be found in the complexity class *EXP* (also known as EXPTIME), which contains decision problems that can be solved in exponential time by a deterministic Turing machine. When discussing this class, we finally accept intractability and explore the set of problems solvable under these relaxed conditions.

Following the notion of NP-completeness, we also introduce the class of EXP-complete problems, which are polynomially reducible to each other. These are the hardest problems in EXP. An example of an EXP-complete problem is generalized checkers [64]: given a position on an $N \times N$ board, decide if there is a possibility for the white player to win. As the number of squares on the checkerboard increases, the duration of one game can grow exponentially, i.e., for a board of $N \times N$ squares, one game may take $O(c^{N^2})$ moves. Potentially, all these games have to be checked to find a possible win for the white player.

Coming back to the idea of space complexity, let us also introduce the *EXPSPACE* class, consisting of decision problems that can be solved using exponential space. The notion of completeness is applicable to the classes PSPACE and EXPSPACE. A decision problem is (EX)PSPACE-complete if it belongs to (EX)PSPACE and every other problem in (EX)PSPACE can be polynomially reduced to it.

A simple example of an EXPSPACE-complete problem is the following task: given two regular expressions *with squaring*, decide whether they describe the same language [48]. "Squaring" denotes a non-standard operation, repeating the given expression: $S^2 = SS$.

Figure 11.5 shows the likely yet unproven relation between the most important complexity classes.

11.6.6 COMPUTATIONAL IRREDUCIBILITY

Before wrapping up this chapter, let's appreciate how profound the phenomena of computability and complexity are. The Turing machine is an entirely artificial construct, an imaginary elaboration of the concept of a "paper machine" able to carry out simple operations. Yet the strong Church-Turing thesis is a general statement that *"resembles a physical law such as the law of gravity: it is consistent with all known empirical observations, could in principle be falsified by experiment, and appears to describe an invariant property of the universe"* [46, Sec. 15.3].

We usually take for granted the deep relationship between the laws of physics and seemingly abstract mathematical structures, but it is not really clear why nature works this way. Eugene Wigner famously called this phenomenon *"the unreasonable*

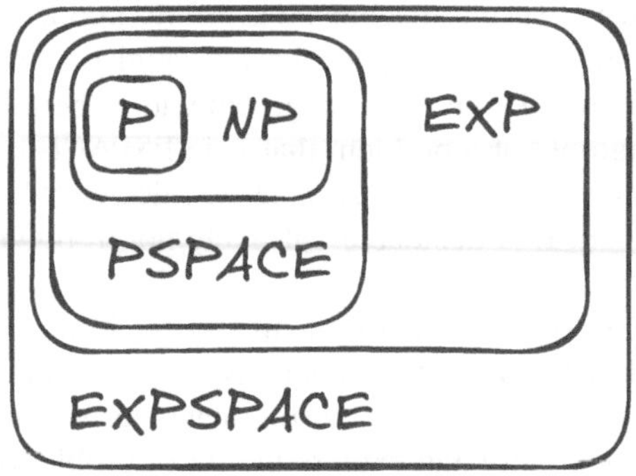

FIGURE 11.5: The complexity classes P to EXPSPACE.

effectiveness of mathematics" [75]. To him, it was far from obvious why the laws of gravity, observed by Galileo in Pisa, would work everywhere on the planet and not only in his lifetime. Some authors, like Max Tegmark, believe that our universe *is* a mathematical structure, so it should come as no surprise that mathematics works so well [71].

Computational complexity is a similar kind of phenomenon. There seems to be something inherent in the problems we discuss that makes them "tractable" or "intractable." I find it particularly fascinating that the border between tractability and intractability is very thin. For example, consider the following problem. A telephone company operating in N cities must build a network to make sure there is a (possibly indirect) connection between any two given cities. Determine whether there exists a network cheaper than K, given the cost of a link between any two cities. This problem, known as a *minimum spanning tree* (MST), can be easily solved in polynomial time [17, Sec. 24.1]. However, a small twist on the task definition turns it into the intractable traveling salesman problem.

An interesting view on complexity is expressed by Stephen Wolfram [76]. Much of his discussion is focused on the relation between "internal" and "external" complexity, aiming to show how simple processes can produce elaborately structured objects. We have already seen how this works while studying L-systems. What is more relevant to our current topic is the concept of *computational irreducibility*. Wolfram argues that classic science owes much of its success to the discovery of certain computational shortcuts. We don't have to trace the trajectory of our planet to find its distance to the Sun on a given day: a simple formula, based on Kepler's First Law, provides a quick answer. However, there is no reason to believe that we will always be lucky enough to discover simple computations that allow us to skip or "fast-forward" underlying natural processes. Wolfram's favorite example is cellular automata, but we can again resort to L-systems. How can one obtain the N-th generation string derived from a given axiom? It seems there is no way to do it directly: we will have to produce all intermediate strings of generations 1 to $N - 1$.

Such observations can provide a reasonable starting point for thinking about intractable problems. It is very likely that brute-forcing an NP-complete problem is similar to producing all intermediate strings of an L-system: there is simply no way around it, no computational shortcut. Under this logic, intractability should be viewed as the norm rather than as an obstacle to be resolved eventually. We are lucky that so much can be achieved with tractable, polynomial-time algorithms.

11.7 TAKEAWAYS

1. Like any other computational device, the Turing machine has its limitations. There are languages it cannot recognize, for example, the language of "string-encoded Turing machines that halt."
2. According to the Church-Turing thesis, what can be computed in principle can be computed with a Turing machine. Presuming this statement is correct, we can use the terms "algorithm" and "Turing machine" interchangeably.
3. According to the strong Church-Turing thesis, all natural processes are based on computation. Essentially, everything, including our thinking, can be modeled on a Turing machine. Conversely, if a Turing machine is not powerful enough to decide a certain problem, we cannot decide it either.
4. All other sufficiently powerful ("Turing-complete") models of computation, such as untyped lambda calculus, are computationally equivalent to the Turing machine.
5. Decidable problems can be classified into certain complexity classes. The most important classes, P and NP, represent decision problems that can be solved in polynomial time by a deterministic Turing machine and a nondeterministic Turing machine, respectively.
6. It is widely believed that P is properly contained within NP. Many NP-class problems are likely intractable, requiring exponential-time algorithms (essentially based on brute-force search) on deterministic computational devices. The classes PSPACE and EXP contain even more computationally demanding decision problems.
7. The Church-Turing thesis and the notion of computational complexity are tightly connected with our physical reality, and many authors treat them as laws of nature.

References

1. Alfred V. Aho and Jeffrey D. Ullman. *Principles of Compiler Design*. Addison-Wesley Series in Computer Science and Information Processing. Addison-Wesley Pub. Co, Reading, Mass, 1977.
2. Alfred V. Aho, Monica S. Lam, Ravi Sethi, and Jeffrey D. Ullman. *Compilers: Principles, Techniques, & Tools*. Pearson Addison-Wesley, Boston Munich, 2nd edition, 2007.
3. David M. Beazley. *Python Essential Reference*. Addison-Wesley Professional, 4th edition, 2009.
4. James R. Bell. Threaded code. *Communications of the ACM*, 16(6):370–372, June 1973.
5. Alexander Bogomolny. Pigeonhole Principle. https://www.cut-the-knot.org/do_you_know/pigeon.shtml.
6. David M. Bourg and Glenn Seemann. *AI for Game Developers*. O'Reilly, Sebastopol, CA, 1st edition, 2004.
7. Ivan Bratko. *Prolog Programming for Artificial Intelligence*. International Computer Science Series. Addison-Wesley Pub. Co, Wokingham, England, 2nd edition, 1990.
8. Chandra Chekuri. A Note on Proving Non-Regularity via Fooling Sets. https://chekuri.cs.illinois.edu/teaching/fooling-sets.pdf.
9. Noam Chomsky. Three models for the description of language. *IRE Transactions on Information Theory*, 2(3):113–124, 1956.
10. Noam Chomsky and Marcel-Paul Schützenberger. The Algebraic Theory of Context-Free Languages. In P. Braffort and D. Hirschberg, editors, *Studies in Logic and the Foundations of Mathematics*, volume 26 of *Computer Programming and Formal Systems*, pages 118–161. Elsevier, January 1959.
11. Nicos Christofides. Worst-Case Analysis of a New Heuristic for the Travelling Salesman Problem. *Operations Research Forum*, 3(1), March 2022.
12. Alonzo Church. *The Calculi of Lambda-Conversion*. Number 6 in Annals of Mathematical Studies. Princeton University Press, 1941.
13. Jens Clausen. *Branch and Bound Algorithms-Principles and Examples*. Department of computer science, University of Copenhagen, pages 1–30, 1999.
14. Keith D. Cooper and Linda Torczon. *Engineering a Compiler*. Elsevier, 2nd edition, January 2011.
15. B. Jack Copeland. The Church-Turing Thesis. In Edward N. Zalta and Uri Nodelman, editors, *The Stanford Encyclopedia of Philosophy*. Metaphysics Research Lab, Stanford University, winter 2024 edition, 2024.
16. B. Jack Copeland. The Rise and Fall of the Entscheidungsproblem. In Edward N. Zalta and Uri Nodelman, editors, *The Stanford Encyclopedia of Philosophy*. Metaphysics Research Lab, Stanford University, winter 2024 edition, 2024.

17. Thomas H. Cormen, Charles E. Leiserson, and Ronald L. Rivest. *Introduction to Algorithms*. The MIT Electrical Engineering and Computer Science Series. MIT press McGraw-Hill, Cambridge (Mass.), 1992.
18. Russ Cox. Implementing Regular Expressions. https://swtch.com/~rsc/regexp/.
19. David Hilbert. Mathematical problems. *Bulletin of the American Mathematical Society*, 8(10):437–479, July 1902.
20. Martin Davis. *Computability and Unsolvability*. Dover Publications, 2013.
21. Penny de Byl. Unity Learn: Finite State Machines. https://learn.unity.com/project/finite-state-machines-1.
22. Bryce S. DeWitt. Quantum mechanics and reality. *Physics Today*, 23(9):30–35, September 1970.
23. Jeff Erickson. *Models of Computation*. https://jeffe.cs.illinois.edu/teaching/algorithms/#models, 2015.
24. Javier Esparza and Michael Blondin. *Automata Theory: An Algorithmic Approach*. MIT Press, October 2023.
25. Abdullah Ezzeddin. Mastering Python Lambdas — A Comprehensive Guide for Developers. https://ezzeddinabdullah.com/post/python-lambda/.
26. Jeffrey Friedl. *Mastering Regular Expressions*. O'Reilly Media, Sebastapol, CA, 3rd edition, September 2006.
27. Erich Gamma, Erich Helm, Richard Johnson, and Ralph Vlissides. *Design Patterns: Elements of Reusable Object-Oriented Software*. Addison-Wesley Professional Computing Series. Addison-Wesley Professional, 1994.
28. William I. Gasarch. Guest Column: The Third P=?NP Poll. *ACM SIGACT News*, 50(1):38–59, March 2019.
29. Diego Giacomelli. Unity Avatar Mask and Animation Layers. https://diegogiacomelli.com.br/unity-avatar-mask-and-animation-layers/.
30. Seymour Ginsburg and Joseph Ullian. Ambiguity in context free languages. *Journal of the ACM*, 13(1):62–89, January 1966.
31. James Gosling and Henry McGilton. *The Java Language Environment*. Sun Microsystems Computer Company, 2550:38, 1995.
32. Dick Grune and Ceriel J. H. Jacobs. *Parsing Techniques: A Practical Guide*. Monographs in Computer Science. Springer, New York, 2nd edition, 2008.
33. David Harel. Statecharts: A visual formalism for complex systems. *Science of Computer Programming*, 8(3):231–274, June 1987.
34. James L. Hein. *Theory of Computation: An Introduction*. Jones and Bartlett Publishers, Inc., 1996.
35. John E. Hopcroft and Jeffrey D. Ullman. *Introduction to Automata Theory, Languages, and Computation*. Addison-Wesley Series in Computer Science. Addison-Wesley, Reading, Mass, 1979.
36. John E. Hopcroft, Rajeev Motwani, and Jeffrey D. Ullman. *Introduction to Automata Theory, Languages, and Computation*. Pearson, Bosten San Francisco Munich, 3rd edition, 2007.
37. Zhenjiang Hu, John Hughes, and Meng Wang. How functional programming mattered. *National Science Review*, 2(3):349–370, 2015.

38. Paul Hudak. Conception, evolution, and application of functional programming languages. *ACM Computing Surveys*, 21(3):359–411, September 1989.
39. Andrew Hunt and David Thomas. *The Pragmatic Programmer: From Journeyman to Master*. Addison-Wesley, Reading (Mass.), 2000.
40. Stephen Kleene. Representation of events in nerve nets. In Claude Shannon and John McCarthy, editors, *Automata Studies*, pages 3–40. Princeton University Press, 1956.
41. Donald E. Knuth. On the translation of languages from left to right. *Information and Control*, 8(6):607–639, December 1965.
42. Philip J. Koopman. A taxonomy of decomposition strategies based on structures, behaviors, and goals. In *International Design Engineering Technical Conferences and Computers and Information in Engineering Conference*, pages 611–618. American Society of Mechanical Engineers, 1995.
43. Vladik Kreinovich and Olga Kosheleva. A Turing Machine Is Just a Finite Automaton with Two Stacks: A Comment on Teaching Theory of Computation. Technical Report University of Texas at El Paso, July 2018.
44. Richard E. Ladner. On the Structure of Polynomial Time Reducibility. *Journal of the ACM*, 22(1):155–171, January 1975.
45. Salvador Lucas. The origins of the halting problem. *Journal of Logical and Algebraic Methods in Programming*, 121:100687, June 2021.
46. John MacCormick. *What Can Be Computed? A Practical Guide to the Theory of Computation*. Princeton University Press, Princeton, New Jersey, 2018.
47. Yuri Matiyasevich. Diophantine sets. *Russian Mathematical Surveys*, 27(5):124, 1972.
48. Albert R. Meyer and Larry J. Stockmeyer. The equivalence problem for regular expressions with squaring requires exponential space. In *SWAT*, volume 72, pages 125–129, 1972.
49. Edward F. Moore. Gedanken-Experiments on Sequential Machines. *Automata Studies*, 34:129–153, 1956.
50. Hanspeter Mössenböck. *The Compiler Generator Coco/R User Manual*. University of Linz, 2010.
51. Chihiro H. Nakajima. Statistical Mechanical formulation and simulation of prime factorization of integers. *Interdisciplinary Information Sciences*, 19(1):51–56, 2013.
52. Dejan Nedelkovski. G-code Explained. List of Most Important G-code Commands. https://howtomechatronics.com/tutorials/g-code-explained-list-of-most-important-g-code-commands/, May 2020.
53. Theodore Norvell. Parsing Expressions by Recursive Descent. https://www.engr.mun.ca/~theo/Misc/exp_parsing.htm, 1999.
54. Robert Nystrom. *Game Programming Patterns*. Genever Benning, 2014.
55. Pascal Ochem and Michaël Rao. Odd perfect numbers are greater than 10^1500. *Mathematics of Computation*, 81(279):1869–1877, 2012.
56. Bryan O'Sullivan, John Goerzen, and Donald Bruce Stewart. *Real World Haskell: Code You Can Believe In*. O'Reilly, Beijing, 2010.

57. Jukka Paakki. Attribute grammar paradigms—a high-level methodology in language implementation. *ACM Computing Surveys*, 27(2):196–255, June 1995.
58. Roger Penrose. *Shadows of the Mind: A Search for the Missing Science of Consciousness*. Oxford Univ. Press, Oxford, 1995.
59. Przemyslaw Prusinkiewicz. Graphical applications of L-systems. In *Proceedings of Graphics Interface*, volume 86, pages 247–253, 1986.
60. Przemysław Prusinkiewicz and Aristid Lindenmayer. *The Algorithmic Beauty of Plants*. The Virtual Laboratory. Springer-Verlag, 1996.
61. Michael Rabin and Dana Scott. Finite Automata and Their Decision Problems. *IBM Journal of Research and Development*, 3(2):114–125, April 1959.
62. Michael Rescorla. The computational theory of mind. In Edward N. Zalta and Uri Nodelman, editors, *The Stanford Encyclopedia of Philosophy*. Metaphysics Research Lab, Stanford University, winter 2024 edition, 2024.
63. Dennis Ritchie. An incomplete history of the QED Text Editor. https://www.bell-labs.com/usr/dmr/www/qed.html.
64. J. M. Robson. *N* by *N* Checkers is Exptime Complete. *SIAM Journal on Computing*, 13(2):252–267, May 1984.
65. Susan H. Rodger and Thomas W. Finley. *JFLAP: An Interactive Formal Languages and Automata Package*. Jones and Bartlett, Sudbury, MA, 1st edition, 2006.
66. Daniel J. Rosenkrantz and Richard E. Stearns. Properties of deterministic top-down grammars. *Information and Control*, 17(3):226–256, October 1970.
67. Walter J. Savitch. Relationships between nondeterministic and deterministic tape complexities. *Journal of Computer and System Sciences*, 4(2):177–192, April 1970.
68. Michael Sipser. *Introduction to the Theory of Computation*. Course Technology, Boston, 2nd edition, 2010.
69. Jonathan Sorenson. An introduction to prime number sieves. Technical report, University of Wisconsin-Madison Department of Computer Sciences, 1990.
70. David Spector. Efficient Full LR(1) Parser Generation. *Sigplan Notices - SIGPLAN*, 23, December 1988.
71. Max Tegmark. *Our Mathematical Universe: My Quest for the Ultimate Nature of Reality*. Popular Science. Penguin Books, London, 2015.
72. David Thomas and Andrew Hunt. *The Pragmatic Programmer: Your Journey to Mastery*. Addison-Wesley, Boston, 2nd edition, 2020.
73. Alan Turing. On Computable Numbers, with an Application to the Entscheidungsproblem. *Proceedings of the London Mathematical Society*, s2-42(1):230–265, 1937.
74. Alan Turing. *The Essential Turing: Seminal Writings in Computing, Logic, Philosophy, Artificial Intelligence, and Artificial Life, plus the Secrets of Enigma*. Oxford University Press, 2004.
75. Eugene P. Wigner. The Unreasonable Effectiveness of Mathematics in the Natural Sciences. In *Mathematics and Science*, pages 291–306. World Scientific, 1990.

76. Stephen Wolfram. *A New Kind of Science*. Wolfram Media, Champaign, IL, 2002.
77. Edward Yourdon and Larry L. Constantine. *Structured Design: Fundamentals of a Discipline of Computer Program and Systems Design*. Yourdon Pr, New York, NY, 2nd edition, 1978.
78. Mark Ziemann, Yotam Eren, and Assam El-Osta. Gene name errors are widespread in the scientific literature. *Genome Biology*, 17(1):177, December 2016.

Index

ε-automaton, 27
ε-closure, 29
ε-transitions, 26
`re` (Python module)
  `findall()` function, 11
  `finditer()` function, 10, 11
  `fullmatch()` function, 6, 11
  `match()` function, 11
  `search()` function, 8, 11
  `sub()` function, 10

accept state, *see* favorable state
acceptance by empty stack, 81
acceptance by favorable state, 81
algorithm, 192
alphabet, 1, 14
alternation operation, 2
ambiguity, 91
ambiguous grammar, 92
animation layers, 66
associativity, 3
asymptotic complexity, 205
attribute grammar, 137
axiom, 152

backreference, 10, 55
backtracking, 55
behavioral state machine, 67
big-O notation, 205
Boolean satisfiability problem (SAT), 207
bottom-up parsing, 96
branch-and-bound, 208
breadth-first search, 85

capturing group, 9
Chomsky hierarchy, 190
Chomsky normal form, 117
Church-Turing thesis, 193
Cocke-Younger-Kasami algorithm, 117
code generator, 126
compiler, 126
compiler generator, 125
compiler-compiler, *see* compiler generator
complement language, 38
complexity class
  EXP/EXPTIME, 213
  EXPSPACE, 213
  NP, 206
  NP-complete, 212
  NP-hard, 211
  NP-intermediate, 212
  P, 206
  PSPACE, 212
computational complexity
  asymptotic, 205
  cubic, 122
  exponential, 37, 205
  linear, 17
  polynomial, 205
  quadratic, 203
  quasilinear, 203
computational irreducibility, 214
computational problem, 70
computational theory of complexity, 189
concatenation operation, 2, 3
conjunctive normal form, 209
context-free grammar (CFG), 71
context-free language, 73
context-sensitive grammar, 166
context-sensitive L-system, 162
context-sensitive language, 166
Cook-Levin theorem, 212
cubic time, 122
currying, 199

decidable language, 189
decider, 170

decision problem, 70, 165
declarative programming, 200
decomposition, 57
decoupling, 57
depth-first search, 35
deterministic context-free (D0L) L-system, 152
deterministic context-free language, 84
deterministic finite automaton (DFA), 12
deterministic finite state machine (DFSM), *see* deterministic finite automaton (DFA)
deterministic pushdown automaton (DPDA), 84
deterministic Turing machine, 170
determinization (NFA), 28
directed graph, 13
directional parser, 93

effective computation, 193
empty string, 2
end-of-string marker, 99
EXP/EXPTIME complexity class, 213
exponential time, 37, 205
EXPSPACE complexity class, 213
Extended Backus-Naur form (EBNF), 127

favorable state, 13
final state, *see* favorable state
finite automaton (FA), 12, 23
  ε-automaton, 27
  ε-closure, 29
  ε-transitions, 26
  accepting/rejecting a string, 16
  complete, 19
  conversion to RE, 48
  deterministic (DFA), 12
  DFA minimization, 17
  favorable state, 13
  final state, *see* favorable state
  NFA determinization, 28
  nondeterministic (NFA), 23
  recognizing a language, 16
  sink state, 19
  start state, 13
  state equivalence, 18
  transition, 13
  transition function, 14
  unreachable state, 18
finite state machine, *see* finite automaton
formal language, *see* language
fractal, 158
functional programming, 200

grammar, 71
  ambiguous, 92
  attribute, 137
  augmented, 99
  CFG to PDA conversion, 82
  context-free (CFG), 71
  context-sensitive, 166
  conversion to LL(1), 116
  left-linear, 73
  LL/LR, 94
  nonterminal, 71
  production rule, 71
  regular, 73
  right-linear, 73
  start symbol, 71
  terminal, 71
  unrestricted, 190
  variable, *see* nonterminal
greedy matching, 8

halting problem, 190
Harel statechart, 67
hierarchical state machine, 66
higher-order functions, 204

inherently ambiguous language, 93
interpreter, 126
intractable problems, 204

just-in-time compilation, 126

Kleene star/closure operation, 3

Kleene's theorem, 44
knapsack problem, 207
Koch curve, 158

L-system, 151
  axiom, 152
  context-sensitive, 162
  deterministic context-free, 152
  parametric, 163
  production rule, 152
  stochastic, 161
Ladner's theorem, 212
lambda calculus (untyped), 198
lambda expression, 198
language, 2
  complement, 38
  context-free, 73
  context-sensitive, 166
  decidable, 189
  deterministic context-free, 84
  inherently ambiguous, 93
  LL/LR, 94
  nonregular, 11
  recursive, 189
  recursively enumerable, 189
  regular, 3
  undecidable, 190
lazy matching, 9
left recursion, 116
left-factoring, 117
left-linear grammar, 73
leftmost derivation, 93
lexical analyzer, *see* scanner
linear bounded automaton (LBA), 189
linear time, 17
LL(1) parsing, 112
LL/LR grammar, 94
LL/LR language, 94
lookahead, 94
lookahead LR (LALR) parser, 123
looping, 170
LR(1) items, 102
LR(1) parser, 96

many-worlds interpretation, 23
Markov chain/process, 62
Markov property, 62
McNaughton-Yamada-Thompson algorithm, 46
minimization (DFA), 17
minimum spanning tree, 214
model checking, 196
Moore's algorithm, 18
multi-head Turing machine, 184
multi-tape Turing machine, 185
multi-track Turing machine, 184

nondeterministic finite automaton (NFA), 23
nonregular language, 11
nonterminal, 71
NP complexity class, 206
NP-complete complexity class, 212
NP-hard complexity class, 211
NP-intermediate complexity class, 212
nullable nonterminal, 97

P complexity class, 206
P versus NP problem, 206
palindrome, 85
parametric L-system, 163
parse tree, 89
parser, 89
parser generator, 96
parsing, 46
  bottom-up, 96
  directional, 93
  leftmost derivation, 93
  LL(1), 112
  lookahead, 94
  lookahead LR (LALR), 123
  LR(1), 96
  recursive descent, 113
  rightmost derivation, 93
  shift-reduce, 96
  top-down, 112
partially decidable language, *see* recursively enumerable language
perfect number, 197

pigeonhole principle, 69
polynomial time, 205
polynomial-time reduction, 209
possessive matching, 9
prime factorization decision problem, 212
procedural content generation, 164
production rule, 71, 152
PSPACE complexity class, 212
pumping lemma, 68
pumping lemma for context-free languages, 166
pumping length, 68
pure function, 200
push/pop operations, 80
pushdown automaton (PDA), 80
  acceptance by empty stack, 81
  acceptance by favorable state, 81
  deterministic, 84
  PDA to CFG conversion, 82
  push/pop operations, 80
  stack alphabet, 80
  stack memory, 80
  two-stack, 168

quadratic time, 203
quantifier, 7
  greedy, 8, 54
  lazy, 8, 53
  possessive, 8
quasilinear time, 203

race condition, 196
raw string, 6
recursive descent parser, 113
recursive language, 189
recursively enumerable language, 189
reduction operation, 198
regex, *see* regular expression
regular expression (RE), 2
  alternation, 2
  backreference, 10, 55
  capturing group, 9
  concatenation, 3
  conversion to FA, 44
  engine, 54
  Kleene star/closure, 3
  quantifier, 7
regular grammar, 73
regular language, 3
repetition operator, *see* quantifier
Rice's theorem, 191
right-linear grammar, 73
rightmost derivation, 93

Savitch's theorem, 212
scanner, 126
selection sort, 203
semantic actions, 128
semi-structured data, 125
shift-reduce parser, 96
Sierpiński triangle, 158
sink state, 19
skeletal animation, 64
stack alphabet, 80
stack memory, 80
start state, 13
start symbol, 71
state equivalence, 18
State pattern, 58
subset sum problem, 210

terminal, 71
threaded code, 136
token, 126
top-down parsing, 112
transition, 13
transition function, 14
translator, 125
transpiler, 125
traveling salesman problem (TSP), 207
Turing completeness, 197
Turing machine, 168
  decider, 170
  deterministic, 170
  equivalence with 2-PDA, 170
  linear bounded automaton, 189
  looping, 170
  multi-head, 184

multi-tape, 185
multi-track, 184
robustness, 184
universal, 187
turtle graphics, 154

undecidable language, 190
universal Turing machine (UTM), 187
unreachable state, 18
unrestricted grammar, 190
untyped lambda calculus, 198

variable, *see* nonterminal

For Product Safety Concerns and Information please contact our EU representative GPSR@taylorandfrancis.com Taylor & Francis Verlag GmbH, Kaufingerstraße 24, 80331 München, Germany